Parting Shots

Parting Shots

MATTHEW PARRIS
AND ANDREW BRYSON

VIKING
an imprint of
PENGUIN BOOKS

VIKING

Published by the Penguin Group
Penguin Books Ltd, 80 Strand, London WC2R 0RL, England
Penguin Group (USA) Inc., 375 Hudson Street, New York, New York 10014, USA
Penguin Group (Canada), 90 Eglinton Avenue East, Suite 700, Toronto, Ontario, Canada M4P 2Y3
(a division of Pearson Penguin Canada Inc.)
Penguin Ireland, 25 St Stephen's Green, Dublin 2, Ireland (a division of Penguin Books Ltd)
Penguin Group (Australia), 250 Camberwell Road, Camberwell, Victoria 3124, Australia
(a division of Pearson Australia Group Pty Ltd)
Penguin Books India Pvt Ltd, 11 Community Centre, Panchsheel Park, New Delhi – 110 017, India
Penguin Group (NZ), 67 Apollo Drive, Rosedale, North Shore 0632, New Zealand
(a division of Pearson New Zealand Ltd)
Penguin Books (South Africa) (Pty) Ltd, 24 Sturdee Avenue, Rosebank, Johannesburg 2196, South Africa

Penguin Books Ltd, Registered Offices: 80 Strand, London WC2R 0RL, England

www.penguin.com

First published 2010
2

The publishers wish to thank The National Archives for permission to reproduce the following
pictures: 1 (ref. FCO 15/339); 6 (ref. FCO 8/2889); 7 (ref. FCO 7/3356); 8 and 9 (ref. FCO 33/3941);
10 (ref. FCO 7/680); 11 (ref. FCO 7/1111); and 12 (ref. FCO 93/1925).

Set in 12/14.75 pt Minion Regular
Typeset by TexTech International
Printed in Great Britain by Clays Ltd, St Ives plc

A CIP catalogue record for this book is available from the British Library

HARDBACK ISBN: 978–0–670–91928–4
TRADE PAPERBACK ISBN: 978–0–670–91973–4

www.greenpenguin.co.uk

Contents

Introduction

Beyond retirement there can be no reprisals. Which of us does not have embarrassing memories of a works leaving-do at which (after perhaps a few drinks too many) the departing colleague decides to say a few words; and says a little too much: really lets rip? It may be venomous, it may be melancholy, it may be mawkishly affectionate or it may take the boss apart, but what distinguishes these occasions is that an individual, offered the chance to take a parting shot, has blurted out all the things he or she always wanted to say about the job, about colleagues, about customers, about the business, or about life generally: things that can now be said without fear of disapproval.

HM Diplomatic Service has, over the centuries, learned to civilize the practice in a most unusual sort of essay. It's an extraordinary beast, called the Valedictory Despatch. How we tracked the beast to its lair you may read in my co-editor's Notes on the Material, at the end of this book – a chapter I recommend looking at before you turn to the material itself, as it sets the species in context. And these animals, surviving into the Millennium, have recently become extinct, hounded from existence by thin-lipped Whitehall mandarins and a vengeful Foreign Secretary.

The creatures in question were simply called 'valedictories' in the FCO. As you will read within, they – and a centuries-old tradition – came to an effective end in 2006 when Margaret Beckett was Foreign Secretary, and some exasperated remarks about the 'bullshit bingo' of the new management-consultancy culture in Whitehall leaked from a valedictory into the press. The Foreign Office's response was so to clip the valedictories' wings by restricting and 'targeting' their circulation, that the free-ranging and indulgent ambit of the despatch, and thus its essential spirit, was lost. With their writers deprived of an audience, the tradition withered on the vine; diplomats who were in post at the time talk of the move simply as 'the ban' (see Chapter 2).

'I thought it was a splendid tradition,' Lord (Chris) Patten, the last Governor of Hong Kong, told us: 'It's important to remember that the final telegram from an ambassador at the end of his career represents the mountain top in this cultural exercise.' Lord (David) Owen called the ban 'absurd . . . one more of those dreadful PC behaviours inflicted on us, flattening out individuality . . .'

But, said Denis MacShane, a Foreign Office minister under the late Robin Cook, 'the days when, once a week, an ambassador would go into a darkened room and write an essay as if they were competing for a Fellowship at All Souls are gone'. What a pity.

But perhaps we should in part blame this sad demise on the very instrument by which we have been able to extract many of the despatches you'll read here from locked archives of material classified under the Official Secrets Act. The Freedom of Information Act has been our tool. Now we have it, 'For Your Eyes Only' is an instruction in which no modern diplomat can any longer place confidence, and it is precisely because most valedictories were more embarrassing than they were threats to national security, that the FCO cannot block their release by using the exceptions allowed to the Act. Yet valedictories, though they were often formally and elegantly printed, and given a circulation wide enough to include (sometimes) Buckingham Palace and the Bank of England, were inherently private documents, written in a personal and private style, for a knowing audience of sometimes-cynical insiders. Paradoxically, they were the more relaxed, indiscreet, knockabout and broad-brush because of it.

I was twenty-five when I read my first. I'd just joined the Foreign and Commonwealth Office, and was serving as a junior officer in Whitehall on the Foreign Office desk dealing with the Scandinavian countries. I read the wires; I opened the post; mine were often the first eyes to see the material arriving from abroad in the FCO's big, Wandsworth-prison-sewn diplomatic bags. And every so often would arrive a despatch that was different from the others, awaited with interest, and – as often as not – circulated fast and with relish. This would be a valedictory, and addressed (in form, at least) direct to the Foreign Secretary, though not all were read, or even shown, at that altitude. The valedictories I processed included final despatches from an ambassador leaving his present post but moving on to another one; and also the more exceptional type of valedictory: a diplomat's last, before he left the Foreign Office for retirement.

In came one such from our retiring ambassador in Oslo. I chortled as I read. His letter was a tirade against the difficulties British diplomats labour under; he warned of the dangers of drink; he recommended regular exercise; he lamented that he had to get up at dawn when VIPs from Britain stayed at the Residence, check whether they'd left shoes outside their rooms – and, if so, clean them himself because you just couldn't get the staff in Norway. I thought this despatch oddly compelling, and argued with my colleagues for its wide circulation – and was overruled: colleagues thought the despatch rather silly.

But I remembered that elegantly eccentric little essay on Service life – and have managed to find it again, for this book.

What exactly is a valedictory? Ambassadors departing their posts abroad write – ostensibly to the Foreign Secretary – a sort of goodbye-to-all-that letter, usually classified (see Notes on the Material) as 'Confidential' or 'Restricted', talking often astonishingly frankly about the country they've been posted to, its inhabitants and its politicians.

They may turn their fire on their own colleagues too, if they wish – or even on their own government, country or countrymen. They may complain about conditions of service, or lavish praise on their long-suffering spouse. Nothing – from the President, to the economy, to the local cooking, to the drains – is off limits. As custom has it the letter is printed and circulated often quite widely within the Foreign and Commonwealth Office and beyond. Then it's locked away in Classified FCO files.

When the post the valedictory-writer is quitting is his or her last before retirement, the missive can be particularly frank – or funny, or sad. British diplomats are often accomplished stylists, and ambassadors (knowing their valedictory will get a wide and interested audience) can take tremendous care to make it good.

I've never forgotten this curious diplomatic tradition, though it did not strike me that, having left the Foreign Office, I would ever be able to retrieve such documents. But I wrote about the custom in *The Times* and the *Spectator*. Out of the blue a young BBC producer, Andrew Bryson, contacted me. He said he thought he could track down a range of valedictories, using the Freedom of Information Act. Maybe we could make a book from them, rescuing the material from obscurity? Maybe we could make a radio series out of the best? As the tradition had recently been (effectively) abolished, why didn't we set about putting together a valedictory to the Valedictory?

Interested, I left him to it. We decided to start with the radio series. If the material we found seemed to support the idea, we could then go on to make the book.

Andrew burrowed. The Freedom of Information Act was by far his most important tool, though a clumsy and time-consuming one. The fruits of his researches started coming in. 'After four years in Hanoi,' wrote our ambassador to Vietnam, 'I shall be overjoyed to leave. Of the six European Community missions here, four live, and three have their offices, in rat-infested hotels . . . Most foreigners in Vietnam, diplomats or not, are on the verge of insanity.'

Both Andrew and I became convinced that this would make a marvellous series on BBC Radio 4 – the commission for which Andrew had set about, finally with success, securing. The programme we made was broadcast in 2009, and was surprisingly well received (greatly assisted by the use of some splendid if somewhat camped-up actors' voices to read the choicest of our selections). We were pleased at the number of listeners, colleagues and friends who encouraged us to carry on and publish a book; and our appetite for the idea had grown as Andrew had worked to edit down the material he had gathered, and shortage of space had forced us cruelly to abbreviate, and often regretfully to abandon altogether, reams of wonderful stuff.

We had learned, too, that many of the despatches we were encountering were more than rude and funny. There was plenty of knockabout stuff, but some of the finest valedictories went far beyond that. These men and women, people of the highest calibre and intellect, had spent the whole of their adult lives in exotic, or dangerous, or pivotal places, often at critical times in history. Their valedictories had been their first and often only opportunity to draw the threads together. You would expect – and we encountered – more than wit.

Sir Peter Jay's valedictory, as he departed Washington in 1979 (see Chapter 6), turned its guns upon his own country, and began 'Our world is dying, and its death is being hastened by errors and myopia in our own ranks . . .' Sir Nicholas Henderson ('How poor and unproud the British have become' – see Chapter 4) had in one magnificent sweep surveyed the relative decline of modern Britain – and perhaps unwittingly set its author up, as it turned out, to be brought back by a new Prime Minister in Downing Street for the most important role in his career.

Our book, as it was emerging in our minds and from the material Andrew was amassing, would uncover some of the more notable essays on modern politics, economics and diplomacy to emerge over the last half-century; many of them important even at the time among the small private audience for which they were written. We were to uncover some of the silliest, too. Now a wider audience would see them all.

For that wider audience it's worth, in this Introduction, placing the valedictory in its context.

'Despatches' have for centuries been the formal method for official communication between Heads of Mission at foreign posts, and senior diplomats based in Whitehall; and with government ministers. The bulk of reporting and commentary is done at a lower level, by letter or (these days) email to the appropriate department at the FCO in Whitehall. A despatch, however, is special. There are First Impressions despatches, written at the start of an ambassador's tour. Ambassadors have also been expected to write an (often tedious) Annual Review summing up their work, accompanied by a catalogue of the year's events, which could read like a school history project.

Then again there are ordinary despatches, the most numerous dealing with matters serious or technical. A big 'set-piece' occasion such as a state visit would justify a special, one-off despatch (if it was a Royal visit, such a despatch, likely to be copied to Buckingham Palace, could be relied on to be sycophantic in its praise of whichever royal personage was sent to patronize the ambassador's patch; these were written, and read in Whitehall, with an unspoken wink).

But valedictories were exceptional: an opportunity for ambassadors to be far more wide-ranging, critical and self-indulgent than usual. They shared some attributes, though, with other types of reporting. Some First Impressions despatches, for instance, contain generalizations about foreigners as funny and damning as in any valedictory. And some 'set-piece' despatches were brilliantly funny and descriptive; Denis MacShane remembers reading a 'splendid essay' from a roving British ambassador in Mexico equal in its descriptive prose to anything by Bruce Chatwin.

Candour is (I found) a quality encountered in refreshing quantity everywhere in the Diplomatic Service – but only in private between consenting adult colleagues. Privately, ambassadors love shooting from the hip, many being the very opposite of the bland diplomatists whom you might imagine handing out chocolates. Some were incredibly brutal and rude about people and events. 'The way the Foreign Office worked – it seems to be for hundreds of years –' (said Denis McShane) 'is [to display] the most brutal frankness on paper.' The valedictory can be the finest flowering of that.

These days, means of communication have changed. Ambassadors write fewer formal despatches; communication by secure email is used, with encrypted messages taking moments to reach Whitehall rather than weeks, as the old diplomatic bag might. And with the advent of social media, diplomats now blog and tweet. Not only has the means of communication changed, so has the audience; the Foreign

Office now encourages its diplomats to write blogs which anyone can read on the internet. In some ways the new forms of communication may be said to give the Foreign Office a more human face: to the outside world, at least. In the process, however, some of the intimacy and sense of honest exchange between colleagues that permeates these despatches has been lost.

Sir Alan Campbell, a former ambassador to Italy and Ethiopia, writing in Gaynor Johnson's useful book of essays *The Foreign Office and British Diplomacy in the Twentieth Century* (Routledge, 2005), says that modern innovations such as air travel, email, photocopiers and faxes made life easier since he joined the FCO in 1950: 'All of this eliminated or simplified many of the tasks which used to be so very time-consuming and boring – the enciphering and deciphering of telegrams, typing and retyping of drafts, the numerous messengers carrying sealed bags or locked boxes, their trolleys thundering down the passages. Then there were metal tubular cylinders that enclosed papers to be sent all over the building by a compressed air system. They sometimes got stuck. But fifty years ago, an expert typist, operating the good old Imperial typewriter, could produce five but no more than five legible copies of a typescript using carbon paper ...'

Faster communication means more communication. Before the advent of electronic mail diplomats could spend days (sometimes weeks) assembling and polishing a despatch; today, however, even a small post might receive sixty official telegrams from the FCO and from other posts in a single day. The painstakingly slow craftsmanship of old nowadays looks like antique office practice.

In the days before email, the printing and circulation of despatches was bound by custom and some ceremony. Despatches which were considered to be important or of wider interest were accorded the honour of printing and a wide distribution, but they had to justify it. Custom, however, dictated that valedictories were printed unless there was a good reason why not. To some extent that limited the power Whitehall had to suppress the spread of contrary views from ambassadors in the field. But Whitehall could still exercise power over the distribution list. Ambassadors would hope to see their despatches printed as Diplomatic Reports. Here the printers would typeset the document and run off several hundred copies on best green paper, to be distributed far and wide. Less favoured valedictories were printed and distributed in what was known as the Departmental Series – a despatch about, say, Brazil would go to other diplomats in the South American department and others with a stated interest in the region. And some valedictories were never printed at all, merely filed away. But not most. Andrew Bryson and I have been surprised at the polite ceremony afforded to a number of astonishingly indiscreet – sometimes plain insulting – valedictories. I have to admit that in putting this collection together, hilarious indiscretion has been, for me, the most fun.

We laughed (as most of our radio series's audience laughed) at the valedictory from a British High Commissioner departing Canada (p. 101), who remarked that 'the calibre of Canadian politicians is low. The majority of Canadian ministers are unimpressive and a few we have found frankly bizarre . . . Anyone who is even moderately good at what they do . . . tends to become a national figure . . . and given the Order of Canada at once.' Not everyone in Canada laughed, however, where the broadcast caused a minor storm, with Canadian columnists manning the barricades on both sides of the argument. Indeed the publication of newspaper commentaries forcefully and eloquently taking the High Commissioner's side went some way (in my view) to proving him wrong. The spirit of self-criticism, and the energy of the debate, showed a less parochial Canada than his own valedictory had suggested.

I will not spoil for you the valedictory from our man in Bangkok, beyond reporting that its broadcast in 2009 forced his present-day successor, a generation later, to issue a statement dissociating himself and HMG from the ambassador's predecessor's remarks.

In Nigeria it seems there were no repercussions following our quotation of a valedictory from Lagos in which our departing ambassador wrote that Nigerians had a 'maddening habit of always choosing the course of action which will do the maximum damage to their own interests. They are not singular in this: Africans as a whole are not only not averse to cutting off their nose to spite their face; they regard such an operation as a triumph of cosmetic surgery.'

I could quote for ever ('There is, I fear, no question but that the average Nicaraguan is one of the most dishonest, unreliable, violent and alcoholic of the Latin Americans . . .') but, instead, why not read on? It is in Chapter 1 that the bulk of these 'poking fun at foreigners' discoveries will be found. Modern readers may perceive racism, or at least a rather unkind tendency to resort to national stereotypes, but it should be remembered that standards were very different in earlier decades.

And, as Chapter 4 ('Friendly Fire') shows, British diplomats abroad were not scared of turning their critical gaze back in the direction of home as well as on the natives abroad. As Sir Nicholas Henderson, author of arguably the most famous of valedictories, put it, 'A representative abroad has a duty to draw the attention of the authorities at home to the realities of how we look.' Diplomats get a privileged vantage point from which to see ourselves as others see us, and, as Andrew Bryson describes in Notes on the Material, Foreign Office records from the 1960s and 1970s provided the richest seam for this collection. It was a period when a British Chancellor of the Exchequer had to go 'cap in hand', as the contemporary cliché had it, to the IMF for financial aid. These despatches reflect the preoccupations of that time – a sense of loss of national prestige, and in the background a nostalgia for the days when a British ambassador had real clout. Our diplomats abroad were remorseless in their reports of how our own country's standing, if not the affection felt for it by many foreigners, had fallen as a result of economic difficulties.

Regularly in the despatches you will see self-doubt. But you will also detect an underlying and defiant pride: a sense that even if we and others had temporarily lost sight of the fact, Britain was still, after everything, Great.

A theme we explore in Chapter 8 ('The Sun Sets on Empire') is decolonization. The empire was recent history, if history at all – some despatches contain accounts of Britain's withdrawal from far-flung colonies even in the late 1970s. The Foreign Office was deeply and directly affected by these events; it was subject to various reviews – Duncan, Berrill, Plowden – designed to trim its scope and budget accordingly, and the bruises felt show repeatedly in valedictories of the time. Indeed the arrival of management consultancy (see Chapter 2) becomes a recurring and increasingly enraged theme. The diplomats know their world is changing, and their role changing, yet they cannot help bridling at its passing.

Readers will often sympathize – I do – but resistance to the measurement of performance can sometimes be self-serving. Nor can the FCO be accused of racing ahead of the times. It is said that when the Churchill War Rooms underneath the Treasury were opened to the public as a museum in 1984 all the curators had to do to fit it out with authentic 1940s furniture was stroll across King Charles Street into the Foreign Office and borrow some of the vintage stock still in everyday use there. As for the office furniture, so for some of the furniture of diplomatic minds and procedures.

But all have been changing, including the attitudes. If not (by the standards of their times) racism, then paternalism is certainly apparent in many of the older despatches. But readers may feel, as I do, that this was benign. Despatches are imbued with a touching concern, particularly for former colonies, a watchfulness for the development of good government in the nation which has been their temporary home-from-home, and a real anguish when things seem to be going wrong.

More than anything, I think you will detect a strong sense of public service running through this book, particularly through despatches written at the end of a long career. The belief in national duty is a sentiment sometimes shyly articulated by diplomats, almost apologetically, as if adhering to an old creed. Some of this is movingly expressed.

Indeed it's often been moving, but at other times depressing, occasionally shocking – but mostly fun – to retrieve and read these yellowing documents. From their pages leap sometimes grumpy, sometimes comical, sometimes prophetic individuals – none of whom, when they wrote, can have had the least idea that their letter to the Foreign Secretary would, one day, be broadcast, and now, in this book, published in print.

There is no need here to take the reader through our chapter headings – they are self-explanatory – or our organization of the material, which is self-evident. Chapter 1, within which we have tried to corral some of the best examples of ambassadors lashing out merrily at the characteristics, conditions and foibles of the nation to which they've been posted, needs no introduction beyond this: within it, we've divided the planet roughly into the four quarters of the compass.

To each of the succeeding chapters I've penned a short introduction to its field. But it's worth conceding that there's a degree of randomness in our attempt to corral valedictories into fields, as they were by their very nature wide-ranging. A large part of this collection could really have been placed in a single chapter, entitled 'And Another Thing . . .' Occasionally we've put part of a despatch in one chapter, another part in a different one; occasionally we've allowed a despatch to ramble off into territory that really belongs elsewhere.

And we have condensed, sometimes brutally, often by excising huge chunks, and bridging with ellipses. For our brutality we apologize to the authors of some of these valedictories, or to their shades. The abbreviating process can make tracts read in a rather summary or jerky way, so some of the non sequiturs or apparently arbitrary pronouncements you'll find in this book are the editors' and not the authors' fault – but we wanted to save our readers wading through material which time has rendered dull, or too narrowly specific.

Whatever the subject-heading, what almost every valedictory shares, from the flippant or comical to the profound, is a wish to make an impression. For many, this was the Big One; for a few it was a bid for fame; for many, too, it was a chance to blow their own trumpet – a final toot, though the tooting is often extremely subtly done. For some it really was an angry or aggrieved parting shot; for others an apologia for those things they ought to have done which they had not done; or ought not to have done which they had. For almost all the valedictory was written in hopes of raising a cheer, a boo, or at least an eyebrow around the Office.

Many of the valedictories we encountered are notable for

their erudition – quoting widely: from a fifth-century Bishop of London to Aristotle's *Nichomachean Ethics*. And there is a good deal of poetry too – where else in a civil service career did one get the chance?

These essays were often very well written: the best British diplomats (and some of the worst) were writing for an audience that would judge style as well as content: it was in part a cultural exercise.

As to their success, you may share the editors' opinion that this collection displays some sharp variations in the calibre of the writer, and of his or her mind. Many of these valedictories are simply magnificent; a few are magnificently pompous; not a few are magnificently wrong and just as many proved magnificently right; but sometimes ambassadors tried too hard, obviously feeling they were expected to push the boat out stylistically for their career-defining final despatch. You can occasionally sense a diplomat moving beyond his comfort zone – and the bounds of his intellectual or stylistic ability.

Not every ambassador submitted a valedictory: the practice was entirely voluntary. Here, in what might be called a valedictory blog (blog-edictory or vale-blog? Foreign Office classicists, of which there were many, would incline to the second), is our erstwhile man in Freetown, Derek Partridge, explaining (in June 2009) why he never wrote a proper valedictory. His blog was prompted by the online posting by another former ambassador, Brian Barder, of his own 1991 valedictory (p. 281) complaining that Africa and its needs had been 'downgraded' by the British government. Partridge agreed. 'I left Sierra Leone' (he blogs)

> on retirement in May 1991 having served five years as British High Commissioner. I did not submit a valedictory despatch.

My Annual Review for 1990, in which I had made the case for more assistance to Sierra Leone now that it was abandoning the one-party state constitution and moving to multi-party democracy, had not been submitted to Ministers. I was told that they were pre-occupied with Kuwait, and Sierra Leone had 'little priority'. What would be the point, therefore, in repeating those arguments in a valedictory despatch? I did in my final call on Lynda Chalker [then Minister of State for Overseas Development] complain at the paucity of aid to Sierra Leone while I knew that we had been content to let Kenya misapply £200 million. I was told that steps were being taken in respect of Kenya. When I paid my valedictory call on Douglas Hurd [then Foreign Secretary] he said that he under-stood that I thought we should be giving more help to Sierra Leone. He would expect a good High Commissioner to think that. Would I tell him why? I did so. It clearly made no impact. I was speaking to a closed mind. My final report on leaving the Service, I was officially told, was that I had done a good job but because I had spent so long in Sierra Leone I had exaggerated the British interest there . . .

Not many years later, HMG found itself sending troops to Sierra Leone.

At the FCO they have a term for that notion – that one has 'spent too long' in a place. They call it 'going native'. Only in one particular area of diplomacy and geography is the vice widely indulged, if teasingly, by the Office. 'The Arabists', as they are known by Whitehall – or, more affectionately, 'the Camel Corps' – are a distinct cadre of British diplomat (see Chapter 5). People are proud to be Arabists.

Otherwise, 'he's gone native' is a sneering charge, and, often enough it isn't until an ambassador comes to write the final valedictory that he dares to acknowledge that there has been any question mark about his objectivity, and to answer back. Time and again the valedictory will explain why its author believes Britain should strengthen its relations with the country he is leaving, and try to understand – even sympathize – more. Time and again an ambassador will exhort ministers not to 'take for granted' the goodwill and cordial relations between Britain and, say, Burundi – even though a dispassionate observer in Whitehall, juggling a myriad of competing and superior priorities, may question the proportionality of that response.

It is hard, of course, not to become seized of the needs and concerns of a foreign nation when sent there to represent HMG, and easy to exaggerate the extent of the British interest in the country's fate. But cool heads (or cold hearts) back in London are quick to spot the edge of the slippery slope to 'going native' – which can end (and, in the British Diplomatic Service, remarkably often does) in marrying a native. We asked Sir Andrew Green (see Chapter 2) whether he had gone native in Saudi Arabia. 'I think there's a very important difference,' he replied, 'between taking a country's point of view and understanding their view . . . If you go native you're finished, but if you don't understand the natives you're useless . . .'

Sir Harold Nicolson, in *Diplomacy* (his classic 1939 manual for the profession), remarks that 'the worst kind of diplomatists are missionaries, fanatics and lawyers; the best kind are reasonable and humane sceptics'. I would add that the best kind of sceptics are indeed reasonable and humane; the worst kind (and the FCO is not without examples) are aloof, dismissive and blinkered by a notion of the national interest that can be self-defeatingly narrow and short-term. The knee-jerk Whitehall response, 'gone native', can be less clever than it sounds. This collection of valedictories offers an antidote.

But there's one despatch we never found: the despatch that helped tip me, finally, and two years after joining after Cambridge and Yale, into resignation from the Foreign Office.

Our man in (I'm almost, but not totally, certain) Reykjavik, quitting as HM Ambassador to Iceland and also retiring, commented bitterly that, looking back over a long Diplomatic Service career, he reckoned he'd given key advice to HMG at perhaps half a dozen or more critical moments. And reviewing the advice he had given, he reckoned he'd been, in retrospect, right in about three quarters of those cases, and wrong in the rest.

But nobody else had ever conducted this review, he wrote, sadly – and nobody ever would. He didn't believe anybody in London had ever checked, later, to see when he'd been right and when he'd been wrong. By the time anyone was in a position to judge, everyone had moved on; many were in different jobs; and it was all water under the bridge. Nobody noticed and nobody cared. Advancement in the FCO, he implied, was largely unrelated to the quality of an officer's decisions or the long-term wisdom of his advice.

To a degree, I think that ambassador was right. But our study of hundreds of valedictories suggests that, in headline cases at least, there was awareness within the Office when the judgement-calls of senior colleagues had gone seriously well or seriously awry after the event. As you will sense from many valedictories collected here, ambassadors would be expected when they quit a post to make predictions about the future – who among the country's politicians should be cultivated, who was likely to endure, who fade, who be shot. In unstable regimes such advice was particularly useful. Diplomats willing to stick their necks out and make concrete predictions in their valedictory were admired for it, but risked being proved wrong.

Some were. We give examples in this book. Not included, however, were the remarks of our ambassador to Malawi, Sir Robin Haydon, who played it almost risibly safe when he said of the then Leader in 1973: 'President Banda could, I believe, go on for as long as he lives or he could be assassinated tomorrow (nice easy non-prediction in a valedictory despatch – but the truth!).' Banda in fact did go on: ruling until 1994, dying, peacefully, in 1997.

Others simply threw up their hands and admitted the impossibility of the exercise: 'Our visitors usually ask, in decent circumlocutions, when the Bahrain revolution will break out. The reply is that the revolution is not due for a year anyway and probably not for two: they should ask again next year, when they can expect much the same answer.' – Alexander Stirling, Ambassador to Bahrain, 1972.

To what, then, if not always for their forecasting skills, was advancement related? That valedictory from Reykjavik did not (to the best of my recollection) go on to say what as a young desk officer I was beginning to suspect: that communicating in the right way, in the right voice, with the right people, in the right order of precedence, was often more important than the objective truth or wisdom of what you communicated.

I can still recall the raised eyebrows and gentle admonition that followed my pinning together a sheaf of documents for internal use, in a manner that left the sharp end of the pin protruding from the top folio. In the FCO, I was advised, you never, ever, used a paperclip: only in the Department of Health and Social Security were such things even glimpsed. Ideally you used (for longer sheaves) a 'green Treasury Tag' (a length of green wool with a metal end-stop at each end) or (for shorter sheaves) a 'red India tag'. *In extremis* ('if you're desperate' is not the way they put things at the FCO) one might indeed use a pin: but it should be placed in the top left-hand corner of the sheaf, aligned at forty-five degrees to the horizontal, proceed from the top folio to the ultimate folio, re-penetrate the ultimate folio, and end its passage with its sharp end safely sheathed between the penultimate and the ultimate folio – lest any senior officer or (God forbid) minister – should run the risk of pricking their fingers when handling the documents.

I exaggerate but do not entirely misrepresent the picture when I say that, in the 1970s at least, questions like this, of presentation, were at least as important as whether the advice contained in the document was in fact sound. You will find within (p. 231) a valedictory from our man in Tehran, freely confessing that he got the most important judgement that his job required him to offer, wholly and disastrously wrong. He went on, no doubt deservedly, to higher things.

No doubt deservedly, I did not – and ended up outside the walls of Whitehall, as a clerk to Margaret Thatcher instead. But I've never forgotten that first valedictory I read from Oslo; and Andrew and I hope you'll find some of what we've subsequently uncovered memorable too.

Matthew Parris
Derbyshire
July 2010

1. Diplomacy as Caricature

Part I: NORTH

Austria

'The average modern Austrian only thinks about his Schnitzel'

SIR ANTHONY RUMBOLD,
HM AMBASSADOR TO AUSTRIA, APRIL 1970

Sir Anthony Rumbold was a diplomat of the old school; aristocratic (the 10th Rumbold, Bt) and patrician. Judging by his valedictories he took an often dim view of foreigners. Diplomacy was in his blood – in Austria he followed in the steps of his grandfather, the 8th Rumbold, Bt, who had joined the embassy in Vienna under Queen Victoria. Sir Anthony's father, Horace Rumbold, was ambassador in Berlin when Hitler came to power. Anthony Rumbold's own career took him to Thailand (see p. 71) as well as Austria. He found the Austrian capital a 'rather sad and mean' place. 'There is no longer much raison d'être *about Vienna,' he wrote, in his first despatch back to the Foreign Office. 'To the small extent that it still exhibits a smiling countenance it is . . . because it no longer has any muscles in its face.'*

. . . [M]ost Austrians have become steadily and uninterrupt-edly better off . . . One would have expected their success to have strengthened their patriotism and their self-confidence. But it has hardly had any such effect. On the contrary, the Austrians still talk about their country in a deprecating way. The fact of being Austrian does not particularly stir them. It is only when ski-championships are involved that they show the slightest signs of chauvinism. They do not know the words of their national anthem. Their attachments have become more and more local and the interests increasingly private . . . I am afraid that the average modern Austrian only thinks about his Schnitzel and his annual holiday . . .

. . . And in addition to the normal sources of human discontent there are one or two specifically Austrian ones. One is the obsessive preoccupation of the Austrians with questions of professional and social distinction. Very few of them are genuine egalitarians. They are always uneasy about whether they are being treated with proper respect by those whom they regard as their inferiors and they fuss endlessly about questions of precedence and correct forms of address. The result is that many of them live in a state of perpetual frustration or offence. Nearly every Austrian would like to be either a professor or the president of some recognizable institution so as to be called Herr Professor or Herr Präsident. If he is a civil servant he aspires to be a Ministerialrat [senior ministerial advisor] or a Hofrat [privy councillor] (this in a country where there is obviously no court and where in theory it is a penal offence for a man to call himself even 'von'). The disease is universal. It affects waiters and street cleaners no less than academics, politicians and industrial leaders. It is smarter, though often less lucrative, to be an employee (*Angestellter*) than to be a worker (*Arbeiter*). There is nothing new in all this. Trotsky was flabbergasted when he came to Vienna to find that Viktor Adler[1] was referred to as Comrade Herr Doktor.

1. *Viktor Adler*: The father of Austrian socialism. Once a medical practitioner, he turned to egalitarian politics shortly before the First World War after witnessing the poverty in the slums of Vienna.

~

The Netherlands

'A tough inner core'

SIR PETER GARRAN, HM AMBASSADOR
TO THE NETHERLANDS, JANUARY 1970

The Dutch are a complex people. Their thought processes and reactions are not always easy to fathom, either for us or for themselves. There is an odd mixture in their make-up of directness and occasional inscrutability, of hard-headedness and emotionalism. They love discussing among themselves how complex and complicated they are and, when a former Spanish ambassador, the Duke of Baena, wrote a rather inferior book about Holland called *The Dutch Puzzle*, the Dutch – most of them – lapped it up. For me, part of the explanation is that the Dutch have a sensitive outer skin and a tough inner core. The complexities and complications are in the outer skin. But the important thing is the tough, sound inner core. That is what makes them such splendid friends and allies. But we must remember the sensitive outer skin and expect difficulties from time to time because of it.

~

Iceland

'They are not a comfortable people to handle'

AUBREY HALFORD-MCLEOD, HM AMBASSADOR
TO ICELAND, AUGUST 1970

CONFIDENTIAL

BRITISH EMBASSY
REYKJAVIK
12 August 1970

Sir,

In preparing this, my final despatch from Reykjavik, I have
had to scrap several drafts and in doing so I have reluctantly
reached the conclusion that this exercise in itself sums up far
better than any words of mine could describe the nature of the
major problem facing one of H.M. Ambassadors to Iceland
(and probably those in other small countries also). There is so
much to say; there is so little likelihood that anyone in London
will have the time to read even the little that he says . . .

The first comment I venture to make concerns the
relative importance of Iceland to us. I believe that the
Office's computer rates Iceland in the same bracket as
Ethiopia and Malawi . . . [W]e take so little trouble about
Iceland because we believe that she has no choice but to be
on our side. This I submit is a very mistaken view.

There is a great reservoir of goodwill towards Britain in
Iceland, fed by decades of personal contacts and commercial
exchanges. Like all reservoirs, however, in the highly
competitive world of today, this reservoir needs topping up
frequently . . . It is true that, alongside their many positive
sterling virtues, [Icelanders] suffer from strong xenophobic

tendencies, are grasping and opportunist, unjustifiably conceited and ashamedly suppliant in the same breath. They are not a comfortable people to handle and there is probably little we can do to change them. But insofar as we need them at all, we can and should, as a major power with the ambitions and capability to influence world affairs, be ready to meet Icelanders rather more than half way. To paraphrase Guicciardini; it is to be expected that a great prince should treat his lesser allies more generously than they him.

Let us examine for a moment our attitudes towards Icelanders. The general public in Britain still labours under the Eskimo/polar bear image . . . The attitude of [Whitehall] would generally seem to be one of indifference . . . I cannot escape the impression that the British official attitude has always been grudging and ungracious . . . The Americans, Germans and French . . . are actively cultivating their links with Iceland and seeking to increase their stake in the country. But so also are the Russians and the other Eastern Europeans. I submit that as Iceland's nearest neighbour and one of her major trading partners we should be something more than spectators . . .

If, as may well be objected, the foregoing picture of Anglo-Icelandic relations seems unnecessarily gloomy, I would reply that during my service in Reykjavik I have received very little positive guidance to assist me in trying to brighten it. I should have welcomed much more overt support from London. As some of my senior colleagues now leaving the Service have remarked, it is not sufficient that H.M. Ambassadors should enjoy the confidence of H.M. Government; it is also necessary that they should be seen to enjoy it.

∾

Switzerland

'Pharisaical self-satisfaction'

HENRY HOHLER, HM AMBASSADOR TO
SWITZERLAND, APRIL 1970

CONFIDENTIAL

BERNE,
20 April, 1970

Sir,

In a despatch which I had the honour to address to you on
7 October, 1969, I have attempted to compare the Swiss of
today with the Swiss as I had first known them more than
20 years ago. I concluded that, although the Swiss had
become richer and more sophisticated, their national
character had remained basically unchanged, as indeed it
had through the centuries. They have created a modern
industrial State, despite their lack of natural resources and,
with the lamentable exception of Lausanne, they have done
this without destroying the charm of their cities or the
marvellous beauty of their land. Nevertheless, the Swiss
have their problems and the *malaise suisse* reflects a conflict
between pharisaical self-satisfaction and an uneasy
awareness that their well-being is at the mercy of forces
which they cannot control. Until comparatively recently
Switzerland has been a poor country and the Swiss have
remained thrifty and hard-working, even though these
qualities may not be as essential as they once were.

The Swiss attach great importance to getting good value
for their money. Twice a week the square in the centre of

Berne, enclosed by four banks and the Parliament building, is bright with the stalls of the peasants who have come in from the neighbouring villages to sell their produce and there you will meet everybody from the wives of the Federal Councillors downwards doing their own shopping. The Swiss are often generous to their friends and munificent patrons of the arts, but their poverty-stricken past comes out in funny little economies and even meannesses. A Swiss politician, who lives on the Lake of Morat, told me he had been horrified by the way the peasants behaved to each other and these, after all, were rich peasants who did not have to split pfennigs. Many Swiss get to their offices at 7 a.m. and it is not until 6.30 p.m. that you have the rush-hour in a Swiss town. People wish you a pleasant Sunday, not a pleasant week-end. Even if your friend from Geneva comes to Berne for dinner and spends the night, he will catch the 6.43 a.m. train, so as not to arrive too late at his work. It took a week to pack up my effects when I left London; it has just taken the Swiss packers three days to do the same job.

∼

'The Swiss love regulating each other'

ERIC MIDGLEY, HM AMBASSADOR TO SWITZERLAND,
FEBRUARY 1973

(CONFIDENTIAL)   *Berne,*
                                              26 February, 1973

Sir,

A despatch bidding farewell to the stable, deeply rooted Swiss is likely to read much like the first impressions of one's predecessor but two . . .

. . . Political institutions reflect a state of general stability
. . . The Federal Councillors are . . . as much civil servants as
they are Ministers and their style is befittingly modest. A
day or two ago, for instance, after I had taken my final leave
of the President outside his office, he climbed into an old
Volkswagen and waved me away ahead in the Rolls.

At the lower level, Swiss institutions may seem excessively
authoritarian. The police are tough. Suspects go straight
into solitary confinement for questioning . . . Up till recently
[unmarried] cohabitation in Zurich was a criminal offence
and still is so in some cantons when it is shown to be a
cause for scandal. The Swiss love regulating each other. On
missing a traffic sign you may find yourself stopped, not at
all in anger, and given a moral lecture 'to make sure you
don't do it again'. I recall with some whimsical pleasure the
occasion when, after ditching my car in the snow and
bursting into a small café to telephone for help I was sent
back to wipe my feet and shut the door . . .

. . . Swiss attitudes are moulded by Swiss institutions and
if these often inhibit they also foster and protect, abroad as
well as at home. Citizenship is primarily citizenship of the
commune and the population of the average commune is
16,000. The scene is parochial. 'Diplomats are not allowed
to reside in our commune,' said a friend who lives in one of
the Berne suburbs. There are picturesque ancient privileges.
I sometimes meet a respectable Swiss gentleman drawing a
small cart full of logs out of the wood which surrounds my
house. He is a member of the Bourgeoisie of Berne exercising
his right to cut down one tree every year.

~

'Neither the prettiest of people, nor the wittiest'

DAVID MCCANN, AIR ATTACHÉ, SWITZERLAND,
APRIL 1978

Air Attachés represent the Royal Air Force overseas, 'attached' to diplomatic missions. During his stint at the British Embassy in Berne, Wing Commander McCann was also expected to drum up arms sales.

. . . [I]n many ways the Swiss are an unattractive lot. They are neither the prettiest of people, nor the wittiest, and the German dialects most of them speak are among the most cacophonous of languages. Life is as serious a business in the highly affluent Switzerland of today as it was no doubt in the mountain communities from which the country originated.

The best Swiss qualities – their integrity, for example, and their conscientiousness, zeal, thrift and self-discipline – are more likely to attract admiration in foreigners, or even envy, than affection. Their parsimony is a byword; it was entirely in character that, when I arrived at the hospital with my wife in labour, we were first asked for the Sfr700 [about £400 today] deposit, before any medical attention was contemplated! However, one soon forgets these general faults when, in time, individual Swiss accept one into their homes and into their hearts . . .

One of the first things that strikes one about the Swiss is how industrious they are, and professional in the best sense; they tend to be perfectionists. Their working hours are the longest in Europe; even parliament begins sitting at 8 a.m. But when it comes to national defence – and, to a certain extent, to politics – the 'professional' approach is dropped and anyone can participate. Indeed they must, if they are fit and male, because service in the militia army is compulsory . . . However, the Army itself, and the few who follow a full career in it, are not held in high esteem. Although some officers are undoubtedly able, others who reach the top ranks would never progress so far in most other armies, let alone in other branches of Swiss life. Swiss 'generals' have a disconcerting habit of not looking like generals, perhaps because they have so little opportunity to behave as such. Swiss soldiers, sadly, are the scruffiest in Europe.

~

Finland

'Flat, freezing, and far from the pulsating centres of European life'

SIR BERNARD LEDWIDGE, HM AMBASSADOR
TO FINLAND, OCTOBER 1972

The letter of thanks from the Head of Department that a valedictory may trigger (often the last official word an ambassador would receive before retirement) ranges from the perfunctory, to the polite, to the genuinely admiring. This last is well illustrated by the note placed on the file quoted below, reading: 'I always expected – and my Department has been taught to expect – a certain stamp of the first-class from Helsinki. Your last despatch was no exception; indeed, I found it a splendid crystallisation of impressions and thoughts. We shall miss the Ledwidge style!'

Finland was Ledwidge's penultimate diplomatic post. Upon leaving Helsinki he was made Ambassador to Israel, which one imagines he found an altogether warmer and more exciting prospect.

(CONFIDENTIAL)

Helsinki,

19 October, 1972

Sir,

It could plausibly be argued that it is a misfortune for anybody but a Finn to spend three years in Finland, as I have just done. Even the Finns who can afford it are happy to make frequent escapes to sunnier climes. Finland is flat, freezing, and far from the pulsating centres of European life. Nature has done little for her and art not much more. Until yesterday the country was inhabited only by peasants, foresters, fishermen and a small class of alien rulers who spent most of their money elsewhere. The rich cultural past of Europe has left fewer traces in Finland in the shape of public and private buildings of quality and the objects of art which adorn them than anywhere else in the Western world save perhaps Iceland. Finnish cooking deserves a sentence to itself for its crude horror; only the mushrooms and the crayfish merit attention.

I came to all this after four sybaritic years in Paris; and I have at times turned with a new sense of fellow feeling to the odes of lamentation which Ovid addressed from Tomi to his friends in Rome. Yet it will be with a distinct sentiment of nostalgia that I shall leave Finland this evening for Israel . . . I have come to appreciate the rare beauty of this remote land, to like its inhabitants, and to admire what they have made of their meagre inheritance since they achieved independence in 1917 . . .

Finland today is of course subject to the same social pressures as other Welfare [Socialist] States, but she suffers from them in a less marked degree than most. The climate and the proximity of the Russians are both factors which, in their different ways, impose realism and discourage extravagant visions of what life can and should offer to the individual citizen. Moreover the Finns have a cohesion which is tribal rather than national. Their unique environment and their unique language set them apart. They feel at home nowhere else in the world. I referred . . . to the rich who enjoy holidays in sunnier climes. They do, but they always come home again; and Finnish women married to foreigners often persuade them to come back and live here. The charm of Finland is difficult to define, but it exists. Some of it certainly lies in the natural surroundings. The broad horizons; the countless islands dotting the Baltic coast; the expanses of nearly empty lake and forest; the ice and snow which prove to be so varied in colour and contour throughout the long winter, all these make their strong appeal to the Finn; and now they appeal to me too.

～

'It is a full time job trying to get to know the Finns'

THOMAS ELLIOT, HM AMBASSADOR TO FINLAND,
SEPTEMBER 1975

(CONFIDENTIAL)

Sir,

Helsinki,
15 September, 1975

President Kekkonen, when I first called on him to present my credentials, was kind enough to inform me that the first British Ambassador to Finland had been murdered . . .

[H]e implied that I should deserve not much less savage treatment if I did not apply myself to learning about the peculiar Finnish attitude to politics and to life, and instead took Finland for granted . . .

. . . I have come to realise that there was a serious point behind President Kekkonen's typically paradoxical warning . . . It is a full time job trying to get to know the Finns. The least arrogant or ostentatious of peoples, they have a self-sufficient reserve that the foreigner cannot easily penetrate. When confronted by what is unexpected or unfamiliar, as well as by the unreasonable, they take refuge behind the barriers of silence or (what is much the same to most people) the use of their language. (Though they make a show of pleasure when foreigners start the daunting task of learning Finnish, they also convey the impression that you may be wasting your time, as well as a little presumptuous, in trying to break their own private code.) It would be right to conclude that all this makes them elusive; but it also gives them as a people an admirable strength.

. . . [M]uch in the Finnish national character can be explained by the fact that they have been traditionally hunters in the forests, not agricultural people. In their wild corner of Europe they survived by lying low and keeping their heads down – while preparing beautifully designed traps for the unwary. (For a time in 1939–40 the technique worked particularly well with the Russians.) . . . [T]he habits and interests acquired in the forests still mean much to many people. Any Finn, no matter how taciturn, will thaw a little if he gets a chance to talk of saunas or fishing or hunting game or collecting berries or even mushrooms. And any Finn, no matter how industrious, will pounce on the first excuse for a holiday and make his way to his country cottage where, as far away from anyone else as possible and as untroubled as

possible by any modern convenience, he will restore his
energies by living a forest life as his ancestors did.

~

Germany

'They almost appear to be blaming us for their losses'

SIR NICHOLAS HENDERSON, HM AMBASSADOR TO THE
FEDERAL REPUBLIC OF GERMANY, AUGUST 1975

*For a British diplomat chasing the top jobs, the embassy at
Berlin (or Bonn, before reunification) came second only to
Washington and Paris. But despite decades of profitable
peace, Anglo-German relations toil today, as they toiled when
this despatch was written, under the weight of memory of
two episodes of total war. Diplomats posted to Bonn or Berlin
were never short of a theme for their valedictory.*

*Sir Nicholas Henderson's 1979 valedictory from Paris (p. 200)
is justly famous as a courageous alarm call that Britain was
falling behind her competitors in Europe and had only herself
to blame. Henderson's other valedictories from his previous
European posts are less well known, but pack a similar punch –
although with retirement still some way off, the ambassador
picks his targets more carefully.*

(CONFIDENTIAL)   *Bonn,*
                                          13 *August,* 1975
Sir,

THE BURDEN OF THE PAST

Thirty years after the end of World War Two the British still
have doubts and preoccupations about the Germans, more

so than about any other people, more so than do many other nations in the West.

There is, of course, a difference between generations. I am struck by how slowly the 'black record' dies, by how often I am asked by visitors from the UK of a certain age, whose business does not bring them into frequent contact with the Germans, whether there is not some lack of balance, and some deep-seated undemocratic, not to say brutal, streak in the Germans that makes them unlike others and of which we should beware. But it is not only the older generation in Britain. Those who are too young to have experienced the Nazis are encouraged by television films and comics to see all Germans as 'baddies'.

The Germans do not understand this. For a representative of Her Majesty's Government in the Federal Republic today it requires great, not to say gymnastic, efforts to try to bridge the gulf between the British people's lively remembrance of the past and the Germans' oblivion about it.

There is no European country that is so governed by its past as Germany, and none that seeks so strenuously to avoid it. To the modern German there are no national heroes, nobody to compare with Washington, Jefferson or Lincoln in the US; or Cromwell, Nelson or Churchill in the UK; or Joan of Arc, Napoleon or de Gaulle in France. Even Frederick the Great and Bismarck are seen mainly as Prussian figures, coming from a part of Germany that is not part of the Federal Republic. When you come to think about it, about the nature of Germany's recent past, there is really no paradox in this. But there is a certain obtuseness in the German attitude, and although I quite understand why they do not think, particularly the younger ones, that they should continue to suffer from guilt about what was done in Germany's name a generation ago, I think it insensitive of them not to realise the difficulties others have in forgetting it. One of my first experiences of this kind occurred soon after I had arrived here from Poland, when some German who, in other respects seemed understanding and aware, told me that he could not see why the Poles continued to bear a grudge against the Germans because the Germans felt no grievance towards the Poles. Likewise, I continue to be surprised by the number of Germans who criticise Herr Willy Brandt for having knelt at the ghetto in Warsaw, a gesture they regard as unnecessarily humiliating. Herr Brandt, perhaps because he has lived abroad more than most of his compatriots, does not appear to have the customary gap that separates the way the Germans see themselves from the way others see them, an airlock in their system that is largely responsible, I think, for our view about their humour.

Then I think it is difficult for the hackles of an Englishman to remain entirely horizontal when he hears, as he does quite often, a German spokesman exhorting others not to forget the lessons of the '30s. I remember Herr Scheel[1] when he was Foreign Minister criticising the idea of the French *force de frappe* as being a Maginot Line. More recently Herr Scheel, addressing the American Congress, said that 'totalitarianism may use arbitrary means, yet in the end freedom will triumph'. For those for whom the Nazi torch-lights still flicker in the mind's eye, it is a little difficult to take, from those who may have borne them in procession, warning about the dangers of the dark. It is a particular theme of Finance Minister Apel's to say that he and his generation feel no responsibility for the war and are not prepared to fork out money now under pressure of guilt. That is all right, but Herr Apel himself does not seem to realise the effect it has when he starts to criticise something, as I have heard him doing, as being a 'Munich'. Of course Herr Apel, aged 43, represents the new Germany whose attitude toward the past differs from that of their elders: the latter try to ignore it; the young dismiss it as none of their business.

I also have been surprised in talking to Germans from different walks of life and of varying ages, how relatively little admiration there is for Stauffenberg[2] and others who resisted the Nazis. When I said to the wife of a very senior German official who had mentioned the horrors of the Nazi time that I assumed that for her and other like-minded Germans, Stauffenberg must be a heroic figure the answer I got was 'No, he tried to undermine his country in a moment of dire need.' Of course, this is not a universal attitude, and certainly among the young there would be admiration for those who had sacrificed their lives in trying to overthrow Hitler, but they are not national heroes by any means. In this same vein, I should also mention how often Germans refer to the sacrifices they have had to make since 1945, *i.e.* in particular, the loss of territory in the East, as being due to the fact that they lost the war, rather than to the fact that they caused it. They almost appear to be blaming us for their losses.

1. *Herr Scheel*: Walter Scheel, President of the Federal Republic of Germany, 1974–9. Like a sizeable minority of Germans of his generation, Scheel was once a member of the Nazi Party. So was his successor as President, Karl Carstens.
2. *Stauffenberg*: Claus Von Stauffenberg, leader of the failed 1944 plot to assassinate Hitler with a briefcase bomb.

∽

'Seriousness, thoroughness, humourlessness,
perfectionism and pedantry'

SIR JULIAN BULLARD, HM AMBASSADOR TO THE FEDERAL
REPUBLIC OF GERMANY, MARCH 1988

*Julian Bullard was the last British Ambassador to divided
Germany; the Berlin Wall fell the year after he retired. It was
not the first time in his career that his lot had been to face
down a Communist regime. As head of the East European and
Soviet Department, Bullard had overseen the very public
expulsion of 105 Soviet KGB agents from London. A further
extract from this despatch is on p. 123.*

BRITISH EMBASSY BONN

7 March 1988

The Rt Hon Sir Geoffrey Howe QC MP
Secretary of State for Foreign and Commonwealth Affairs
Foreign and Commonwealth Office
London SW1A 2AH

Sir,

TAKE TROUBLE WITH GERMANY

I have the honour to send you my thoughts on leaving the
Federal Republic of Germany after 3 periods of service at
Bonn spread over 25 years.

Introduction
It used to be said that the Federal Republic was a country
where the Government worked badly and the economy well,
and where the first knew better than to interfere with the
second. In the last year or two the Government in Bonn has
at times worked so badly as to cause serious qualms at

home and abroad, while many doubt whether the economy is as well equipped for the 1990s as it showed itself to be in the 1960s and 70s. Does this matter? I think it does, because the health of Germany matters to Britain, and because I believe the Federal Republic to be a less stable and less 'normal' country than may appear at first sight.

Constants

Certain constants have operated here throughout my time. There are the regional differences, which become more evident as one learns to recognise the surnames, accents and facial characteristics which go with certain attitudes of mind. But I think it is still possible to talk of German national characteristics, and one of these is the seriousness, thoroughness, humourlessness, perfectionism and pedantry which have made the German the butt of so many anecdotes. (To quote a true one, the artist Philip Ernst painted the view from his window, leaving out a tree which spoiled the design: that night he was attacked by remorse, got up from bed – and cut down the tree.) 'Ordnung' has a high status here, and to some Germans the rule of law seems to mean more than the rule of conscience.

On top of this comes patriotism, but of a peculiar kind. It attaches itself unhesitatingly to German sporting champions, but begins to have misgivings at the sight or sound of anything that echoes the Third Reich. An influential book of 1987 called *Die verletzte Nation* ('The wounded Nation') showed how especially younger Germans recoil from what in other countries are self-evident propositions about loyalty to the State. This is one of the reasons why even some of our best friends in Bonn found it hard to understand the Falklands episode.

The other main constant is the structure of the Federal Republic, in the form given it by the victorious allies and

German constitutional lawyers. 'Designed to be inefficient', this system has been called, and the brakes built into it are indeed powerful. In a federation, and with proportional representation, elections come round at an average rate of 3 a year, and more often than not they produce coalitions. Another check on policy is the apparatus of administrative and constitutional courts which can block, perhaps for months on end, anything from American chemical weapons to a plan to build a test-track for Mercedes cars. These checks and balances seemed to do Germany no harm during the years of the economic miracle: indeed they were thought to promote the consensus on which that was based. But in recent years it has been clear that difficult decisions would be taken and put into effect more quickly if there were not so many in-built ways of holding them up.

Special Factors
Two things are special about the Federal Republic. The first and more obvious is that we have here a state not co-terminous with the nation which lives in it. In saying this I have in mind not only the 17 million Germans in the GDR, but also the German communities in the Soviet Union and in every East European country except Bulgaria, numbering perhaps another 4 million altogether . . .

The second and less obvious peculiarity of the Federal Republic is that it rests on a crust of history only 40 years thick, beneath which a hot fire can still burn. We saw this over President Reagan's visit to Bitburg[1] in 1985, and we are starting to see it now as journalists look for parallels between the cases of President Waldheim and von Weizsäcker.[2] Herr Werner Höfer,[3] a kind of German Sir Robin Day, lost his post in 1987 when a magazine reprinted something he had written in 1943. The Historians' Debate of 1986/87, which was about the historical context in which Hitler's crimes should be seen, has given way to a Philosophers' Debate about how much of a Nazi Heidegger was. I have known Germans shy away from statistics on handicapped children, from boarding schools and even from an auditorium holding 2000 people, simply because of their historical echoes. Earlier and safer periods of German history are studied with interest, but not with anything like the emotional bond which unites so many people in Britain with the nation's past.

A corrective is needed here. Outside the province of the state, Germany is rich in traditions which go back a long way and do not seem to be uneconomic. In large country houses meals are still served by what are obviously family retainers in uniform, and I know one Schloss near Coburg which still sends the best tablecloths to be washed at a place in Holland where the water is thought to be specially soft. At the other end of the social scale, the fruit and vegetable market still brings the grower into direct touch with the buyer in the town square, and there seems to be no shortage of skilled manual craftsmen, whether it is a question of laying cobblestones in elegant fan patterns or of reducing a tree trunk to a squared baulk of timber in about 10 minutes. There is continuity too in the barracks built by Hitler which now house (among other things) Ministries, Universities and an Agricultural Research Institute near Brunswick – where incidentally the starting point for today's research into non-food crops was the work done by Hitler's scientists on import substitutes in the 1930s, in preparation for the Second World War and the inevitable allied blockade. It is the Federal Republic itself, not life inside it, that lacks history.

1. *Bitburg*: President Reagan accepted a German invitation to visit the Bitburg military cemetery as part of the events to commemorate the fortieth anniversary of VE Day. Then the White House realized that Waffen SS were among the 2,000 Nazi soldiers buried there. Reagan went ahead with the visit despite the controversy.

2. *von Weizsäcker*: Carl Friedrich von Weizsäcker worked on nuclear research for the Nazis under Werner Heisenberg in the 1940s. The Americans beat them to the secrets of chain reaction. After the war, the German physicists said this was a deliberate failure – they did not want the Nazis to be first to the atomic bomb.

3. *Herr Werner Höfer*: Höfer wrote an article in 1943 in support of the execution of the pianist Karlrobert Kreiten, who was hanged after a Gestapo informant overheard him criticizing Hitler. Höfer was forced to resign from Germany's equivalent of *Question Time* after *Der Spiegel* published the story.

~

'German television makes Des O'Connor look like alternative comedy'

SIR CHRISTOPHER MEYER, HM AMBASSADOR
TO GERMANY, OCTOBER 1997

When New Labour stormed to power in 1997 some diplomats found themselves out of step with the times. High-ranking diplomats had served Tory ministers for more than a decade, and enough of them lived up to the Foreign Office stereotype as public-school Telegraph *readers to kindle the suspicions of left-wing MPs on the back benches. The difference between the two sides was largely one of culture and outlook. In the lead-up to the election a group of nervous diplomats sought out Denis MacShane, who rose to become Minister for Europe under Tony Blair, to ask him what might be on the incoming Foreign Secretary Robin Cook's agenda. He told them to try reading the* Guardian.

But there were also deep policy differences; Labour orthodoxy in opposition was that the Foreign Office was guilty of supporting apartheid South Africa and of appeasing Serbian aggression in the former Yugoslavia. And a few diplomats did get the chop when Labour came to power. But the best of them were able to adapt to the changing political weather. Sir Christopher Meyer, recently appointed ambassador in Bonn, was New Labour's pick for Washington. In promoting Meyer to the most high-profile job in the service, Robin Cook was giving a huge vote of confidence in the Foreign Office's political neutrality; Meyer had once been press secretary to John Major. The ambassador repays the compliment in this valedictory, with a glowing account of the impact in Germany of Tony Blair's landslide election on 1 May 1997. The valedictory also makes reference to the victory in the French parliamentary elections a month later of another European Socialist, Lionel Jospin (Prime Minister of France, 1997– 2002.)

RESTRICTED

BRITISH EMBASSY BONN
10 October 1997

The Rt Hon Robin Cook QC MP
Secretary of State for Foreign and Commonwealth Affairs
Foreign and Commonwealth Office
London SW1A 2AH

Sir,

GERMANY: HELLO AND GOODBYE

As the shortest serving British Ambassador to Germany since the War, and probably ever, first and last impressions become one. I offer the Chief Clerk a new concept in value for money: the combined first and farewell call.

My time falls into two distinct parts: before 1 May and after 1 May. Labour's massive win has transformed Britain's position in Germany for the better. The job is to turn this into a long-term increase in British influence.

Before 1 May Britain was in German eyes a tiresome irritant. Kohl felt personally offended by the last Government. In the EU we were a problem to be got round. Nobody was terribly interested in our views. Nobody wanted to admit that Britain knew something about restructuring and tackling unemployment that Germany did not.

For two months before the General Election I preached a constant message. There was an unsung solidity in British–German relations. There was a natural coincidence of interests across a wide range of issues. It was not possible to build a stable Europe without Britain.

The message fell on barren ground. Instead, three questions were repeatedly put to me: who would win the election; and if Labour did, would Britain's European policy change and would I be sacked? My replies were on all counts suitably reserved.

The election result, in its decisiveness and drama, knocked the Germans' socks off. It has even to a degree destabilised German politics.

As early as Mr Blair's visit to Germany in 1996, the cry went up: where is the German Tony Blair? This rose to a crescendo after 1 May and it was the smooth-talking Gerhardt Schroder, SPD leader of Lower Saxony, who stepped forward. I once sat in the back of a car with him waiting for the Duke of Edinburgh to arrive at Hannover airport. The conversation consisted of my answering

questions, as best I could, on how New Labour had come
into being.

The attempt to Germanize New Labour has sharpened
the competition between Schroder and Lafontaine to run
against Kohl next year. Lafontaine once said to me in
exasperation that after the French elections he would have
to market himself as Tony Jospin – better, I thought to
myself, than Lionel Blair . . .

More important for us, 1 May has made it respectable
openly to admire Britain: our political system, the speed
with which the new Government has grasped the reform
agenda, and the extent to which we have already
restructured . . .

. . . This is a complex, multi-layered country. I have visited
11 out of 15 Bundeslander and only scratched the surface.
Germany has astonishing variety and regional differences.
It is like having 18 Scotlands, plus the complexity of
proportional representation. The most stultifying
conservatism sits alongside a strong radical and anarchist
streak. As the burghers of small town Germany tuck into
coffee and cakes on a Sunday afternoon, the anarchists of
Berlin burn a few cars and a supermarket. Variety shows on
German television make Des O'Connor look like alternative
comedy. But by 11.30 many channels are deep into medium-
hard pornography. Ancient 1970s British rock bands rumble
like Chieftain tanks across the North German plain, while,
to wild applause, three naked male Japanese ballet dancers
stand motionless on a Hamburg stage, while a fourth crawls
backwards and forwards dressed in a nightie.

Part II: SOUTH

Nigeria

'They make their blunders with an engaging air'

SIR DAVID HUNT, HM HIGH COMMISSIONER
TO NIGERIA, MAY 1969

Sir David learned to read and write aged three, and by twenty-four was a Fellow at Magdalen College, Oxford. He served as Private Secretary to both Clement Atlee and Winston Churchill; and during a spell in the Commonwealth Relations Office he drafted Macmillan's famous 'winds of change' speech. Yet Hunt became best known for his appearance on a TV quiz show. He won the BBC Mastermind 'champion of champions' competition in 1982.

The Nigerians certainly deserve a happy and united future after all they have gone through. I have a great affection for them because they are generally cheerful and friendly in spite of their maddening habit of always choosing the course of action which will do the maximum damage to their own interests. They are not singular in this: Africans as a whole are not only not averse to cutting off their nose to spite their face; they regard such an operation as a triumph of cosmetic surgery. But at least they usually make their blunders with an engaging air.

∾

Senegal

'Possibly the only people to have made no use of the wheel'

IVOR PORTER, HM AMBASSADOR AT DAKAR (SENEGAL, MALI AND MAURITANIA), AUGUST 1973

... [M]ost Africans of my region are still basically animists – many still practicing ... [T]hey tend to accept rather than to combat Nature and to rely on ritual and association with their natural environment rather than on tools with which to destroy it. They are possibly the only people to have made no use of the wheel and in a mechanical sense they are still well below par. At the same time they have gained in emotional and existential qualities – as evidenced by their dance and music – they have retained the warmth, dignity and stoicism which are declining in the more developed urban societies ...

As part of Nature they accepted sex, and the image of the sex maniacal buck nigger, which the Christian slave traders planted so effectively in our subconscious, seems to be no more true than the image of the noble African perpetrated in paperbacks during the '50s. He prefers palaver [talking] to violence or fanaticism as much as, if not more than, the European ...

... [T]heir main preoccupation is in fact with the community rather than the individual. Hence their irritating cult of dialogue and consensus, which has turned the UN into so much of a talking shop. 'Nothing came of it', we say of an OAU[1] or a UN meeting, though for people brought up to believe that consensus is essential to the preservation of the village community, it is perhaps not the meaningless resolutions that matter so much as the process of compromise which led up to them ...

They are quite good linguists, often speaking several African and one European language . . . [O]ral historians can be found in the countryside today who are still accurate for about two centuries back. Their over-reliance on personal contact and memory often of course leads to bureaucratic nonsenses. Our offer of 25 buses to Guinea two years ago seems to have disappeared without trace, when the Minister with whom I had almost completed the negotiation was locked up during Sekou Touré's latest purge.

In spite of his ineptitude with paper and under-development in other respects, the individual African of my region does not suffer from an inferiority complex towards the European. He believes his way of life to be inferior to ours in many respects; he accepts without apparent resentment the European's disregard of his own qualities. He responds to an interest in his problems but only if it is an intelligent interest; any sign of paternalism causes him to withdraw, still talking pleasantly enough but to the European instead of to you.

1. *OAU*: Organization of African Unity.

~

Liberia

'It is extremely difficult for them to keep working or even to stay awake'

HAROLD BROWN, HM AMBASSADOR TO LIBERIA, MARCH 1963

In moments of stress – and they occur, for one reason and another, almost every day here – I have sometimes turned for refreshment to the following which appears in a confidential

Foreign Office *Peace Treaty Handbook* on Liberia dated March, 1919:

> The British Consul-General at Monrovia stated in 1910 that 'labour is scarce and expensive, and probably the worst in the world'. This sweeping statement seems to be justified with regard to the majority of the tribes at present known in the interior ... No supply of labour need be expected, from the descendants of the colonizing element (the Americo-Liberians) ... They despise manual labour, and have shown no competence even in matters to which they mainly devote themselves such as politics and religion.

It was easier to make sweeping statements about Liberians forty or fifty years ago than it is now but in at least one respect what was true in 1910 is still true today; labour was then and is now scarce ... [M]ost skilled labour has to be imported while unskilled labour must be continuously supervised. The diet of most Liberian workers is inadequate and it is extremely difficult for them to keep working or even to stay awake during working hours. We have found with our own servants, however, that properly fed they need much less sleep and have more energy. I have no doubt that this is true for the working population as a whole and that with an adequate diet they could do as well as, say, the people of Ghana, but it will take time.

The Americo-Liberians still generally despise manual labour, as they did when the Handbook was written, and have no incentive to acquire a taste for it. Some of them are now becoming doctors, dentists, engineers and the like and often show considerable competence. In politics and the law, as in journalism and literature, standards of performance are surprisingly low probably as a result of Liberia's isolation for many years from neighbouring and other countries. Liberia is by no means isolated now, and standards in consequence are gradually going up. In a few years' time it may be possible for a foreigner to keep a straight face in court or to read the local newspapers or a serious Liberian poem without shaking with laughter but I am grateful that solemn stage had not arrived during my time.

~

'It would be difficult to fall in love with the country or its people'

MALCOLM WALKER, HM AMBASSADOR
TO LIBERIA, JUNE 1967

There is of course, much in the life of Monrovia which is absurdly pompous. I really find the Liberians' pleasure in funerals impossible to swallow. Many of the functions I have had to attend have been hilariously funny – indeed 'hilarious' is a word which I have heard used about Liberia by a number of people. The press is often decorated with unbelievable misprints and tales that in England would not be printable. I have with regret to record that many of the people, particularly the women, are arrogant and ill-mannered. It has been a disappointment to me that there is not more natural gaiety among the people. I find it irritating that the English language should be so debased as it is here . . . [I]t is a strange place, still in some ways a more plausible site of 'Black Mischief' than Ethiopia. I think it would be difficult to fall in love with the country or its people . . .

~

Brazil

'Still a tremendously second-rate people'

SIR JOHN RUSSELL, HM AMBASSADOR
TO BRAZIL, JUNE 1969

After leaving São Paulo, John Russell was given the embassy in Madrid, where one of his juniors was Christopher Meyer (see *p. 42),* *at the start of a career that would end as ambassador in Washington. Meyer remembers Russell as a great stylist who took enormous pride in his despatches, and whose valedictories and Annual Reviews were famous – or infamous, according to taste – within the Foreign Office for their quirky tone, clever phrasing and shrewd analysis.*

Not everyone enjoyed them. Madrid was Russell's last posting before retirement, but his final valedictory failed to impress his Head of Department, who wrote: 'This is not a profound despatch and some of the judgements in it are debatable.' The ambassador's personal thoughts on the improvement of the Diplomatic Service were described as a 'random collection of reflections ... ranging from the eminently sensible to what might charitably be described as puckish'.

But Russell's Brazilian valedictory (below) did find favour. It was given priority printing and warmly reviewed by superiors in Whitehall: 'In this very readable and highly personal despatch Sir John Russell outlines the extraordinary character of Brazil and casts the occasional well-deserved brickbat at its people.' Russell overshot his Brazilian population forecasts, however: the 2000 census saw a population of 169 million; and he was perhaps a little hasty in his prediction of an imminent dissolving of all racial difference into a coffee-coloured melting pot.

DESPATCH   BRITISH EMBASSY
                                             RIO DE JANEIRO

CONFIDENTIAL.

22 August 1969

Sir,

This is to be my valedictory despatch on Brazil. But how can any passing stranger pretend to write with truth and regard about a country so vast, so varied and protean as this? How on the basis of less than three years' acquaintance should I presume to forecast the future of Brazil? The clue, I think, is not to generalise but to try to pick the significant out of the gross.

At one end of the Brazilian rainbow you have stone-age Indian tribes living in the green depths of the rain-forest who still practice cannibalism and human sacrifice and who have yet (happily for them) to meet their first white man. It still takes 25 days by Booth Line[1] from Liverpool to Manaus, the capital of Amazonas, as it did in 1890: and there is still no access to Manaus by land. In seven tenths of this country life is lived today almost exactly as it was on the Western frontier of America in the years immediately following the war between the States. Slavery was abolished within living memory.

At the other extreme of the time-scale you have São Paulo, which has just passed the six million mark and is now the third largest city of Latin America (also unchallengeably the ugliest) . . .

Demographically Brazil presents an extraordinary

picture. Around ninety-two millions today, the population is growing at the rate of 3.4% per annum and will be around the 225 million mark by the year 2,000. And 42% of the population is under 15 years of age . . .

One problem at least is on its own way to solution without benefit of planner. Within a generation or two the racial issue will have ceased to exist. By then there will be neither identifiable whites nor identifiable blacks. In the United States a drop of black blood makes a white man black: here a drop of white blood makes a black man white. (A little money does the same for him.) Fusion is the order of the day and differences are shading over fast.

A very few years more will also see the disappearance of the last of the forest Indians, finally overwhelmed in their unequal struggle against the white man's greed and brutality, his guns, his lethal gifts, his exploitation, his diseases. For all the noble work of the early Jesuits, of General Rondon[2] and the Villas Boas brothers[3] the Brazilian Indian is fast going the sad way of his brother of the North American plains . . .

. . . Brazil owns one sixth of the world's forests and one third of the world's known reserves of iron ore: and produces more hydroelectric energy than any other country in the world. Wherever I have been in the country I have felt an urgent, irresistible prosperity: to the layman like me Brazil's future appears set irresistibly at fair.

Why then, you may well ask, is Brazil not already rich and prosperous? The short answer is, because the country is damn badly run – because there are five different gauges on the railways: because Guanabara has more civil servants than New York, and Petrobras in the State of São Paulo alone employs more chemists than Shell does in the whole world; because you can buy anything from a driving licence to a High Court Judge: because the Rector of the Federal University of Rio is paid $500 a month, whilst house-rents here are three times those of London and Rio's hotels are among the world's most expensive (also among the world's worst run): because there are only 18,000 miles of paved highway in the country: because in 1968 the Brazilians killed 10,000 people on their roads – rather more than the total of U.S. casualties in Vietnam during the same period: because, as Peter Fleming[4] put it, 'Brazil is a subcontinent with imperfect self control' . . .

. . . And now, further to confound the existing administrative confusion, they are about to transfer the whole governmental machine to Brasilia, that wantonly remote and quite unworkable monument to one man's, President Juscelino Kubitschek's, corrupt and ruinous vanity. This move can hardly fail to divorce the government still farther from reality.

The students are repressed . . . The Communists are few and ill organised and the only thing about them that is not underground is Che Guevara's ghost – although many of the now almost daily bank hold-ups are widely believed to be fund-raising exercises for the party . . . (In São Paulo it is now said to be quicker and safer to rob a bank than to try to cash a cheque in one.) The Church is split . . . The Press is muzzled: the intellectuals exiled or disheartened: Labour weak and inarticulate . . . The expanding middle-class plods indifferently on acquiring the good material things of life. The rich continue very private-spirited. And the poor . . . ?

There used to be – maybe there still is – an inscription bearing the date 1767 on the mill at Hawarden, Mr. Gladstone's old parliamentary seat in Flint, which ran: 'Wheat was in this year 19/- and barley 5/- a bushel. Luxury was at a great height and charity extensive. But the poor were starving, riotous and hanged.' The poor of Brazil have not quite got there yet: but it is now open to question how much longer they will be content to go on hoeing their hopeless row . . .

But now my sands are running out and I must wind up my Brazilian ledger. How does the account stand today as compared with three years ago? Materially the country has galloped ahead: politically it has gone backwards. The flat-earth hard-line colonels have arrested the spiritual development of what is potentially a brilliant country of liberal creative instincts and the most lively intellectual capacity. I like to hope that the check is only temporary.

But if the government of Brazil has hardened, I think that I must have mellowed a little in the same interval. No longer, as in my First Impressions despatch, do I feel moved to caustic comment on the shortcomings of the Brazilian character. The Brazilians are still a tremendously second-rate people: but it is equally obvious that they are on their way to a first-rate future. Maybe I have yielded something to Rio's tropical insidious charm: maybe I have just learnt to soften my dour northern standards, to see things a little less primly in this warm forgiving climate. I like to believe that the more indulgent eye gets the truer perspective . . .

I have the honour to be,
With the highest respect,

Sir,
Your obedient Servant,

John Russell.

1. *Booth Line*: A passenger service sailing from European ports to Brazil. The company's posters from the 1920s show incongruously large steam-ships towering over native canoes, advertising 'Tours 1,000 miles up the River Amazon'.

2. *General Rondon*: Candido Rondon (1866–1956) founded Brazil's Indian Protection Service. His expeditions laid thousands of miles of telegraph wire across the Amazon jungle, mapping the interior, despite frequent opposition from local tribes.

3. *Villas Boas brothers*: Orlando, Claudio and Leonardo Villas-Boas dedicated their lives to defending indigenous rights; in 1961 they succeeded in getting the entire upper Xingu River, a tributary of the Amazon, legally protected for the tribes.

4. *Peter Fleming*: Brother to the James Bond creator, Ian. In 1932 Peter Fleming answered a personal advertisement in *The Times* seeking recruits for an 'Exploring and Sporting expedition' to Brazil. The purpose was to investigate the fate of a previous expedition which never returned; the sport would be shooting whatever animals loomed into view on the riverbank. The amateur mission ended in acrimony and failure, but Fleming's account of the trip, *Brazilian Adventure*, sold well.

~

Argentina

'A fairly ungovernable lot'

SIR MICHAEL HADOW, HM AMBASSADOR
TO ARGENTINA, DECEMBER 1973

In the first place, there is the land – a huge expanse extending from the semi-tropics of the Chaco to the semi-Antarctic of Tierra del Fuego. It contains one of the largest concentrated areas of natural agricultural wealth in the world. Yet it pays to remember that one half of it is desert or semi-desert . . . As one travels through the lush pastures of the huge provinces of Buenos Aires, Entre Rios, Santa Fe and Cordoba with their noble avenues, high windbreaks and woodlands, it is as well to reflect that only 100 years ago there was not a tree to be seen in that whole vast area except an occasional, solitary treelike growth known as the 'Ombu'. Indeed, the first officially appointed British Minister to the Argentine Republic in bewailing his fate in what was then an insalubrious back-water ended his Jeremiad to one of your distinguished predecessors, Sir, with the words: 'And were there but a tree to be found, I would gladly hang myself thereon' . . .

. . . All I knew of Argentines before coming here was that they were generally disliked by all other Latin Americans as unduly pretentious, snobbish upstarts. Their pride in their 'Europeanness' is certainly justified if it means that they are 'white' and lack that essential Hispano/Amerindian mixture which goes to make up the basic Latin American. They are a melting pot of European races with Italian predominating even more than Spanish. They have not yet found a sense of nationality or patriotism except through vocal outbursts of xenophobia. They are probably desperately unsure of themselves yet want to be admired and loved. The per capita outlay on deodorants in the Argentine is the highest in the world . . .

Politically, the Argentines are probably a fairly ungovern-able lot. One of my predecessors described them in the words of Pope 'with too much quickness ever to be taught, with too much thinking to have a common thought'. I myself have described them more briefly as the Bandar Log.[1] Lacking a true feeling of nationhood, they have in recent years gone through cycles of trying to solve the problem between having 'democratic' government with all the worst features of the French Fourth Republic or a self-imposed military rule which brings for a time order, efficiency and relative incorruptibility but which is not 'democratic'. The problem is worse con-founded by the fact that the military are all democrats at heart, are sensitive to public disapproval and after a period in power yearn to return to their barracks . . .

. . . The Bandar Log yearn for a strong leader and admire

totalitarianism (it was democratic governments before Peron who backed the Axis in World War II). In a recent film when the scene showed young Storm Troopers singing the *Horst Wessel Lied* – meant as an ironic touch for European audiences – half the audience here applauded with real enthusiasm. But at the same time they yearn for no governing hand at all. A hundred yards from my house I noticed on the day of my arrival scrawled across a wall the heartfelt cry '*Anarquía es orden*' (Anarchy is order). It is still there.

1. *The Bandar Log*: Kipling's monkeys in *The Jungle Book*. Irresponsible and foolish, they constantly talk up their abilities: 'We are great. We are free . . . We are the most wonderful people in all the jungle! We all say so, and so it must be true.'

~

Bolivia

'*. . . but when you leave you also weep*'

SIR FREDERICK HERBERT GAMBLE, HM AMBASSADOR
TO BOLIVIA, APRIL 1967

There is a saying here among foreigners that when you first arrive in La Paz you weep but when you leave you also weep. It all depends on what makes you weep, but I would say that there is much truth in this. Whether you arrive in La Paz by air or by train you will first come to El Alto which, situated at over 13,000 feet, can be very bleak and forbidding. From there your first sight of La Paz spread out in a vast crater over 1,000 feet lower down will fill you with amazement, but as you wind down the road to the centre of the city you may well be depressed by the shabby little houses on either side of it and, if you are unlucky, you may also be feeling distinctly dizzy from the effects of the altitude. In most cases these effects will wear off quickly and before long you will become interested in the many-sided problems of what is still a very undeveloped country . . .

. . . [T]here are good opportunities for the future. The question is whether the Bolivians will be able to take them. Unfortunately they are not very good at working together. As soon as one gets to the top all the others eventually try to pull him down. Perhaps this is something which comes from their Indian background, something which causes fear and suspicion . . . And the central government does not give them much help. With a few exceptions, the standards of efficiency in the various Ministries are deplorably low and the employees notoriously underpaid. Corruption exists at all levels, even, and perhaps particularly, at the highest, and I fear that the longer you stay in the country the more you are conscious of this. It is something which must make you weep not only when you arrive and when you leave but at all times. You could weep also for the miners who still work and live in such pitiably poor and miserable conditions and for the villagers whose colourful fiestas only too frequently degenerate into drunken orgies. You could weep in sympathy with the few people who in the face of so many difficulties are trying to work for the betterment of these people, and you could certainly weep at the thought of leaving this country of wide variety and spectacular beauty, of blue skies and billowing white clouds, of dark green tropical rivers and the lovely snow-capped Cordillera Real.

I have the honour to be,
Sir,
Your obedient Servant
F. H. Gamble

~

Uruguay

'Nearly all the faults and none of the virtues of Spain'

SIR KEITH UNWIN, HM AMBASSADOR TO URUGUAY,
JUNE 1969

(CONFIDENTIAL)   *Montevideo*
                                                  16 May, 1969

Sir,

In the 34 years since my first foreign posting I have spent
three years nominally in the United Kingdom . . . Of the
remaining 30 to 31 years, 17 have been passed in Spanish-
speaking countries . . . I have wondered at times whether so
much living among people whose approach to work, meals,
politics and punctuality is so different from ours, had not
unfitted me for dealing with my own people; and there was
a time 16 years back when I reflected that the English were
just as tiresome as any other foreigners. My final posting has
to some extent reassured me. After living now for over two
years among people who call themselves Orientals and who
seem to have inherited nearly all the faults and none of the
virtues of Spain (though they have many minor virtues of
their own), I look forward to returning to what I conceive
to be, at least by contrast, the speed and efficiency of my
own country.

In Uruguayans, efficiency may inspire respect but not
emulation; and sometimes a perverse refusal to adapt
their pace at all. Requests for assistance or advice do not
necessarily imply a desire to accept the advice or use the
assistance; the donor or adviser must also be a first-class

salesman and may well have to start by explaining to his hosts why he has come, and persuading them of the need to do what they asked him to come for . . . If he cannot do all this he may work alone; he needs the patience of Griselda and the qualities of a scoutmaster – but if he has only these he may find that he is despised by those he came to help . . .

Under the collegiate system most of the more prominent politicians got themselves elected as joint presidents . . . The collegiate pattern, with time, became repeated at lower levels . . . the rot spread downwards through political patronage to such an extent that five men had to be appointed to do one job at every level, in order to prevent discontent in the ranks. This has been recently defended on the ground that it prevented unemployment. At my arrival in Uruguay the 'First State Airline', PLUNA, had between 800 and 900 staff on the ground, to attend to the movements of four or five aircraft, but could not put one in the air . . . I was advised that a first decision in a legal action might take 10 years; to take it through all the possible stages of appeal would occupy a lifetime.

Part III: EAST

India

'A colossal amount of humbug'

SIR JOHN THOMPSON, HM HIGH COMMISSIONER
TO INDIA, JUNE 1982

BRITISH HIGH COMMISSION

NEW DELHI, INDIA
21 June 1982

The Rt Hon Francis Pym MC MP
Foreign and Commonwealth Office
London SW1

Sir

INDIA: CONCLUSIONS AND
RECOMMENDATIONS

India has become fashionable, yet few people in the West understand the realities in this country. The truth is elusive, never more so than in India, but some recognition of the good and the bad aspects of modern India is essential to the formulation of sensible policies . . .

The bad things are more familiar than the good. An appallingly large population increase . . . a high and growing level of corruption . . . Communal rioting occurs in many parts of the country, law and order are slow and precarious and there are serious doubts about the honesty of the police. The situation in educational institutions, including many of higher learning, seems likely to perpetuate these deplorable conditions. It is not uncommon for a thousand students to have been detected cheating in the exams of a single university, but it is rare that anything effective is done about it . . .

It is not surprising that such blemishes in the ethos of Indian society are reflected in the physical environment. Her children have inflicted ugly scars on the face of Mother India. Half or more of all the trees in India have been cut in the past 35 years with frightful consequences for soil erosion, silting, flooding and climatic conditions. Following the felling of their forest homes many of the 40 million or so tribal people are in a pitiable condition and the situation of the urban slum dwellers is degrading.

I came to India with the familiar and depressing outlook described above but to my surprise I found that the good points outweigh the bad. India is a remarkably contented society, more so than any in which I have lived. The underlying, mostly unconscious reason is the Hindu ethic, which has grown out of the circumstances of Indian life. It allows this undisciplined self-centred people to exercise their individuality and hedonism while at the same time inducing in them a philosophical acceptance of things as they are. Such an attitude to life is encouraged by the physical richness of India: the necessities of life are simple and available. The country has abundant sun, a lot of excellent soil which is at present under-used, and a sufficiency of water . . .

Whether the promise will become performance depends upon the human resources. There is an enormous amount of brain power, a readiness to work hard and a considerable mechanical aptitude. India has arguably the best administration of all newly independent countries. Despite constant political fluctuation (which the Indians enjoy) the country is secure and relatively stable. Democracy is more deeply rooted than in any other member of the new Commonwealth. There has, since independence, been a notable increase in self-confidence amongst Indians. The intelligentsia complain that standards are low and that opportunities are being lost. They are right, but they are largely ineffective. There is no discussion of national issues or long-range programmes in Indian politics. Instead, a colossal amount of humbug is spoken and acted out, though for the most part not really believed. Anyone who has a regard for India understands the feeling of Mr Sompath – a character in a novel by R K Narayan: 'The possibilities of perfection seemed infinite though mysterious, and yet there was a terrible kind of pig-headedness in people that prevented their going the right way.' Very true, but at the same time there is a great deal of inventiveness and drive. It is entirely possible that the Gujaratis and Sindhis now settling in New York will hold their own with the Jews and Armenians there . . .

[A] problem in the Indo/British relationship is the quality of media coverage . . . No wonder there is still an illusion in Britain that India is a land of maharajahs, snake charmers, Oxfam babies and the ogress Mrs Gandhi.

~

Pakistan

'Proud and touchy'

JOHN BUSHELL, HM AMBASSADOR TO PAKISTAN,
APRIL 1979

Pakistan has many of the characteristics of mid-Victorian England – few, unfortunately, of the better ones. Power lies essentially in the hands of a small ruling elite. Ownership of land is the normal basis of power and respectability. As a general rule women are kept firmly in the home, and the middle class, though it is coming up, is not yet of much significance. Education is making only a slight dent in illiteracy. Population is growing fast, while contraception is hardly a matter for public discussion. Religion maintains its strong and binding force; only a daring intellectual or eccentric would question it . . .

For Pakistan, internal fragility is aggravated by alarming external changes, for the most part still in the course of evolution. Neighbours look dangerous or liable to be dangerous

. . . There is another aspect to this. Pakistanis are not only short of real friends in the world, as I have often commented, but also proud and touchy – a pretty awful combination.

~

Nepal

'Riddled with superstition and astrologers'

TERENCE O'BRIEN, HM AMBASSADOR TO NEPAL,
MARCH 1974

(CONFIDENTIAL)   *Kathmandu,*
                                    20 March, 1974

Sir,

'An undistinguished invitation card in Devnagri script was
delivered at the Residence on Sunday night. Since all our
servants are illiterate and my 'nagri non-existent, I left its
translation until Monday morning. This brought surprises
when my P.A. rushed in saying that I had five minutes
to get into diplomatic uniform and attend the Prince's
wedding. I completed my dressing in the Austin Princess
as we swept into the courtyard of an old Rana Palace. A
fusillade of shots greeted us. I emerged cautiously from the
car and was relieved merely to find a motley collection of
soldiers strolling about the grounds with flint-lock muskets
indiscriminately firing *feux de joie* into the air. Two bands
were riotously playing totally different and incompatible
bits of music. Some ceremonial elephants had been
corralled in the carpark and were busily eating the canna
lilies that had just been planted out. As I hustled into the
Hindu marriage service, Nepalese courtiers murmured that
the auspicious hour had struck (which was odd as it was
then exactly seventeen minutes past nine). My only
satisfaction was that my other diplomatic colleagues had
been similarly caught off balance. It is the first time I have

seen a French Ambassador in morning coat but with a bright pink shirt and a sportif tie . . .' (Extract from a letter to my wife after my first arrival 10 days ahead of her in Kathmandu.)

It has been very tempting to report in like fashion to the Office. The Ruritanian aspects of the Court of Nepal, riddled with superstition and astrologers, make Lawrence Durrell's diplomatic memoirs read like a White Paper. Just the sort of place to provide endless copy for despatches that would enliven the darkest and coldest day that Whitehall might suffer. And it isn't just the Court. There was the occasion when the Nepalese Air Force was grounded because the rats that live in its aircraft had eaten all the insulation off their electric cables. Or the time that Nepal's rival merchant navies . . .

∼

Mongolia

'A curious feeling of timelessness'

MYLES PONSONBY, HM AMBASSADOR TO MONGOLIA,
MARCH 1977

Mongolia was at this time virtually a Soviet puppet state.

. . . [T]he Mongols are a proud and independently-minded race still virtually unaffected by the march of so-called progress and to a great extent untainted by the political ideologies imposed upon them . . . [T]he Mongolian leadership must be profoundly grateful for the work done for their country by Russian construction troops, skilled labour being at a very high premium . . . But I very much doubt that the

ordinary Mongolians feel the same way about the Russians . . .
They do not mix with the Mongolians who dislike their
arrogant and contemptuous behaviour. Stones are often
thrown at them and there have been stories of muggings. All
this is hardly surprising. Mongolia is to all practical purposes
an occupied country and occupiers are rarely liked by the
occupied.

Despite the delightful cheerfulness that one sees on the
faces of the ordinary people in the streets, shops and at the
theatre or circus (the latter are always sold out especially
for Mongol productions) the men and women at work in
the factories present an altogether different projection of
the collective persona. The present day Mongolian dislikes
factory work. The monotony is utterly alien to their nature.
(I once asked the Director of the Second Department of
the MFA[1] why he was constantly moving from one office
to another. He replied with a deprecatory shrug, 'No Mongolian likes working – or living – in the same place for very
long.') . . .

Another stark contrast is the instantly identifiable difference between those Mongolians either young or not so young
who are party members or activists and those who are not.
Many, especially in the younger generation, are easily spotted
by their predilection for the permanent use of dark glasses. It
seems to be a kind of required uniform. A totally expression-
less face and never the vestige of a smile completes the make
up. They are known in this Embassy as 'boot-faces' and
treated accordingly . . .

A number of little vignettes of my service in Mongolia will
always be engrained on my memory. The first was the security precautions taken for the arrival of Mr Brezhnev in
November 1974 . . . [I]t seemed strange to me that security

dictated that an armed policeman should be stationed on the steppe by the roadside every 100 yards or so from the airport to the city when no humans were visible (they had all been herded into the city for a 'spontaneous' welcome). The only potentially dangerous creatures were some very cold cows.

Approximately once a year all Ambassadors attend a session of the Great People's Khural when the elected representatives of the people gather together to listen to long, boring speeches telling them what has already been decided upon by the Central Committee of the MPRP.[2] Whether or not one can understand a word of what has been said is beside the point, and of no consequence. It has all been said before. What is really intriguing is the absence of any attention to the two hour monologue. The members of the Great People's Khural, apart from a tiny minority of assiduous note takers, seem singularly disinterested. I observed one lady attending to the <u>coiffe</u> of her neighbour in front. Snuff was passed and snuff-bottles admired. Sweets and even nose-drops were passed around. Some gave up the unequal struggle to keep awake and either slept on their hands or sitting upright. I actually saw one of the latter, no doubt in the middle of some Mongol dream, rear up and crash into the aisle. No one took the slightest notice. He was heaved back into his seat and the proceedings continued.

There is a curious feeling of timelessness about the country. Not so much of time standing still, but time not really being of importance. Mongolair's internal service is a typical example. The so-called scheduled flight planners give detailed ETDs and ETAs, but the pilots scarcely heed them. Aircraft – and cars/trucks are treated like horses: fuel them, flog them, start and stop them. (The Mongolians have devised a unique system for getting up an icy slope. It is simply to engage gear, rev up the engine and let the back wheels spin until the heated rubber melts the ice. Proceed a few feet and repeat the process until the summit is successfully reached.) . . .

The Mongolians are almost pathologically concerned about their progressive image, and strangely anxious to show a Western Ambassador (or his wife) only those examples of their activities which they believe will make a good impression. It was only after involving the wishes of Mme Tsedenbal-Filatova[3] herself that my wife was permitted to visit a school and the music and ballet academy. Requests to visit the children's hospital initially met with no success. There was vague talk of an apparently permanent flu epidemic. It was only after I had twisted the Minister of Health's arm after presenting him with a large quantity of drugs donated by Beechams that permission was forthcoming. In the event it was a pretty harrowing experience and the wives returned thoroughly shaken. The so-called intensive care unit contained rows of very sick premature babies, several dead and some clearly dying.

And yet . . . and yet. Despite all the difficulties, the frustrations and the rag-bag of absurd and petty annoyances, there is something very engaging about many (certainly not all) of the Mongolians that I have met. The children – those that survive – are particularly attractive. (The one that threw a stone accurately at my wife, mistaking her for a Russian, grinned wickedly as he fled.)

One will remember the people for their extraordinary cheerfulness and their sometimes overwhelming hospitality, for their infinite capacity for making promises they know they cannot keep and for their tendency to say nothing: unable to say yes and unwilling to say no . . .

The ground here is cold and stony: the row fairly hard to hoe.

I am sending copies of this despatch to Her Majesty's Ambassadors at Moscow, Peking and Washington.

I have the honour to be
Sir,
Your obedient servant,

Myles Ponsonby

1. *MFA*: Ministry of Foreign Affairs.
2. *MPRP*: Mongolian People's Revolutionary Party.
3. *Mme Tsedenbal-Filatova*: Anastasia Filatova, the formidable Russian wife of Mongolia's Communist leader Yumjaagiin Tsedenbal.

∽

Thailand

'Licentiousness is the main pleasure of them all'

SIR ANTHONY RUMBOLD, HM AMBASSADOR
TO THAILAND, JULY 1967

Sir Anthony's valedictory from Thailand caused quite a stir. Not for the opinions within it, which are, to put it mildly, rather old-fashioned, but because it reached a far wider audience than was ever intended. Not least because it questions the sanity of the Thai Foreign Minister, the despatch, though selected for printing, was supposed to go to a narrow 'Q' distribution. But the clerk's handwriting was indistinct, and when it reached the printers the despatch was mistakenly given the much wider 'A' distribution. The Foreign Services of more than fifty countries across the Commonwealth received a copy, including Malaysia and Singapore. Whitehall realized its mistake only after the amused staff of the New Zealand Embassy in Washington – so far had word of the notorious telegram spread – asked their counterparts at the British Embassy there for a copy.

Perhaps this despatch is jinxed, for when in 2009 the editors of this book included it in their BBC Radio Four series, Parting Shots, the current British Ambassador in Bangkok found himself obliged to issue a press release distancing himself from his predecessor's opinions.

It's hard to fault Anthony Rumbold's style (his final Austria telegram, on p. 21, is another masterful put-down sketch). But his powers of prophecy have proved imperfect. He predicted elsewhere in this (abridged) despatch that Thanom and Prapass, the two military leaders then ruling Thailand, would stay the course, avowing that 'the days of the coup d'état are probably over for good'. But by the time Arthur de la Mare, Rumbold's successor-but-one in Bangkok, came to write his valedictory, there had been a popular uprising (in 1973) when the two dictators were to be found 'fleeing the country like thieves at dead of night, on their way to igno-minious exile'. And far from being 'over for good', Thailand saw its most recent military coup in 2006.

GOODBYE TO THAILAND

Sir Anthony Rumbold to Mr. Brown (Received 18 July)

(No. 19. CONFIDENTIAL)

Bangkok,
13 July, 1967.

Sir,

I am on the point of leaving Bangkok after a stay of two and a half years and have the honour to set down some thoughts about Thailand . . . There is a theory that the Thais are rather easier for Europeans to understand than are other oriental people. I do not believe this theory. It seems to me that Sino/Indian/Malay/Thai ways of thought are so alien to ours that analogies between events in South-East Asia and events in Europe are nearly always misleading, that forecasts based on such analogies are bound to be wrong, that the motives of Asians are impossible for us to estimate with any exactness, and that Thailand and the Thais offer no exception to these precepts. The general level of intelligence of the Thais is rather low, a good deal lower than ours and much lower than that of the Chinese. But there are a few very intelligent and articulate ones and I have often tried to get some of these . . . to come clean with me and to describe their national characteristics as they see them themselves . . . [but] [s]omething always seems to be held back . . .

. . . The traveller Henri Mouhot described the whole of Siamese society in the mid-19th century as being 'in a state of permanent prostration, every inferior receiving his orders from his superior with signs of abject submission and respect' . . . But I would go so far as to make the unfashionable assertion that the most steadying feature in the body politic of Thailand, irritating and even repulsive though it may be, is precisely this sense of his place in society possessed and accepted by each and every individual. The god-like position of the King is questioned by nobody . . . Below the King, very far below him, the individuals who control the nation are ranged in their respective places, each one knowing exactly how he or she stands in relation to each other. These relationships are perfectly clear to the Thais themselves . . .

Since the revolution of 1932 which put an end to the absolute monarchy, though scarcely affecting the veneration owed to the monarch, proximity to the source of military power has been the most important factor in assuring influence and position . . . Money is another important factor. All Thais love money and the possession of it is regarded as a sign of virtue or merit. They call it vitamin M. The amount of it and the use made of it is of more significance in their eyes than the method by which it has been acquired. Family connections are very important. Even good birth is still a factor to be reckoned with . . .

The more important Thai leaders are worth considering individually. The one with whom I have had most to do has been the Foreign Minister, Colonel Thanat Khoman . . . [H]e is vain, touchy and disputatious. Most of his colleagues in the Government dislike him for his intellectual arrogance and because he lets everybody including themselves know that he despises them. He keeps everything to himself and is beastly to his subordinates . . . His obsessions about 'liberals', about the French and about Cambodia sometimes make one wonder whether he is altogether sane. But he is not entirely repulsive. He quite likes the British, indeed he worked with us in the war, but he regrets our present weakness and our tendency to appeasement as he sees it . . .

I have very much enjoyed living for a while in Thailand. One would have to be very insensitive or puritanical to take the view that the Thais had nothing to offer. It is true that they have no literature, no painting and only a very odd kind of music, that their sculpture, their ceramics and their dancing are borrowed from others and that their architecture is monotonous and their interior decoration hideous. Nobody can deny that gambling and golf are the chief pleasures of the rich and that licentiousness is the main pleasure of them all. But it does a faded European good to spend some time among such a jolly, extrovert and anti-intellectual people. And if anybody wants to know what their culture consists of the answer is that it consists of themselves, their excellent manners, their fastidious habits, their graceful gestures and their elegant persons. If we are elephants and oxen they are gazelles and butterflies . . .

I have, &c.

A. RUMBOLD.

~

'Latter-day version of Sodom and Gomorrah'

SIR ARTHUR DE LA MARE, HM AMBASSADOR
TO THAILAND, NOVEMBER 1973

In the National Archives and after declassification, sections of despatches are occasionally blanked out; in their place a red stamp informs the reader that the full document remains closed until some specified future date. The redacted material may threaten to damage Britain's relations with foreign countries even after thirty years have passed. Sir Arthur de la Mare's valedictory, declassified in 2004, is rare however, in that it is the opening paragraph, where the ambassador typically sets the scene, which has been obscured. Doubtless it contains more caustic comment on the Thais. The full document will be declassified in 2014. For now we can only speculate: it is possible that the redacted section contains a negative reference to the King. Even today, anyone making an offhand reference to the Thai Royal Family can expect to cause offence, or face a minimum of three years in jail if they are unwise enough to do so in Thailand, where strict lèse-majesté laws apply.

FAREWELL TO THAILAND, TO EAST ASIA AND TO THE DIPLOMATIC SERVICE

Her Majesty's Ambassador at Bangkok to the Secretary of State for Foreign and Commonwealth Affairs

(CONFIDENTIAL)   Bangkok,
                                              15 November, 1973

Sir,

CENSORED

It does. Decayed garbage left for months on the side of the roads; stagnant canals that serve both as cesspools and as the dumping ground for dead dogs; buses and lorries that belch uncontrolled clouds of diesel fumes; scarcely a pavement without potholes and open manholes to break the legs of the unwary; bag-snatchers in every block; assault and violence a way of life; prostitution and every form of natural and unnatural vice on a scale astonishing even in Asia; a city of 4 million with only one park, and that littered with refuse and infested by thieves; unplanned hideous ribbon development; no proper drainage, so that in the rainy season large areas of the city remain flooded for weeks on end; and the whole set in a flat mournful plain without even a hillock in sight for a 100 miles in any direction: this is Bangkok, the vaunted Venice of the East. A small section, the old city with its palaces and temples, retains some of its oriental charm, but it is but a poor compensation for those who have to live in this 'improved' latter-day version of Sodom and Gomorrah.

But why do I begin this farewell despatch from a post which in spite of its many frustrations I have greatly enjoyed with so uncomplimentary a description of its capital city? I have often had occasion to remind London that Bangkok is not Thailand, nor Thailand Bangkok. That is true, but most Thais do not realise it. Bangkok to them is not only all that counts in their country, it is all that counts in the world.

There are reasons for this. There are here no Manchesters, Birminghams or Liverpools to share the industrial and commercial loads with the capital. The two Thai towns next largest to Bangkok, Chiang Mai in the North and Haad Yai in the South, though both growing rapidly are country villages by comparison. If it was ever true that a man who is tired of London is tired of life it is equally true that a Thai who given the choice prefers to live outside Bangkok is looked upon as an eccentric. I have often asked Thai friends why when they retire they do not go to live in more pleasant and salubrious areas such as Chiang Mai or Songkhla. The question astonishes them: 'But we couldn't live anywhere but in Bangkok!' Civil servants or business officials sent to man posts in the provinces regard it as demotion and as loss of face . . .

. . . [L]ike other people including ourselves the Thais tend to gauge their status by the past rather than by the present. Inordinately vain and race conscious by nature they look upon themselves as the elite of South East Asia. After 37 years' acquaintance with them and the last three in their own front yard I cannot say that I find their pretensions entirely justified. Except for those who have Chinese blood they are indolent and feckless. Their charm is proverbial, but it is often no more than a polite pose and I am quite sure that of all the Asians of various nationalities whom my wife and I have known and whom we call friends it is the Thais who will most quickly forget us. Trying to determine whether a Thai really means what he says is one of the most difficult tasks I have encountered in my diplomatic life. And, charming and friendly as they are, to do business with them is a constant frustration. They cannot make up their mind; everything has to be referred to a higher authority; and even the highest authority of all, the King, is so shackled by protocol and precedent that though he will speak his mind with refreshing directness he will seldom intervene even in situations which only he can resolve . . .

. . . Some two years ago I bethought myself that I would address you on the subject of the Thai way, and got as far as setting pen to paper. But after wrestling for some weeks with a draft I abandoned the project, deeming it prudent not to give you further cause to doubt my sanity. But since it is now immaterial whether my superiors consider me better fitted for a lunatic asylum than for a diplomatic post I shall try to describe the Thai way as it has been vouchsafed and revealed to me.

First the idiom. If I were a Thai official in the presence of my superior I would stand at deferential attention while he spoke, then when he had finished would bend low and hiss in his ear the one word: 'Crap!' For in Thai this basic four-letter word is not only the appropriate but the mandatory expression of total submission. And, on another plane, what can one make of a language where the word for dentist is 'more fun' or where, at least to the foreign ear, the words for 'near' and 'far' are exactly the same?

But why not? Distance and proximity are matters of the mind, and so is time. Shortly after my arrival here I paid a courtesy call on a senior Minister. I was advised that it should take only 15–20 minutes to get to his office but that as traffic was unpredictable I should allow 30. I did, and arrived at the Ministry flustered and embarrassed

35 minutes late. The Minister heard my apologies with blank astonishment. 'But my dear Ambassador, it's true that in principle our appointment was for four o'clock but it is only four thirty-five and I didn't expect you until about now.' And then as he remembered my British provenance his eyes twinkled and he added: 'If I may offer a word of advice to you as a newcomer don't worry about punctuality. It is a British fetish but we Thais don't suffer from it.'

So here is there and near is far and a watch merely an ornamental bauble. There are indeed separate and distinct expressions for 'yes' and 'no' but since it is impolite to use the latter the former is used for both. It is then up to the person addressed to decide whether yes is to be interpreted as a flat no or as a no which he may convert into a yes by putting his request in another form or to a higher authority. But usually it means that his request will receive favourable consideration, which in turn means that no action will be taken upon it. If you invite a Thai to dinner and he accepts you must not deduce therefrom that he will be there, for by accepting he has done you a courtesy; he has thus transferred the obligation from himself to you and is therefore under no necessity to turn up. If you know him well enough to remonstrate he will be taken aback: 'But I accepted, didn't I?' It is then no good replying: 'Yes, mate, so you did, and that's why I expected you', for he will go away confirmed in his assurance that the thought-processes of the farang (Westerner) are quite beyond comprehension.

$\sim$

Japan

*'An intensely emotional people,
given to suicide'*

SIR FRANCIS RUNDALL, HM AMBASSADOR
TO JAPAN, JULY 1967

(CONFIDENTIAL)   *Tokyo*
                                                  6 July, 1967

Sir,

It was suggested in a policy planning paper recently in the
Foreign Office that, in our dealings with the Japanese, we
must always remember that their character is such that they
require unusually careful and delicate handling. In this my
valedictory despatch I have the honour to offer my own
observations on this . . .

. . . Whilst good manners demand an impassive exterior
and concealment of one's real feelings, the Japanese are an
intensely emotional people, given to suicide and with at
least their fair share of crimes of violence. They are a very
hard working people with an ingrained sense of loyalty to
their employers and to authority which has come down
from feudal times. They are an Asiatic people and share the
general Asian preference for the oblique rather than the
direct approach to a problem. This is true also of their
speech; many a visiting businessman has been misled by the
polite Japanese agreement which has no firmer basis than a
desire not to contradict the honourable foreigner. I do not
myself feel that the Japanese can be described either as a
militaristic or as a pacific people. They respect military
power, certainly, and throughout their history effective

power has always been sought and maintained by force of arms, but they are also the world's greatest pragmatists and would adopt the means, military or otherwise, most suited to gain their ends . . . as a senior Japanese General said not long ago, 'The war was wrong because we could not possibly have won it.' . . .

. . . The Japanese have many lovable characteristics; a genuine capacity for friendship once one is accepted; a code of politeness in social intercourse which, though confusing to the foreigner, is helpful and agreeable once one knows the rules; and an almost overwhelming sense of obligation for favours done. If one approaches them properly, with due politeness and without resorting to high-pressure tactics, they are often extremely co-operative. Above all, once a personal relationship has been established with them it brings with it the ethical obligation of an entirely different approach. No people are more inconsiderate to those they do not know – one need only drive in Tokyo traffic to discover this – but few are more considerate to their friends. It should therefore be the aim of every visiting businessman to reach this relationship; he will not achieve much until he does. We must furthermore seek to exploit this trait at national level. The Japanese will listen to their friends and they realise that they have still much to learn about how to conduct political and economic relations with other countries. If they see in us a friendly country, and if personal contact can be established amongst statesmen and officials at the highest level, we can exercise an influence beyond their estimation of our national strength. We can, at the least, enlighten their self interest.

Though irrelevant to the subject at issue one is allowed to be subjective in the last paragraph of one's final despatch. I have had nearly 37 very happy years in the Consular,

Foreign and Diplomatic Services, with interesting work and excellent colleagues. Sitting in a comfortable and air-conditioned office I can contrast my last days in the Service with my first introduction to it, attempting to cope with an unruly mob of seamen in the earth-floored stable which served as a Shipping Office in the Consulate-General at Antwerp. We have come a very long way since those days and both our work and our conditions of Service have changed out of all recognition. But I feel that we have kept up with the times and I am confident that we shall continue to do so.

I have, &

F. B. A. RUNDALL

~

'The general lack of a coherent philosophy of life'

SIR HUGH CORTAZZI, HM AMBASSADOR TO JAPAN,
FEBRUARY 1984

JAPAN YESTERDAY, TODAY AND TOMORROW

Her Majesty's Ambassador at Tokyo to the Secretary of State for Foreign and Commonwealth Affairs

Tokyo
8 February 1984

Sir,

I leave Japan on retirement shortly, I first came in contact with this country over forty years ago and I propose to comment in this despatch on some relevant aspects of Japan as it was, as I see it today, and as it may be in the future . . .

I began to learn Japanese in London in 1943 as an aircraftsman. I am still learning about this country . . . All in all, I have spent some fifteen years of my life in Japan and much of my time in London has also been spent on affairs Japanese. During my time as Ambassador, I have travelled officially through all Japan's forty-seven prefectures and tried through numerous speeches and articles in Japanese to put over our views.

I was never directly involved with war crimes trials but I remember stumbling in Singapore in 1945 on some facts about one of the many unpleasant incidents in the Japanese occupation of Singapore. I also had relations who suffered on the Burma/Siam railway. So, I cannot ignore this side of Japanese life but Japan, like Germany where I have also served is a complex society and there is good as well as bad in every country's history. In any case, Japan is a force of major importance in the modern world and it behoves us to get on with the Japanese. I am glad to think that we have got away from the era when, so story has it, whenever a paper about Japan was submitted to one of your predecessors he used simply to write on it 'I do not like the Japanese.' I confess, however, that I still have the impression that Ministers as a whole tend only to focus on Japan when a problem arises with it . . .

The Japanese are much more diverse than they and the world at large like to think. But history, geography, ethnography and culture have induced certain general characteristics in their society. Japanese arrogance is matched by Japanese sensitivity and resentment of discrimination against themselves; Japanese language and culture, as well as their long history of seclusion, have meant that they were isolated from the rest of the world for too long. The contacts of the last hundred and thirty years have gone deep and have changed Japan beyond recognition, but have left the Japanese – at heart at least – less internationally-minded than the people of most of the advanced countries . . .

. . . Despite all its success in producing a highly educated people capable of performing the tasks of a modern industrial society, the Japanese education system has a number of built-in weaknesses as well as strengths. The strengths include the fact that literacy (despite the complexity of the written language) and numeracy are among the highest in the world . . . Moreover, Japanese education, with its emphasis on performance, is highly meritocratic and thus provides incentives for success. The weaknesses, however, are equally real. The meritocratic emphasis puts a premium on getting on to the right escalator from kindergarten upwards. It also involves the 'exam hell' with its occasional suicides and the phenomenon of the 'education mama' whose task it is to force young Taro or Emiko to do their homework properly and, if necessary, to send the children to crammers. Those who do succeed are often exhausted by the time they get to University and regard their years at University as a welcome holiday. The 'holiday' may enable them to recharge their batteries for the next highly competitive step of getting a good job and then climbing the ladder. One danger in this process, however, is that the need to conform in order to get promotion (combined with the slog to pass examinations) could lead to a decline in creativity and independent thought. This will not matter if nevertheless Japan continues as hitherto to produce the sort of dynamic leadership which still marks its top companies. I suspect that such leaders will be found among those who rebel against the system and work up through medium and small scale enterprises.

At the same time, however, smaller families with fathers frequently out late have led to a decline in parental discipline, while the general availability of what would at one time have been regarded as luxuries has resulted in a move away from the frugality of the past. One result has been a growth of juvenile pilfering. Another has been the development of the phenomena of school violence against teachers, as well as fellow pupils. There are also signs of an increase in the numbers of drop-outs or opters-out. The temptations of the easy life – more leisure, more holidays, more luxury goods – have been a contributing factor. Drugs fortunately have not yet been a major problem, but gang revelry in noise, drink and way-out behaviour can all be found in Tokyo and other parts of Japan. The problems are compounded by the general lack of a coherent philosophy of life and the breakdown in or lack of ethical teaching.

~

Vietnam

'This is still a rugged country'

TIMOTHY EVERARD, CONSUL GENERAL IN
NORTH VIETNAM, NOVEMBER 1973

In North Vietnam carefulness and patience are rugged qualities . . . An electrician testing for short circuits in the power supply is more likely to use damped fingers than a voltmeter. Those who test lorry brakes (in the pleasant but busy old avenue where our office stands, which is also used by turns for foxholes, football pitch, firewood supply and rifle-range) screech to a halt in the middle of the road, and emerge to measure and study the skid marks. Occasionally this is unnecessary, if the brakes pull unevenly and the lorry has already hit a tree or it is on its side. Yet they carry on, and we have, so far, seen many failed brakes but no casualties. This is partly a tribute to the agility and vigilance of Vietnamese pedestrians and cyclists. This is still a rugged country and its policies and practices, even when 'peaceful' and 'patient' have a vigour and rigour of their own.

~

'The Viet-Namese . . . have, within the last five centuries, destroyed within their present territory two cultures . . . whose artistic achievements were vastly superior to their own'

FRANCIS BROOKS RICHARDS, HM AMBASSADOR
TO SOUTH VIETNAM, FEBRUARY 1974

LAST THOUGHTS FROM SAIGON

*Her Majesty's Ambassador at Saigon to the
Secretary of State for Foreign and Commonwealth Affairs*

(CONFIDENTIAL)   *Saigon,
27 February, 1974.*

Sir,

Claudel observed that five years in Asia are enough totally to inhibit a European from putting pen to paper. I have served in Saigon for little more than two, but that is enough to have bred at least a sense of caution. The complexities of this three-ways divided country, the limitations of what one does not, and cannot, know are daunting enough: what, one is bound also to ask, will anyone in London at present find time enough and light to read about a place which most of the world asks only to forget; and where policy is minimum commitment at minimum cost.

Claudel's cycle of Cathay and mine moved at different paces. I set about this attempt to round up valedictory impressions not in palanquin or sampan but in mid-air, at what my Air Attaché judges an altitude unlikely to tempt that revolutionary weapon, the hand-held heat-seeking missile. The sun is coming up out of the South China Sea, throwing the Annamite Cordillera into silhouette. Those lucky enough to move much about this spectacularly beautiful country by aircraft, and by helicopter in particular, see unexpected aspects of that beauty – the herring-bone patchwork of vegetables; the viridian of young rice; the cerulean of the sky reflected in flooded paddies – as well as the scars of defoliant and many millions of tons of ordnance . . .

Cultural originality and, indeed, creative achievement in the broadest sense have not been strong suits with the Viet-Namese. The taste of the court at Hue was as curious, as eclectic and, to me, unsatisfactory as that of Ludwig of Bavaria, its contemporary. The Viets appear to have had no music and perhaps even no verse of their own before they absorbed from their contact with the Chams a non-Chinese instrumental tradition and a melancholy style of epic poetry . . . The Viet-Namese would find it difficult to rebut the charge that they have, within the last five centuries, destroyed within their present territory two cultures, the Cham and the Khmer, whose artistic achievements were vastly superior to their own. They appear, indeed, to have something of a bad conscience about the Chams: I have more than once been told by educated Viet-Namese that the present misfortunes can be considered punishment for their ancestors' misdeeds in this respect . . .

The women are important: though industrious and often decorative, they are mercantile and rapacious. Even three centuries ago, travellers noted their skill in business: they were used by foreign merchants as factors and it was normal for the wife of an aspiring mandarin to keep the family while he prepared for the triennial examination. Today, far too many of the wives of those in positions of public responsibility are feathering their nests on the grand scale. One hears it said that particular women drive their men hard to satisfy their lust for talismanic jade or gold or real estate.

∾

Indonesia

'A natural tendency towards violence'

SIR JOHN FORD, HM AMBASSADOR TO INDONESIA,
FEBRUARY 1978

Sir John's focus on the violent side of Indonesian (or 'Javanese') character was inspired by his ringside seat during the bloody seizure of East Timor in 1975. By the time the Indonesians withdrew in 1999, some 200,000 East Timorese had been killed. The UK government was in a bind over what line to take. In public London opposed the invasion, but behind the scenes the picture was more complicated. A 1975 telegram from Sir John had counselled tacit support for Suharto: 'The people of Portuguese Timor are in no condition to exercise the right to self-determination . . . Certainly as seen from here it is in Britain's interest that Indonesia should absorb the territory as soon and as unobtrusively as possible; and that if it comes to the crunch and there is a row in the United Nations we should keep our heads down and avoid siding against the Indonesian Government.' Today East Timor has achieved its independence from Indonesia. History was not, as it turned out, on the ambassador's side.

Like the Balinese volcano Gunung Agung which bottles up its energy until the pent-up force within breaks out, so within the Javanese it seems as if a natural tendency towards violence is pent-up; cruelty is ever near the surface; and all hell breaks loose when restraints collapse. There is something particularly repulsive about the propensity to cold cruelty of the Indonesian. This explains partly why firm government is so necessary if unchecked emotions are not to lead to a loss of control most horrible in its manifestations . . .

. . . For the Javanese as for so many Orientals, feelings are so much more important than reasons. The Javanese is waiting almost expectantly for his feelings to be injured by the high and mighty foreigner. The Javanese smiles and resents and remembers and grudges. The Javanese is hide-bound and traditional, mystical and devious. The well-educated Javanese remembers Raffles with respect and regrets that Britain handed back the East Indies in 1816. And so a Britain which is no longer seen as high and mighty but yet as traditional and somewhat mystical in its attitude to [our] Crown and somewhat devious in its policies can have some appeal and exercise some beneficial influence. A special responsibility thus falls on all Britons – diplomats, technical co-operation staffs and businessmen – who serve out here.

Part IV: WEST

United States

'One of the most egotistical men I have met'

LORD HARLECH, HM AMBASSADOR TO THE UNITED STATES
OF AMERICA, MARCH 1965

*Lord Harlech (David Ormsby-Gore) was not a career diplomat,
but a political appointee, which used to be common for the
Washington job. A former Foreign Office Minister under
Harold Macmillan, Harlech achieved a level of closeness to
the White House unsurpassed by any other envoy before or
since; a long-standing close personal friend of John Kennedy,
with whom he dined at the White House once a week,
Harlech also romanced the President's wife. Harlech and the
widowed Jackie Kennedy reportedly became lovers after the
ambassador, who lost his wife in a car crash in 1967, stepped
down from the Foreign Office. There was briefly speculation
that the two might marry. Relations, however, were not quite
so cordial with the Johnson White House. The new President, it
is said, took a dislike to the ambassador's patrician manner.*

*Harlech's valedictory deserves attention as a masterly and
well-phrased thumbnail sketch of a particular president, his
instincts, his capabilities and his shortcomings. A British Prime
Minister or Foreign Secretary who took ten minutes to read
this letter might have gained a better grasp of the essential
LBJ than might be imparted by reams of briefing papers. Time
and biography have since rendered this the standard picture
of Lyndon Baines Johnson, but at the time it was prescient.*

But the despatch also indicates the perils of forecasting.

Lyndon Baines Johnson was not, in the event, to serve 'eight more years' as President. In March 1968, three years after Lord Harlech's despatch, LBJ told a stunned nation: 'I shall not seek, nor will I accept the nomination of my party for another term as your President.' Domestically, LBJ was caught between hawks, wanting total commitment to American military victory in the Vietnam War, and doves, wanting a peace settlement; both abandoned LBJ when their aims were frustrated.

March 1965 saw the start of the aerial bombing campaign Operation Rolling Thunder. Harlech was mistaken in judging this to be only 'temporarily more belligerent' behaviour by the Americans, it was in fact a significant slither down into the quagmire. Belying his determination, as reported in this despatch, to avoid a 'dangerous escalation', Johnson in fact increased American troop numbers from 16,000 in 1963 to more than half a million in 1968.

The Administration was indeed talking of limited war, but Harlech was perhaps listening too credulously: it was the disconnect between the Presidential speeches and the grisly reality on the ground in Vietnam – a disconnect which introduced the term 'credibility gap' to the political lexicon – that so fuelled public discontent.

Harlech proved no better a doctor than political forecaster. His optimism about the state of Johnson's heart in the eight years ahead was confounded seven years later. LBJ had a stroke in 1972. A repeat heart attack which killed him in January the following year came just two days after the end of what would have been Johnson's second term in office.

Our ambassador to Washington received, in turn, despatches of his own from British consular posts around the United States. In the archives Harlech's despatch sits alongside two interesting accounts from western states, which also *feature below. The first, which is essentially about the phenomenon of Texas, is today lent poignancy by the subsequent phenomenon of George W. Bush.*

I now confront the difficult task of attempting to prophesy United States policy in the future under the leadership of a very different type of man, President Johnson. Barring some unforeseeable disaster or a collapse in his health Mr. Johnson is likely to preside over the fortunes of this most powerful nation on earth for eight more years. There are those who think it most improbable that a man, who has had serious heart trouble and who possesses an inability to relax, can physically survive so long, but I am bound to say that up to now he seems to be thriving on the presidency. Perhaps the frustrations for him of supreme power are less than the frustrations of not having supreme power. For he is one of the most egotistical men I have met. His political talents are undoubtedly of a high order and his 'populist' approach to the problems of his country is in tune with the broad traditional instinct of Americans – certainly more so than the slightly sceptical, highly sophisticated and almost aristocratic approach of President Kennedy. He believes in low interest rates, thinks there is no real conflict of interest between business and labour, feels uncomfortable with intellectuals, hardly ever reads a book, has little interest in the history or affairs of other countries, but he does have a tremendous loyalty to his conception of the American dream and a driving determination to make it come true under his guidance. Hence his programme to create 'The Great Society'. How successful will he be? I would judge pretty successful . . .

When I turn to the prospects in the international field under President Johnson I feel I must record a large question mark. He is of course in favour of peace, disarmament, expanded trade and every other sort of desirable objective. He is naturally cautious . . . and he has around him, at least for the time being, intelligent and hard-working advisers. But basically he has no feeling for world affairs and no great interest in them except in so far as they come to disturb the domestic scene. He has little sensitivity to the attitude of foreigners, as witness a statement of his that on the basis of his globe-trotting as Vice-President he was convinced that in every country he visited the people would prefer to be Americans. The thought of the impression he would make in a *tête-à-tête* with General de Gaulle is too horrendous to contemplate. He seems most reluctant to concentrate his mind on long-term policy and prefers to arrive at a course of action after an intricate search for a consensus involving much behind-the-scenes manoeuvring and general obfuscation. I doubt therefore whether we can expect much inspired leadership from the United States under Mr. Johnson but I would be surprised if he made many mistakes in reacting to situations not of his making. I see no sign, for instance, that he will give a lead to the American people over the recognition of Communist China or its membership of the United Nations. On the other hand I think he is determined to avoid a dangerous escalation over Viet-Nam despite the temporarily more belligerent American behaviour in that part of the world.

∾

PETER HOPE, CONSUL-GENERAL IN HOUSTON,
JANUARY 1965

CONFIDENTIAL AND GUARD

British Consulate-General
1005 World Trade Center
1520 Texas Avenue
Houston, Texas 77002
January 5, 1965

My Lord,

It is some while since a general report on the Southwest of
the U.S. was submitted and since I am shortly to be posted
to the United Kingdom Mission to the United Nations in
New York, this may be a convenient moment to offer Your
Lordship some random observations on one of the more
remote areas of the U.S. which until comparatively recently
was labelled the Great Southwestern Desert. Moreover,
Texas in particular has come into the news, not only because
of the appalling story of the assassination of President
Kennedy last year in Dallas, immediately followed by the
murder of the assassin, but also because there has been
recent publicity about commercial prospects for Britain
in this area . . .

The Southwest is not much smaller than Western Europe,
and this Consular District stretches from some of the
highest and wildest mountains of the Rockies where peaks
reach nearly 15,000 feet across a vast upland of sage, cactus
and a few waterholes, to the steaming swamps and bayous
of the Gulf of Mexico where the temperatures and humidity

compare evilly on occasions with Freetown and other tropical ports.

Over the past thirty years the territory has seen a series of explosions of wealth and population. In spite of the myths of cowboys and Indians, bad men and cattle stampedes, the initial wealth came from lumber, cotton, rice, sheep and goats, since in most of the district, acres were counted to the cow rather than cows to the acre. (The clever intermarriage of Hereford and Brahma cattle has now produced the Santa Gertrudis breed which copes well with heat and flies, and produces bulls over one and one half tons in weight). World War I gave the economy a considerable fillip since once-poor farmers who had discarded waterholes fouled with oil became rich overnight . . .

Stories of the present wealth of Texas abound and though many at first sight appear apocryphal, there is a sound basis for most. In this vast area, it is understandable that men of wealth and their companies use airplanes like cars. There must be two or three times as many private aircraft on Houston's six airfields as there are in the whole of Western Europe. Several oilmen have their private jet aircraft. Sheep farmers in the vast ranges of west Texas and New Mexico save money by herding animals with helicopters – so the Neiman-Marcus store offers them as Christmas gifts. In each of the cities of Houston and Dallas there is more money on deposit in the banks than the total gold and foreign currency reserves which back the sterling area; the Humble Oil Company has the largest tanker fleet in the world; the King Ranch is larger than the English County of Kent – examples are endless.

Money in the Southwest still breeds money, and this rich area, which owed its initial success perhaps more to natural resources than the intellectual brilliance of its present millionaire leaders (to say nothing of their education since most were once roughnecks who left school before their teens), is now for the first time face to face with the outside world. The ramifications of petroleum, the petro-chemical industry, space age projects, the aircraft industry and even banking are leading a proud but basically chauvinistic and inward-looking people along international highways into the complexities of foreign affairs – and they find this experience basically disagreeable . . .

It has been an interesting though not always satisfying experience to watch the almost daily expansion of this great area and the way in which its people are reacting. The hard core still remember with nostalgia both the frontier freedom of the West and the Deep South way of living. Most High School children drive themselves to class – many with pistols in the glove compartment. Nearly all of the many millionaires (and they are legion with more than sixty living in permanent apartments in one hotel in Houston, the Warwick) have made their wealth in one generation, learning to ride before they could walk and starting work as roughnecks . . .

These men of newly-obtained wealth have cleverly banded themselves together effectively to operate a very closed society – under the guise of civic associations. Their word is law, so that the press, news media, civic authorities and even Courts of Justice inevitably follow their wishes. Their generosity is almost unbelievable and their pride in the State is such that the rank and file tolerate this situation for the benefits which accrue to them both through such things as the huge medical centres, the air-conditioned Domed Stadium, and the like. These men have also attracted vast projects of Federal origin to the State, like the Manned

Spacecraft Centre . . . bringing employment and wealth to many.

In-born conservatism largely explains why Dallas accommodates so many rich extremists of the Right and why it was labelled in the world press as the city of hate. It also explains a fierce antagonism to Central Government in Washington which limits freedom of action to take oil from the ground for more than so many days a month; which imposes legislation regarded here as an infringement on the sacred rights of the State and which in general terms asks the oligarchy to modify its way of life. But the evils of what amounts to an 18th Century Whig oligarchy in modern guise are, however, only too observable. Absolute power has tended to corrupt absolutely and to misquote Burke, injustice is often done and even more frequently seen to be done.

To me, however, the most disagreeable feature of this brash, new and selfish society is not the way in which one man likes the White House enough to copy it for himself or another reproduces a French Chateau most incongruously in the centre of a petro-chemical city, but the manner in which open corruption seems to be tolerated . . . Crimes of passion regularly occur, but when the oligarchy is involved they never even reach a Grand Jury. Disregard of law is most flagrant in politics. Ballot boxes are switched or disappear. Names from graveyards are included when necessary in the list of voters. It is indeed a common joke that Texans have a vote whether alive or dead.

I expect, however, that this displeasing aspect of the Southwest will slowly fade as the area is diluted by immigration and internationalises itself. Already Houston is more civilised in this respect, and Dallas more so than West Texas. It is a bitter pill to the oligarchs because essentially these selfish men here had their own way and in their own words 'hate being corralled'. They are only now beginning to understand why, unlike themselves in their own parish, the Federal Government is unable to have its own way with the Red Chinese or in South Vietnam. They still only dimly realise that their country is inevitably involved in the world, but they resent it strongly. They hope for relief from their Texan President and even more to be able to direct him. In this, events are, I am glad to say, so far proving them wrong.

~

'There are <u>some</u> nice people here'

PETER DALTON, CONSUL-GENERAL IN LOS ANGELES,
NOVEMBER 1965

BRITISH CONSULATE-GENERAL

3324 Wilshire Boulevard
Los Angeles
California, 90005

29 November, 1965

Sir,

In my despatch No. 14 of the 19th of December, 1964, to your predecessor, I had the honour to submit some 'first impressions' of Los Angeles. It may seem otiose, only a year later, to submit a valedictory despatch. Nevertheless, it may be of some interest, for the record, to report that, in the intervening year, my impressions have not greatly changed. I still find Los Angeles, on the whole, a disagreeable city and life here, at any rate for a foreign consular officer, not one to which I, personally, find myself attracted . . .

. . . [A]s Mr. Bob Hope put it, in welcoming Her Royal Highness Princess Margaret during her recent visit, 'After your visit to San Francisco, welcome to America.'

But if Los Angeles is politically, and in many ways actually, a great city . . . it is still largely an unplanned mess. Amenities have, hitherto, been sacrificed to material progress, and, while one may travel for miles on the world's finest freeways, there is little to please the eye, or, indeed, any other sense, in doing so. The city has, therefore, at present, little physical attraction.

For the foreign representative, Los Angeles is, I find, unrewarding also in its formlessness and lack of warmth. Southern Californians seem to want to be loved, or, at any rate, reassured, but they do not know, or, in many cases, are too busy to worry about, how to make themselves agreeable. It is not, I find, the distances that divide one from the people as much as the casualness and preoccupation with their own affairs. Many have no time to be cultivated, while others appear to have no wish.

In such circumstances, it is difficult at times to determine in what direction, as a foreign representative, one should address one's efforts, or, indeed, whether what one tries to do makes any impact at all. For the present, I am inclined to think that the most profitable line might be to concentrate on the commercial work . . . and, by and large, let 'society' (including the 'Hollywood fringe') go hang. (The large, demanding and generally, rather low-level British community will, however, always be a millstone round the Consul-General's neck, not easy to shake off.)

One cannot, however, altogether withhold admiration for such a brashly growing place, and, although, at this post, I must say that I leave it with no regrets, I shall certainly be interested to see how it has developed in ten or fifteen years' time and, in the meantime, shall probably not be able entirely to stifle some friendly curiosity about its progress, for, when all is said and done, there are <u>some</u> nice people here.

I am sending copies of this despatch to H.M. Principal Secretary of State for Foreign Affairs and to the Acting British Consul-General at San Francisco.

I have the honour to be,

With the highest respect,
Sir,
Your Excellency's obedient Servant,

P. G. F. Dalton

~

Canada

'He is almost incomprehensible to a great number of "far away Canadians"'

SIR PETER HAYMAN, HM HIGH COMMISSIONER
TO CANADA, OCTOBER 1974

... [A] commentary on Canada must begin with an analysis of that curious man, Pierre Elliott Trudeau. The swinging image has virtually disappeared, although the fifty-five-year-old Prime Minister, sometimes with beads round his neck and other sartorial fads, still tends to look too much like 'mutton dressed as lamb'. But 'trendy Trudeau' was a foolish public relations gimmick that did not reflect the real man.

He is much more interesting . . . [but] [h]e is almost incomprehensible to a great number of 'far away Canadians', the prairie farmers, Albertan oil men, British Columbian lumber-jacks.

~

'One does not encounter here the ferocious competition of talent that takes place in the United Kingdom'

LORD MORAN, HM HIGH COMMISSIONER
TO CANADA, JUNE 1984

Further extracts from Lord Moran's valedictory can be found on p. 366.

Further extracts from Lord Moran's valedictory can be found on p. 366.

OTTAWA
12 June 1984

Sir,

In a few days' time my wife and I leave Ottawa and I become a private man. For the past three years we have travelled all over this vast and disunited land, covering altogether some 130,000 miles – equivalent to five times round the world – by everything from a jumbo jet to a canoe. We have been several times to all the main cities and to places like Prince Rupert, Annapolis Royal and Medicine Hat, but, sadly, not to Moose Jaw, Joliette or Flin-Flon. On countless occasions we have munched those inevitable salads, stood for the singing of 'O Canada' and drunk The Queen's health in iced water. We shall miss, in their different ways, the cry of the loon, as characteristic of Canada as the fish eagle's is of Africa, and the cheerful shop girls and waitresses of North America, who send us on our way with 'Take care' or 'Have a nice day'.

I have sent you and your predecessors my thoughts on Anglo-Canadian relations, Canadian foreign policy, Mr Trudeau, the monarchy in Canada, Canada north of sixty, and French and English Canadians. Now that my sojourn in Canada is nearly over, I would like to record a few last personal impressions on a rather wide variety of subjects.

Mr Trudeau

Although I like him personally and he has been kind to us, it has, I am sure, been a disadvantage that Mr Trudeau has been Prime Minister throughout my time in Canada because, with some reason, he has not been greatly respected or trusted in London. He has never entirely shaken off his past as a well-to-do hippie and draft dodger. His views on East/West relations have been particularly suspect. Many of my colleagues here admire him. I cannot say I do. He is an odd fish and his own worst enemy, and on the whole I think his influence on Canada in the past 16 years has been detrimental. But what he minded most about was keeping Quebec in Canada and his finest hours were the ruthless and effective stamping-out of terrorism in Quebec in 1970 and the winning there of the referendum of sovereignty/association ten years later. For the present, separatism in Quebec is at a low ebb. Mr Trudeau has maintained that only by an increase in Ottawa's powers could Canada develop as a strong state. He treated provincial premiers with contempt and provincial governments as if they were town councils . . .

Lack of Ideology in Politics; Patronage

I have been struck by the marked absence of ideology in Canadian politics. People in the United Kingdom join the Conservative or Labour parties with very different ideas about the kind of society they want to see. In Canada the philosophic differences between Liberals and Progressive Conservatives are scarcely perceptible. The main motive for joining one of these parties is to acquire power or a lucrative job. So political patronage flourishes. Highly paid and long-lasting jobs in the Senate and chairmanships of public enterprises are used almost entirely to reward party hacks. Canadians are surprised to learn that an active member of the House of Lords is unpaid and receives less in expenses than a Canadian on welfare. No one would pretend for a moment that Mr Don Jamieson is the most suitable man to represent Canada in London. He is there because he is an old Liberal war-horse who wanted one more job before he retired (and was disappointed of Washington). Party appointees fill scores of federally appointed posts. Politics run on 'jobs for the boys'. And Canadian ministers arrange for large amounts of federal money to go to their constituencies. In Nova Scotia 40% of all federal grants go to the riding of the Deputy Prime Minister, Mr MacEachen. And provincial governments behave in exactly the same way.

Low Calibre of Canadian Politicians
One result is that the calibre of Canadian politicians is low. The level of debate in the House of Commons is correspondingly low; the majority of Canadian ministers are unimpressive and a few we have found frankly bizarre . . .

But Canadian politicians look after their own – and one another. When, for example, Mr Jamieson (a Liberal) goes home from London, he tells me that a helicopter, provided by the provincial (Conservative) government (at the taxpayers' expense) is at the airport to fly him to his country house in Newfoundland. Ministers and the Leader of the Opposition have free passes on Air Canada – which most of the candidates for the Liberal leadership have been using shamelessly to campaign across the country . . .

Canadian Characteristics
Canadians are a moderate, comfortable people. Not surprisingly, they share many characteristics with ourselves. In a world where we have to deal with the Qadhafis, Khomeinis and indeed the Shamirs[1], and with many others who are happy to ride roughshod over our interests, it seems to me sensible to cultivate decent and reasonable people like this, quite apart from the fact they have such close historic ties with us and dispose of such immense natural resources. Canadians are mildly nationalistic (but perhaps less shrilly so than Australians), <u>very</u> sensitive, especially to any expressed or implied British sneers about Canada as 'boring', and perhaps somewhat lacking in self-confidence. Mr Charles Richie[2] said not long ago: 'We are not the same type of country as Britain – our country is based on accommodation, compromise, and conciliation – and I think that is reflected to some extent in the manner in which we conduct our foreign policy.' My late Chinese colleague, a perceptive man, told us that he thought the friendliest Canadians were in Alberta, Saskatchewan and the Atlantic provinces, and this has been our impression. The most difficult, prickly and unforthcoming are undoubtedly some of those who work for the Federal Government in Ottawa.

Canadians go to church more than we do but their lives are no longer subjected to a stern Presbyterian moral code. About 35% of Canadian marriages end in divorce. One big difference from the United Kingdom is that there is very little here of that strong public opinion which has so far exacted a price from public men or women who fall below accepted standards. The Canadian public expects very little of politicians and tends to shrug its shoulders when the press or television report another scandal. Memories are short. Even ministers who resign after serious misdemeanours, such as forging signatures and trying to influence judges, reappear in Cabinet after the briefest of absences.

Absence of Competition

One does not encounter here the ferocious competition of talent that takes place in the United Kingdom. Many gifted Canadians still seek wider opportunities elsewhere . . . Anyone who is even moderately good at what they do – in literature, the theatre, ski-ing or whatever – tends to become a national figure. Even some Canadian representatives overseas . . . are written up in the newspapers, and anyone who stands out at all from the crowd tends to be praised to the skies and given the Order of Canada at once.

1. *Shamirs*: Yitzhak Shamir, Prime Minister of Israel (1983–4 and 1986–92).
2. *Mr Charles Richie*: Canadian High Commissioner to the United Kingdom (1967-71).

≈

Nicaragua

'The average Nicaraguan is one of the most dishonest, unreliable, violent and alcoholic of the Latin Americans'

ROGER PINSENT, HM AMBASSADOR TO NICARAGUA, JULY 1967

More from Pinsent's despatch can be found on p. 300.

LAST GLANCE AT NICARAGUA

Mr Pinsent to Mr Brown. (Received 7 July)

(No. 13. Confidential)   *Managua,*
10 June 1967.

Sir,

I have the honour to submit in this despatch my impressions of Nicaragua on leaving the country. I regret that there was not time to complete it before I left, owing to the political and social turmoil of the last few weeks . . .

    I did not submit a report on my first impressions of Nicaragua after my arrival at the end of 1963 . . . partly . . . because my first impressions would probably have been too unfavourable to print. In this report therefore I will try to give a balanced view of the country and people as seen on departure . . .

    . . . [T]he approaches to the towns are squalid to a degree that shocks the visitor from Europe or the more sophisticated countries of South America. On arrival we unwittingly caused some offence by enquiring the name of the first village we passed through on leaving the airport, which turned out to be the capital city of Managua. The present Embassy residence on its windy cliff edge looking towards Lake Managua has, if little else, perhaps the finest prospect of all Managua; it happens also to be on the high road to Costa Rica.

These contrasts go right through Nicaraguan life. If ever there was a country where the private affluence of the few is flaunted in face of the public squalor of the many, it is Nicaragua. It is distressing that still to-day after thirty years of *Somocismo*,[1] which has undoubtedly brought stability and prosperity to the country as a whole, the conditions of living for the vast majority of Nicaraguans are little less than sordid: over half the population have no proper housing, little in the way of medical services and the sketchiest form of education. And while the country is undoubtedly progressing . . . the average Nicaraguan, like Thursday's child, has far to go before reaching the standard of even his South American brothers. Even Government offices, with a few exceptions, exhibit a squalor only comparable to certain 'third rooms'[2] in the Foreign Office. Yet, in spite of the low standard of education and general illiteracy, Nicaragua must have one of the highest standards of poetry in Latin America and has as its national hero the poet Ruben Dario, who is considered by many authorities to be possibly the greatest of all Hispano-American poets.

In his excellent valedictory despatch No. 39 of the 23rd of July, 1963, my immediate predecessor, Mr. Patrick Johnston, opined that the Nicaraguan character probably acquired its main characteristics from the Andalusian heritage of the original Spanish colonisers. I regret that I do not entirely subscribe to this view. In my opinion, the Nicaraguans show little of the charm of the Andalusian Spaniard, and certainly lack his talent for music, art and spectacle . . . [T]he true Nicaraguan is a *mestizo* of mixed Spanish and

Indian blood and his culture is the result of nearly five centuries of *mestizaje*. This *mestizo* culture has produced some remarkable poets . . . but it has also produced a large number of corrupt politicians. There is, I fear, no question but that the average Nicaraguan is one of the most dishonest, unreliable, violent and alcoholic of the Latin Americans – and after nearly 21 years of Latin American experience I feel I can speak with some authority on this subject. Their version of Spanish is quite the least attractive I have come across. The Nicaraguan prides himself on his hospitality and will provide it generously to his friends, probably with oceans of contraband liquor. But apart from a thin upper-crust of society most of whose members have been educated in the United States, Canada or Europe, and to whom my strictures do not apply, I must confess that the Nicaraguan generally is not an attractive character and appears to have little natural courtesy: he will not give way to women or children unless he knows them personally; and he exhibits all the worst features of '*machismo*' or the demonstration of virility by competitive discourtesy. The late Argentine Ambassador to Nicaragua on arrival here about three years ago, having rarely left Buenos Aires in his life, remarked to me that this was 'a country of savages' and that Managua appeared to him to resemble what the city of Buenos Aires must have been like in the 1850s (at around the time when British engineers building the Argentine railways were liable to be attacked by Indians with bows and arrows). As a non-career diplomat he was even more outraged than other colleagues about some of the treatment meted out to the Diplomatic Corps in Nicaragua.

I fear that this is a rather jaundiced view of the Nicaraguan character: it is true that we know many charming

Nicaraguans who do not betray the more unpleasant characteristics outlined above; while the Nicaraguan of the Atlantic coast, with his British and negro heritage, is quite different; gayer, better educated and more honest than those they describe as 'them Spaniards from Managua'. There is no doubt also that the better Nicaraguan business man is energetic and full of ideas and initiative . . . But in matters of commerce the fault of the Nicaraguans is not just that they give too little and ask too much, but that they can be as sharp as the famous fresh-water sharks of Lake Nicaragua.

1. *Somocismo*: President-Somoza-style dictatorship.
2. *'third rooms'*: Third Secretaries (Matthew Parris was one) occupy the lowest rung on the Diplomatic Service career ladder. The third room – their domain – is generally a byword for undergraduate-style untidiness.

~

'The standards of local efficiency are the lowest I have ever met'

GEORGE WARR, HM AMBASSADOR
TO NICARAGUA, JUNE 1970

I do not gloss over the dark side. Managua is a very unattractive city and the persistence of the heat throughout the year can be very trying though the horrors of the climate are considerably mitigated by air-conditioning . . . Building the Embassy house, which I have done since I came here, was a prodigious labor for my wife and myself simply because the standards of local efficiency are the lowest I have ever met. But . . . [t]here are compensating factors . . . The most important of these is that there is no xenophobia, or as little as I have ever met. I have served in the USSR and in Turkey where inefficiency is often coupled inextricably with deliberate malice directed towards the foreigner. In Nicaragua the inefficiency is pure and all Nicaraguans suffer from it equally with foreigners.

~

Honduras

'The problem is what I call the "scavenger complex" of Honduran society'

LAURENCE L'ESTRANGE, HM AMBASSADOR
TO HONDURAS, APRIL 1972

Soccer, which Mr L'Estrange mentions as a tension between Honduras and El Salvador, in fact precipitated war between the two countries. The four-day Football War of 1969 followed a pair of qualifying games between the two countries for the 1970 World Cup. Both games saw fans riot but, as L'Estrange records, the underlying dispute was over land, not football – specifically, Honduran efforts to evict the several hundred thousand El Salvadorean immigrant farmers within their borders. The fighting, though short, was brutal. The El Salvadorean Air Force, lacking heavy aircraft, dropped 100lb bombs out of adapted passenger jets. Honduras retaliated with napalm.

It might be asked why Honduras is so poor and what her prospects are. The answer is to be found by probing more deeply than accepting the obvious renowned lethargy of the people or the propaganda (often inspired by El Salvador) which makes the case that this is a potentially rich country whose resources, the people, are too lazy, ignorant, poor or too few to develop. The fact is that only 15% of the area of this largely perpendicular country is arable . . . The main natural resources are the lovely pine forests which thrive on the poor rocky soil, so that when these are plundered, as is occurring on an appalling scale, no worthwhile crop will grow in their place . . . Nor is the banana King any longer in this original Banana Republic. Export prices have dropped and costs of production have risen to such an extent that the contribution of that industry to the balance of trade and to the budget in the form of taxes has been steadily dropping . . .

Honduras is also beset by enormous social problems. Outside the capital and the few large towns educational facilities are abysmally low and medical services distressingly inadequate, if they exist at all. The illegitimate birth rate is high by Latin American standards and seems to be rising. Alcoholism is a national problem and accounts for the ubiquity of Alcoholics Anonymous who seem able to do more about this problem than the church . . . [L]and tenure is . . . a great problem in a country where 1% of the farmers own 46% of the arable land . . . The key to the problem here is what I have come to call the 'scavenger complex' of Honduran society. As an example when a large landowner dies his estate immediately becomes vulnerable and years are spent by the executors recovering lands for the rightful heirs, litigation is endless and the courts are corrupt . . . [T]he exodus of the Salvadoreans was caused as much by the rising wave of propaganda over the first football match between the two countries as by the opportunity this gave to Hondurans to relieve the industrious Salvadoreans of their homes and farms, more so as the harvest was about to be gathered . . .

Sir, I leave this post on retirement. It will be the second time I leave the Service and I therefore feel the more honoured to end my career as one of Her Majesty's Ambassadors and pleased to have had the opportunity of doing so in an area with which I am so familiar. That it was beset by so many problems, insoluble as many of them continue to be, has been an exhilarating challenge. To meet it by cultivating the friendliest relations possible and by displaying a genuine sympathy in their predicament has evoked a satisfying response from Hondurans which belies their renowned dullness.

~

Jamaica

'The Caribbean islands are perhaps dangerous only to themselves'

JOHN HENNINGS, HM HIGH COMMISSIONER
TO JAMAICA, FEBRUARY 1976

The Caribbean countries are not like many others in the world which, after a period of imperial rule, have rediscovered their own internal reverences. They are manufactured societies, and they have for long been dependent upon an external source for their law, their language, their institutions, their culture and even their officials. Dependence has become a habit, and little that has been generated locally is widely accepted as having a validity comparable with the erstwhile metropolitan influences. The self-conscious quest for identity, which can amuse and infuriate the outside observer, both reveals and masks this sense of uncertainty as to what the people of the Caribbean really are. It adds, too, to the difficulty of creating an acceptable autonomous system of government deriving its strength, its self-confidence and its ability to pursue wise, rather than populist, policies from the assurances of a mandate from a cohesively structured body politic. There are resemblances between the Caribbean situation and that of Latin America after the break-up of the Spanish Empire. The pity of it is that the countries of the Caribbean – small, black and certainly poor when weighed against their people's aspirations – are also intrinsically unimportant, so that if disaster comes they alone will be hurt. The Caribbean islands, after all, are perhaps dangerous only to themselves.

In a book which he wrote in 1859 after a visit to the West Indies, Anthony Trollope delivered himself of the cynical judgment that 'If we could we would fain forget Jamaica altogether.' In my time here, a number of Jamaicans, perhaps not altogether without self-pity, have alleged this loss of interest against us. Jamaicans have many endearing qualities – gaiety, colour, an enviable ability to live for the day – but they are hardly a serious-minded people, and, despite a patina of sophistication, their sense of values is that of a small parochial island society. Despite the many good things that do go on here, they seem content with much that is second-rate, in the values of their educational system, in work discipline and in economic output. The tropical climate and a hitherto uncomplicated economic structure connive at an easy-going way of life, and have perpetuated an improvident family system under which private promiscuity co-exists with the faithful outward observances of a metropolitan society of 50 years ago or more. And indeed many who note the inconsistency are often more concerned to defend the improvidences as a legacy of slavery or as the forerunner of the lately acquired permissiveness of the developed world than to reduce them as impediments to economic development and the creation of a modern cost-effective society.

Jamaicans for all their charm – and it is great – can be demanding and costive friends. Their immigrants to Britain rightly demand acceptance, but they tend to argue that their hosts must take them as they are, and that the host society must adjust to them rather than they to it. In matters of trade, too, and in the concepts of the new international economic relationships to which they seek to persuade the developed world, it is difficult at times to suppress the thought that they cherish a persistent belief that what they seek is their due as an act of atonement.

~

Barbados

'Government in the hands of . . . a half-naked intelligentsia'

DAVID ROBERTS, HM HIGH COMMISSIONER
TO BARBADOS, SEPTEMBER 1973

At the time of the Changing of the Guard, I have the honour to report that I leave Barbados much as I found it. Indeed, to judge from the history of Barbados, things do not seem to change very much here, although each generation has lamented the decay in morals and foreseen the dissolution of society through the idleness and loose-living of the young. At my age I also incline to this view . . .

. . . It is now the exception rather than the rule for a young and outstanding Barbadian to be educated at Oxford or Cambridge. Thus, through death, retirement or more lucrative employment, the generation of men who read greats, economics or law in the UK, acquired an affinity with our way of thinking and an acceptance of our social values, and came home to govern Barbados, will pass away. They will leave Government in the hands of young men educated at the University of the West Indies, from which a half-naked intelligentsia is already coming forward. The new generation have largely been instructed by university teachers who could not hold down a reputable job elsewhere. A small country which badly needs carpenters, plumbers, engineers and so forth is turning out third-rate lawyers and sociologists by the dozen. It is good inflammable material for a political bonfire.

~

Puerto Rico

'Quite inaccurate idea of Puerto Ricans as a rather degenerate race of small brown people"

RICHARD THOMAS, CONSUL IN PUERTO RICO,
OCTOBER 1965

I have found during my two and a half years at this post that if anybody in the United Kingdom thinks about Puerto Rico at all (and few do) it is as a rather slummy place owned by the Americans where all those characters in *West Side Story* come from . . .

. . . In the glorious years of the <u>conquistadors</u> Puerto Rico was for Spain a possession without gold or other wealth . . . [I]n Spanish eyes Puerto Rico was merely the place where only the unfortunate or unambitious settlers remained. It was a poor island which was hardly touched by the stories of revolutionary glory that came out of the Spanish mainland territories.

When the Americans came in 1896 the campaign here was a sideshow to those in Cuba and the Philippines. There was no fighting beyond skirmishes and there the Americans were; stuck with a colony they did not know what to do with. And it was just about nothing they did do with it for the next five decades. So poor was the island in the early forties that

Rexford Tugwell, one of the few remembered and a much respected American Governor, entitled his book about Puerto Rico *The Stricken Land*. I have read an account of a visit by an American yachtsman written as late as 1948 in which he described his eagerness to get away from Puerto Rico as fast as possible. The picture he drew was of a sink of poverty where good American dollars had gone down the drain to no avail . . .

And yet, only a few weeks ago I attended a Chamber of Commerce dinner . . . What has inspired this confidence, this quite unprecedented feeling of optimism and self respect? It is not merely the benefits of the American rule. Essentially it was the belated exploitation by the Puerto Ricans themselves of the connexion with the United States. And also there can be little doubt that one man, Luis Muñoz Marin,[1] was the mainspring . . . Today Luis Muñoz speaks standard American English and it would be difficult to fit him in with the common and quite inaccurate idea of Puerto Ricans as a rather degenerate race of small brown people of mixed origins. He is a great personality by most standards . . .

1. *Luis Muñoz Marin*: The first governor of independent Puerto Rico (1949–65); nowadays he is remembered as the father of the nation tens of thousands of Puerto Ricans turned out for his funeral in 1980.

2. Settling Scores

Discussed briefly in the Introduction is the 2006 decision by the FCO so to curtail the impact within the Office of a valedictory despatch that (diplomats have told us) the whole tradition has effectively been ended.

Most potent among the reasons for this move (the editors have surmised) was not the occasional embarrassment caused to HMG when disobliging remarks about foreign countries, or indiscreet remarks about British foreign policy, leaked from a valedictory. No, it was the way the despatch has sometimes been used to turn a retiring ambassador's guns on the FCO itself, and the way the Office is run, that had really enraged Whitehall mandarins, and even ministers. This, as you will see from some of the material that follows, was the one time a civil servant could round on his or her masters. Worse (from Whitehall's viewpoint), some despatches were written to be read by a wider audience – and their authors were less than horrified when they appeared in the press.

But most only wanted their criticisms to be seen by internal eyes. Still, they meant it; it would sometimes be recognized as carrying an element of truth; and it stung. This is perhaps most sharply true of some of the more modern despatches here, all of which we obtained through Freedom of Information. Some of the authors were a little displeased to hear that we had got our hands on them.

We put it to Sir Peter Ricketts, who was then the Permanent Under Secretary – the head – of the Foreign Office, that the valedictory had been effectively banned. There was, he countered, a 'growing tendency [for] valedictories to leak, and they were doing real damage to the confidence and trust that has to exist between ministers and officials . . . I felt that that trust was breaking down.' He went on to say that the Office still wanted 'full, frank, hard-hitting advice – and we don't just want it on the day [diplomats] leave . . . So we were suggesting that people send in their advice in different ways and at different times . . .'

'In fact,' he said, 'the world has moved on, and by and large people don't send despatches anyway . . . The valedictory despatch risked becoming a caricature of itself . . . I don't think [it] did great things for the reputation of the Foreign Office.'

We found this reaction sad. Sir Ivor Roberts (the author of the valedictory that preceded Sir Peter's baleful edict) suggested to us that his despatch was only really an excuse, triggering a change the Office had been waiting to make. He pointed to 'the leaking of some of a valedictory from Iraq from our ambassador a few months earlier which had been quite negative about the direction things were going, and naturally was not regarded as being helpful to government policy. And the fact that the Foreign Office were mulling over whether to suppress valedictories may well have been in the air, as it were, and my valedictory may have been the last straw.'

Sir Christopher Meyer (see Chapter 1) was emphatic. The valedictory, he said, is 'an ancient and noble tradition, which requires an ambassador . . . to put down in a personal, succinct and clear way the conclusions that he's drawn . . .' The ban on valedictories, he said, was 'a cringing, defensive, unworthy posture . . .' and 'to limit their circulation in response to a leak is pitiful'.

Lord (Robin) Renwick (our man in Washington – see Notes

on the Material) called the ban 'a wholly bad thing. It's a pusil-lanimous response designed to protect ministers against criticism they fear might leak. The system was not abused; a lot of worthwhile things were said. These despatches were read with great interest and often real amusement; and it was the one time ... when career civil servants could say what they really thought, and some of them did, and to stop them doing it is absurd.'

Roberts's valedictory comes later in this chapter. We start with a despatch that probably caused less harm to its intended target in London than to the reputation of its author.

∼

'A disconcerting feeling of being watched by critical and potentially unfriendly eyes in London'

SIR PATRICK REILLY, HM AMBASSADOR
TO FRANCE, SEPTEMBER 1968

Sir Patrick Reilly represented Britain in Moscow, and twice as ambassador in Paris. In 1967 General Charles de Gaulle humiliated the British foreign policy establishment by blocking, for the second time, the UK's application to join the European Economic Community; and in May 1968, student riots brought France to a standstill. As one would expect, most of Reilly's valedictory was given over to a serious analysis of the situation on the ground.

Some of the passages included below, however, are more personal in tone. The modern reader may feel that Sir Patrick is here driven by sadnesses or anger that disturb the flow of his argument, leaving the uninitiated a little bewildered. The despatch has some of the qualities of an ill-considered speech at a company leaving-do. The 'special trials' to which Reilly *refers were the result of a falling out with George Brown, the mercurial and alcoholic British Foreign Secretary. Brown was once rude to Reilly's wife, in public, at the French Embassy in London, and the personality clash between the shy, cultured ambassador and the pugnacious Foreign Secretary – for whom the euphemism 'tired and emotional' was coined by Private Eye – cast a pall over the rest of Reilly's time in Paris. His valedictory was addressed to Michael Stewart, Brown's more emolient successor. A covering note from the Department warned of its contents: 'parts of it are controversial and outspoken . . . Sir P. Reilly has made fullest use of the licence which the occasion gives him for speaking frankly.'*

The result is rather sad because in these passages the despatch, striking out wildly in various directions, fails to achieve the coherence for which Sir Patrick must, in an important composition like this, have hoped.

De Gaulle did (as Reilly suggests) eclipse all other French politicians of the time. Nevertheless, Reilly's estimation of the prospects of two (then) also-rans has proved overly pessimistic with the passage of time: Valéry Giscard d'Estaing and François Mitterrand both eventually became President (1974–81 and 1981–95 respectively).

CONFIDENTIAL

BRITISH EMBASSY
PARIS
11 September 1968

Sir,

This last despatch of my official career has been written at a moment when it is exceptionally difficult to see ahead in Paris. France has just emerged from a startling and extraordinary crisis . . . [E]veryone is conscious of the clouds ahead. The dozen or more Ministers on whom I have called in the last fortnight have given me the impression of being very chastened men . . . On the morning of the 30th of May the French seemed hypnotised and paralysed in the face of what was in fact a tiny minority . . . [T]he foremost of the many factors which contributed to this extraordinary affair was the change in the character of political authority in France and the devaluation of all institutions under the Fifth Republic except for the Presidency itself. General de Gaulle thus bears a heavy responsibility for the crisis. Yet for all his failings, being still the one man in the Western world with greatness in him, he was able, having once recovered his will, to reverse the whole situation in a few minutes . . .

The lamentable weakness of the non-Communist Opposition starts with its leaders: Mitterrand, Mendes France, Mollet, Defferre, Bijleres, Lecanuet, Duhamel. Only the last seems to me to have any real future now, but his electoral base is too small. M. Mitterrand arouses astonishingly widespread mistrust. I cannot now see him as a plausible candidate for the Presidency or indeed see the Federation lasting under his leadership. (It is in fact already breaking up.) . . . Outside the Gaullists proper I can at present only see two possible candidates from the majority. M. Giscard d'Estaing, who is only forty-two, will certainly be a strong contender. He is able and experienced, and intensely ambitious. In the May crisis, however, his judgement went wildly astray; and for a man of his age to make a charming wife as miserable as she has appeared lately suggests to me a flaw somewhere. I am not inclined to put much money on him in the years immediately ahead . . .

Nearly all the speeches which have been made to me

before my departure have contained friendly references to the difficulties of mine in Paris. I have often caught myself listening to these phrases with surprise . . . In actual fact, in many ways life is made easy for a British Ambassador in Paris . . . In my experience it is in London that the difficulties arise. I am not of course referring to the special trials to which, like others of our colleagues, my wife and I have been subject during our time in Paris, and which have left deep scars. There is nothing very new about the situation I have in mind. In the 'thirties a senior member of the Service with exceptional experience of Paris astonished his wife by saying that he would never want the Embassy there because he knew too well how the Ambassador was always being shot at, often by people who wanted his job. I know that feeling well. Perhaps it was often illusory and of course for half the three years of my effective mission there was a special situation in London which has probably coloured my impression of my whole time here. Nevertheless I suspect that a disconcerting feeling of being watched by critical and potentially unfriendly eyes in London, most of whose owners are in fact completely ignorant of what is being done here, is the lot of most British Ambassadors in Paris . . .

I have concluded this despatch with . . . perhaps unusual reflections because my experience here has been unusual. A French newspaper described my last French speech, in which I had thought it right to do some plain speaking, as 'oscillating between emotion, some rancour and much bitterness'. I hardly think that the writer could have heard me make it: but the comment is interesting as showing how difficult it is, however carefully you choose your words, to talk frankly to the French without making hackles rise. It is certainly not in this spirit that I am leaving Paris. My mission here has covered the unhappiest time in the history of the Service. It was inevitable that we in Paris should suffer with it ...

I am sending copies of this despatch to Her Majesty's Ambassadors at Brussels, The Hague, Luxembourg, Bonn, Rome and Washington, and to Sir Bernard Burrows, Sir James Marjoribanks, Sir Eugene Melville and Sir Edgar Cohen.

I have the honour to be
with the highest respect,
Sir,

Your obedient Servant,

D. P. Reilly

~

'A harsh and boastful note has crept into British diplomacy'

SIR JULIAN BULLARD, HM AMBASSADOR TO THE FEDERAL REPUBLIC OF GERMANY, MARCH 1988

In the early 1980s, Bullard served as the Foreign Office's first Political Director, a job created to help Britain work more closely with its new European partners. His criticism below of a 'harsh and boastful note' in the tune Britain was playing in Europe in the later Thatcher years would, therefore, have struck (in some quarters) a chord; in others, a nerve.
Extracts from this despatch also appear on p. 38.

Extracts from this despatch also appear on p. 38.

Saying goodbyes up and down this country, I have encountered certain recurrent attitudes. Deep admiration for Britain – for things we take for granted, like our democracy and our Monarchy, but also for things not universally admired, nor even much in evidence, in Britain today. Great respect for the Prime Minister and for the turn-round in the British economy, achieved under her leadership, but stopping short of a desire to apply the same methods here. And a deep wish that Britain would be more present, more engaged, more active in Europe, in everything from space research to youth exchanges, both for our own merits and because many Germans are uncomfortable in the slightly synthetic special relationship with France. It is to this theme that I should like to devote what remains of my allocation of words.

I think we should try to avoid living down to the hard things that have been said about the British in the past. I need not quote Napoleon, but here is Nietzsche: *Die Engländer haben schon einmal mit ihrer tiefen Durchschnittlichkeit eine Gesamtdepression des europäischen Geistes verursacht* ('With their profound averageness, the British have already once caused a general depression of the European spirit'). I wrote last November to the Permanent Under-Secretary, calling for more vision and a different style in British policy in Europe. I received a reply nearly twice as long, asking what we actually lose by our present methods. In a way that illustrates my point. Not everything unquantifiable is unimportant. There will continue to be important decisions to be taken on Europe, perhaps one day on Central Europe, and the CDU will not necessarily always be in power in Bonn, nor the Conservative Party in London. I should not like the British voice to be weak because we had appeared to lose interest, or ignored because listeners had come to resent its tone. Once or twice recently a harsh and boastful note has crept into

British diplomacy, a note which I do not recognise. Or rather, I do recognise it, because it reminds me of a telegram from London which reached us in Amman during the Suez crisis of 1956, which began: 'When we are in control of the canal, which will be very soon now . . .' We all know what happened after that.

My message is a banal one: Take trouble with Germany. Be punctilious over Anglo-German meetings, from Summits down to the humblest expert bilateral, and allow time for those involved not just to read out their briefs, but to unpack some of their mental (as well as their physical) luggage. Europeanise Westminster and Whitehall, not with PR and coalitions but with ever more awareness of the continent, our continent. Where we see a chance for Britain to lead, do so in European colours. And treat the instruments of Anglo-German relations as allies, not as tiresome interruptions in the working day.

Among the best of these instruments are the Embassy in Bonn, British Military Government in Berlin and the Consulates-General, to all of whom I here express my grateful thanks. There is little wrong with any of them except over-administration, most of it dictated from above. To choose a current example: the taxpayer has to pay the cost of transferring a 1st Secretary and his family from Bonn to Riyadh; why should he also pay a Treasury official, who of course has no intention of ever going to Riyadh himself, nor anywhere like it, to tell that 1st Secretary how many cubic metres his baggage should amount to? Among the main sufferers from such attitudes are the Diplomatic Service wives, to whom I also pay my tribute, and especially to my own, whose career moreover need not have been sacrificed to mine if it had been the Treasury official that she married.

I am sending copies of this despatch to HM Representatives

at NATO and EC posts, Moscow and East Berlin; the GOC Berlin, the career Consuls-General in the Federal Republic; and the Commanders-in-Chiefs' Committee (Germany).

I am, Sir,

Yours faithfully,
J. L. Bullard

∾

'How does the "blustering buffoon" sign off for the last time?'

SIR DAVID GORE-BOOTH, HM HIGH COMMISSIONER
TO INDIA, DECEMBER 1998

A charismatic high-flyer, Gore-Booth often courted controversy. He pulls no punches in his valedictory over the treatment he received at the hands of the Scott Inquiry into arms-to-Iraq. Defending the information supplied by the Foreign Office in answer to MPs' parliamentary questions, his rather elusive comment that 'of course, half the picture can be accurate' has entered Whitehall folklore.

Gore-Booth was hauled before another committee to defend his role in what he calls 'the Surtees case'; the sacking in 1994 of Paul Surtees, a British Aerospace employee. Gore-Booth, then Ambassador to Saudi Arabia, had complained about Surtees to the company. The ambassador was rebuked by the head of the Diplomatic Service, John Kerr, and accused of 'extraordinary arrogance' by the Labour MP Peter Bradley.

The valedictory was addressed to Robin Cook. It is he who is praised for 'filleting' the government while in opposition. Nevertheless, the barb about 'the gradual erosion of trust', and the charge that ministerial responsibility was being 'blatantly prostituted', would have hit their mark. It was inevitable that a despatch this critical, circulated to hundreds of readers around Whitehall, would leak. Gore-Booth's despatch quickly found its way into the pages of The Times under the headline 'Labour in turmoil: angry envoy blames ministers'.

Sir David's father, Paul Gore-Booth, had the High Commission in Delhi in the 1960s and eventually became Permanent Under Secretary, the head of the Diplomatic Service. His son seemed destined for similar heights, but David Gore-Booth's career eventually foundered upon an ill-starred state visit by the Queen in 1997 to India. Gore-Booth had already had to mop up the damage caused by an unsolicited offer from the Foreign Secretary, Robin Cook, to mediate in the dispute between India and Pakistan over Kashmir, but that was only the start of his problems. During the visit Britain was to express regret for the 1919 Amritsar massacre, one of the empire's darkest days, when troops under the command of Brigadier-General Reginald Dwyer opened fire on a crowd of 10,000 Indians protesting against the extension of First World War detention laws. A Royal visit to the site heightened tensions, especially after the Duke of Edinburgh was overheard commenting that a plaque commemorating the victims exaggerated their number by counting the wounded. (The Duke's timing may have been unfortunate but his sources were impeccable: General Dwyer's son had served with him in the Navy.) Britain's decision not to offer a full apology for the massacre enraged some Indians further. Gore-Booth's reported description of Delhi bureaucrats as being 'incompetent bunglers' for forcing the Queen to cancel a planned speech in Madras added to the damage.

Gore-Booth's falling out with the Foreign Secretary, as much due to a clash of personalities as the embarrassment of the state visit, saw him recalled from India, and he resigned from the service soon after. Alistair Campbell's carelessly *unthinking suggestion that 'plummy-voiced old Etonians' in the Foreign Office might no longer best represent modern Britain summed up the prevailing mood.*

Controversial to the end, Gore-Booth managed one final kick at the conventions shortly before his untimely death in 2004, after Jack Straw was photographed mistakenly shaking hands with Robert Mugabe at the United Nations. 'It was quite dark in that corner,' Gore-Booth told BBC Radio 4's Today *programme. 'Here are a lot of people and quite a lot of them are black, and it's quite difficult to sort them out.'*

SUBJECT: KEYDOC: GORE-BOOTH: VALEDICTORY

I leave India tomorrow and the Diplomatic Service on New Year's Eve. It is no secret that I had hoped to leave the DS[1] from New York on 14 May 2003. But the dice fell another way. So I shall see in the Millennium as Special Adviser to the Chairman of a major financial institution instead.

As the son of a diplomat, I promised myself not to be one (my wife, a diplomatic daughter, swore she would never be so stupid as to marry into the career!). Yet abroad was in my veins, as was a sense – old fashioned though it seems now to say it – of duty . . . I joined the FO on 3 September 1964 and was despatched two weeks later to learn Arabic at the Middle East Centre for Arabic Studies (MECAS[2]) in Lebanon.

The choice of Arabic (made for, not by, me) turned out to be pivotal. In Baghdad for the June 1967 war, in Tripoli for Colonel Quaddafi's overthrow of King Idris, in London for the October 1973 war, in Jeddah in the early 1980s for the height of the oil boom and the depth of the *Death of a Princess*,[3] in London again for the crisis with Iran over Salman Rushdie, Saddam Hussein's invasion of Kuwait and the subsequent Gulf War; and in Saudi Arabia a second time for its aftermath. A posting to Zambia, two multilateral assignments in UKREP Brussels and UKMis New York[4] and spells in Financial Relations Department and as Head of Planners were testing, if welcome deviations from what had become the norm. As, when I had mined the seam of Arabism to its richest point in Riyadh, was India, controversy over State Visits and nuclear tests notwithstanding.

Arabists were trained for colonial tours of duty in the Gulf and Aden: they were described – even if they did not see themselves – as latter day Lawrences. But before most of my generation could ply their trade, withdrawal from the East of Suez had changed the nature of the task: the rise of the oil price and power meant that the Gulf remained as important to the UK as ever and Saudi Arabia began to eclipse Egypt as Britain's most substantial interest in the region. Above all, the two Arab/Israel wars of 1967 and 1973 meant that Arabists had more than enough to do, not as apologists for the Arabs but to persuade London (and indirectly Washington) that Palestine was a running sore that needed to be treated if the entire Western position in the Middle East was not to be undermined. That danger remains.

To follow one's father's passage to India, three decades on, was as tricky as it was (I think, though I have not checked) unprecedented. At first, social Delhi – a formidable force – queued up to congratulate London on having finally accepted the dynastic principle. Later, as things soured after the 1997 election and the ensuing State Visit, socialites wrote off socialists and began taking pot shots at Her Majesty's messenger. The Indian press is commendably free, but it abuses that freedom to make mincemeats of personalities. I have never held a rein, a gun or a rod in my life – yet I am regularly described here as a hunting, shooting, fishing aristocrat of a type inconsonant with Labour, old or New.

As I learned during the Scott Report saga, the British press is no less proficient than its Indian counterpart at creating stereotypes only to demolish them. One of the great failures of the Diplomatic Service has been its inability to cast off its image as bowler hatted, pin-striped and chinless, with a fondness for champagne. It does not help when Ministers earn themselves a cheap thrill by colluding in the notion that the FCO is elitist and fuddy-duddy. Or that Eton is a dirty word. A Foreign Office Career is one of the best levellers – upwards or down – that has been devised. It is also testing. Bubbly is far from the mind when burning confidential documents on the roof of the Embassy in Baghdad, battening down the hatches against stone throwing mobs outside the High Commission in Lusaka or the Embassy in Tripoli, grinding out texts at all-night sessions in Brussels or New York, paying incognito visits to Syria or doing bumps and jumps in an RAF Tornado over Kuwait. Indeed cocktail parties are death as I am sure 99 per cent of DS colleagues would agree. Whoever it was who suggested an international treaty banning National Day receptions should be canonised.

I know that you filleted the Conservative Government on the issue, but in truth Sir Richard Scott's Inquiry was a travesty in its origin, procedure and output. I am not surprised that you decided that Sir Thomas Legg[5] should conduct his in private. No civil servant should be put in a position where he or she is pilloried in public – and mimicked on the radio, TV and stage – without the chance to defend him or herself. The gradual erosion of trust between officials and Ministers is one of the saddest consequences of the dumbing down of the media and the focus on personalities as opposed to policies. If the doctrine of Ministerial responsibility is to be so blatantly prostituted then civil servants will have to man their own ramparts for rightful remedy. I believe that, as a first step, the Diplomatic Service Association (which I hope will soon be open to all who accept the mobility obligation) should retain the services of a lawyer. He, or she, should advise Foreign Servants on how to protect their fronts – and their rears. Such advice would have been handy not only during the Scott episode but, more recently, the Surtees case in which ill-judged but widely publicised comments by the present FCO Legal Adviser helped to fuel a report which was as inflammatory as it was prejudicial to my personal and professional reputation . . .

Having spent the last six years in Duncan's Outer Area[6], I have to say that I think he got it totally wrong. Saudi Arabia and India are both countries where the UK has extensive interests that can only be promoted by British diplomats. And these must be possessed of abundant reserves of talent, resilience and humour. Saudi Arabia is a cheerless confine, India is a cacophonous cauldron. Serving in the Third World is quite different from serving in the First and, increasingly, the Second; as well, in most cases, as being further from home. Such service needs to be rewarded on a totally different scale, with a much larger quality of life element. I am glad to hear that Hornby[7] marks a step in this direction – though, from the projections I have seen, not a large enough one. Distance, dirt and danger are the key variables.

So how does the 'blustering buffoon' of Francis Wheen's[8] imagination sign off for the last time? Not without thanking my wives; the first for giving up under the strain after only a few years; the second for making the last 21 years a joy above and below deck. And scores of colleagues, whether UK based or locally engaged, who have helped keep this particular show on the road. I have hugely enjoyed a career that has always been colourful and at times controversial. But now it is time to go home.

GORE-BOOTH

1. *DS*: Diplomatic Service.
2. *MECAS*: The first generation of post-war British diplomats trained at the Middle East Centre for Arabic Studies in the mountains overlooking Beirut gained such astonishing proficiency in the language that their successors still speak of the establishment with reverence today. MECAS had regional notoriety as a 'spy school'; the CIA also sent trainees there.
3. *Death of a Princess*: The broadcast of this 1980 drama-documentary on ITV depicting the execution of an Arab princess and her lover for adultery spiralled into a major diplomatic incident. Saudi Arabia banned Concorde from her airspace and James Craig, then Ambassador to Riyadh, was asked to leave the country (see p. 325 for his earlier despatch from Dubai). The film, based on the death of Princess Masha'il in 1977, has never been re-broadcast in the UK.
4. *UKREP Brussels and UKMis New York*: Diplomatic posts at the European Union and United Nations, respectively.
5. *Sir Thomas Legg:* Head of a 1998 inquiry into the British company Sandline International involving allegations of arms sales to Sierra Leone.
6. *Duncan's Outer Area*: Duncan Review Committee on Overseas Representation (1968–9). One of several post-war reviews tasked to trim costs, the Duncan Review proposed a scaled-down and less lavish network of embassies and residences. Duncan divided the world into an Area of Concentration (Europe and North America) and an Outer Area where the axe might fall.
7. *Hornby*: A review of overseas allowances designed to compensate staff for the additional cost and hardship involved in living overseas. The Hornby System allows for eight return business-class flights over a typical three-year posting, but diplomats can also save up their allowance for personal travel if they take fewer trips or slum it in economy. Some do very well out of it; a 2009 *Daily Mail* exposé described a diplomat taking the long way home from a posting in Kuwait via Bangkok, Australia, Washington and Poland, among other places, totalling 35,000 miles.

8. *Francis Wheen*: *Private Eye* journalist. Sir David was known to readers of the satirical magazine as 'Gore-Blimey of the FO'.

∽

'Today's applicants to join the European Union will find Europa's paps all but dry'

SIR ADRIAN BEAMISH, HM AMBASSADOR
TO MEXICO, 1999

SUBJECT: MEXICO: VALEDICTORY

The Valedictory belongs to the genre Complaint: the Poet complains to his Mistress (i.e. the DS). After thirty-odd years, it is perhaps not surprising if, in this context, the Bard's 'age shall not wither her nor custom stale her infinite variety' evokes no more than a cautious if courteous 'ahem'. My purpose is not to complain but merely to make a few points without, I hope, being misunderstood.

But there is another difficulty. The venerable convention is that I address you, Sir, but the competition for space in your box becomes daily more pressing. If not you, then who? Senior colleagues, the gallery, or, via a leak, a prospect we cannot be unmindful of these days, the Press? Is the game worth the candle? Just, I think.

Those of us shuffling into the wings about now were boys in the 40s, teenagers (then a scarcely recognised concept) in the 50s, and joined the Service in the 60s. The world we grew up in, overshadowed by the Second World War, was a time of hope and generosity. The 1944 Education Act, the Marshall Plan, the National Health Service and, later, substantial and enthusiastic overseas aid programmes and the European Common Market all were animated by positive convictions and important commitments to widely shared community goals. But as time passed, changes came. A more hard-nosed approach installed itself at the personal, national and international levels. For example, today's applicants to join the European Union will find Europa's paps all but dry: a sharp contrast to the bounty of the sixties and seventies when the founder members fattened so blithely. The Service could not have expected to remain immune from these changes. Nor has it.

Five years ago, everyone knew how much the PUS[1] was paid. Few do today. Five years ago . . . there were four grades in the senior structure. Today there are about 15. These developments, in keeping with modern management philosophy, divide members of the Service one from another and reduce transparency. Twenty years ago, a member of the Service leaking a document would have infringed not only the Official Secrets Act, but, more gravely, the sense of solidarity and *esprit de corps* arising from the Service's cohesiveness. Today, the reaction is likely to be 'what do you expect?'. In short, in these different ways, reflecting national trends, the Service has become less cohesive.

1. *PUS*: Permanent Under Secretary of State for the Foreign Office (also head of the Diplomatic Service). The UK's top diplomat; a civil servant who runs the Foreign Office under the Foreign Secretary.

~

'Men have forgotten God; that's why all this has happened'

SIR ANDREW GREEN, HM AMBASSADOR TO SAUDI ARABIA, JUNE 2000

Here comes a rant par excellence *– a missive which must have vastly cheered the ambassador who sent it and got it off his chest.*

Part of a diplomat's job is to show ministers back in London how Britain is seen, by foreigners, from the outside. This can mean presenting an unflattering picture. With considerable aplomb but in unapologetically provocative style, Sir Andrew Green acquits himself of this responsibility in his valedictory, describing the clash of cultures when the permissive West meets Saudi conservatism.

But in the year 2000, confronted by Sir Andrew's own conservatism, Whitehall was not in a listening mood. The New Labour government had recently employed the (then celebrated) idea of setting out a 'mission statement' for the FCO, relaunching British foreign policy with an explicit 'ethical dimension'. In a memorable speech the late Robin Cook, then the new Foreign Secretary, declared the Labour government would put 'human rights at the heart of our foreign policy' and support 'the demands of other peoples for the democratic rights on which we insist for ourselves'. By 'ethical' it is unlikely that Mr Cook meant theological.

This valedictory caused a stir: Sir Christopher Meyer remembers word spreading around the embassy in Washington, where he was ambassador: 'People were saying – "phew! bloody hell, have you seen Andrew's despatch,"' he recalls. 'It certainly seized everyone's attention.'

Readers will make up their own minds about Sir Andrew's

views on women and ethnic minorities in the Diplomatic Service.
Some of his comments are simply statements of fact (although
it takes courage to commit them to paper in an age impatient
with such thoughts): it is true, for instance, that the bulk of the
work in bringing up children tends to fall on mothers, not
fathers, though Sir Andrew's critics would say that women are
able to take this into account before applying.

Sir Andrew remains an iconoclast in retirement, as founding
chairman of the pressure group Migration Watch.

SUBJECT: VALEDICTORY TO SAUDI ARABIA AND THE SERVICE

One valuable tradition, not yet abolished by the modern-
isers, is the Valedictory Despatch – an opportunity to record
some reflections on a lifetime of service.

I leave with no complaints whatsoever. I have had a wonderful time, enjoying everything I have done in the course of
7 years in Saudi Arabia, 16 in the Middle East and 35 in the
Diplomatic Service. It has been a challenging and fulfilling
career. I recommend it to any man, but not to every woman,
for reasons explained below.

Saudi Arabia
Handling our relationship with Saudi Arabia will always be
tricky. The gap between our cultures is more like a chasm,
and Western ability to comprehend foreign cultures is in
sharp decline. It is not easy to explain Sharia criminal procedures to a Western press fixated on the possible execution of
British nurses. Nor is it easy to explain to Saudi Princes the
apparently unlimited freedom permitted to Arab dissidents
in London. The knack, I believe, is to keep Saudi Arabia out
of the British press, to see difficulties coming, and to settle
them quietly behind the scenes.

Recent campaigns based on the Western concept of human rights miss the mark and engender hostility. We should focus on the undoubted weaknesses in the administration of justice recognising that the bulk of the Saudi population reject many of our concepts on both religious and social grounds. They are aware of the rate of divorce, abortion, fatherless children, drug abuse and crime in Western societies and do not accept that we can give them lessons in how to organise a society. But, even more important to them, they see us as a Godless society.

Whatever the Saudis' faults – and, after seven years here I need no instruction in their streaks of pride, avarice and indolence – they do live in the presence of God. It is, perhaps, hard to do otherwise when the entire country stops five times a day for prayer. For some, this is religiosity with a large dose of hypocrisy. But not for most. This is a deeply religious society and, because Islamic, deeply conservative. There are those, including the Crown Prince and Foreign Minister, who favour cautious reform but visible foreign pressure undermines their efforts. The fact is that the West's secular approach to life is deeply offensive to many here. Nor are the Saudis necessarily wrong. I recently came across Alexander Solzhenitsyn's verdict on what went so terribly astray in Russia under communism. Written in 1983, it is worth quoting in full:

Over half a century ago, while I was still a child, I recall hearing a number of older people offer the following explanation for the great disasters that had befallen Russia: 'Men have forgotten God; that's why all this has happened.' Since then I have spent well-nigh fifty years working on the history of our revolution; in the process I have read hundreds of books, collected hundreds of personal testimonies, and have already contributed eight volumes of my own toward the effort of clearing away the rubble left by that upheaval. But if I were asked today to formulate as concisely as possible the main cause of the ruinous revolution that swallowed up some sixty million of our people, I could not put it more accurately than to repeat: 'Men have forgotten God; that's why all this has happened.'

I note in passing that, in Britain, the so-called Millennium Prayer made no mention of God . . .

HM Diplomatic Service
It is not terribly British but it is worth stating for the benefit of newcomers, that our Diplomatic Service is one of the finest in the world. American economic and military power puts them in a class of their own. But, in my experience, only the French can match us, with the Germans and the Japanese a pace or two behind. The problem for the State Department is that there are so many players in Washington that, however good their advice, it is frequently not taken. We too risk a similar fate as government focuses ever more intently on the management of the press rather than on the formulation of policy.

Kosovo was a classic example. A whole series of political misjudgements as to how the Yugoslavs would respond to the threat and use of force led to military action which only narrowly avoided degenerating into a very costly ground campaign. The outcome appears to be ethnic cleansing of Serbs rather than Albanians while several thousand British troops remain stuck in Kosovo indefinitely. Yet our propaganda machine projected this as a magnificent victory; Goebbels must be grinning in his grave. After the last diplomatic failure on this scale (Tehran 1979) a full report was written and the necessary lessons learned and applied. Has anyone dared to enquire as to what advice was offered on Kosovo, to whom, and when?

If we are to avoid similar 'victories' in future, we must

improve the political/military interface at policy level in Whitehall. With the demise of the Soviet Union our defence forces have become increasingly an instrument of foreign policy. This makes it the more important that the political consequences of military action (and threats of action) be thoroughly thought through before we set in hand events which take on their own momentum. My views on Desert Fox[1] are well known. Here I simply note that Saddam has not been significantly weakened; the Inspectors have been withdrawn and have not returned; the Security Council is, in reality, split and we are left with a war of attrition in the air. All, except for the last, were consistently forecast from here throughout 1998.

Whitehall battles are the stuff of bureaucracy; a martial art of their own. But our role will be vacuous if it is not founded on thorough local knowledge. It is instructive that, over the last fifteen years, the endless grinding of our administrative wheels (nowadays described as 'modernization'), although maintaining the necessary resources has otherwise had no effect whatever on the actual task here. The key requirements are experience and access so as to get the 'feel' of an opaque and secretive society, and to make the judgements on which the furtherance of our interests depends. The Service is now moving in the right direction – towards greater continuity and expertise. They certainly count. At one point I had more experience in the Middle East than all my EU colleagues put together. And this Embassy still has more Arabists than all the other Western Embassies combined. That is why we are in a class of our own.

I have viewed with dismay the spread of 'Political Correctness' in recent years. Intellectual honesty is the foundation of our Service; Political Correctness its antithesis. 'Diversity' is the latest of several rather fatuous fashions. The truth is that diversity is irrelevant to diplomacy. No foreigner I have ever met knows or cares whether the Service has fifty per cent women, ten per cent homosexuals and five per cent ethnics. His (or her) only interest is whether a diplomat has something useful to contribute. Furthermore, 'targets' are but a thinly disguised form of positive discrimination; this undermines the fundamental principle of the public service that promotion should be based on ability alone. The risk is that 'minorities' will be promoted because they are (just) credible, not because they are the best; if so, they will become symbols, not of inclusion but of incompetence. The Service should cease to be invertebrate in the face of this politically motivated interference.

I am well aware that I (again) fly in the face of fashion in suggesting a franker approach to the conflict between career and family which is so difficult for women officers. Those of us who have seen a full career know the strains of children at boarding school, of their transition to university, and of parents whose health is failing. The brunt of these pressures tends to fall on the mother, emotionally if not also practically. All these pressures are magnified by distance and by the mobility obligation and they come at a time when, for senior staff, the stresses of a demanding job are intense. Taken together they are a great deal to bear. A woman officer should not, therefore, count it a failure, and nor should we, if in her thirties she decides that there are far more important things in life than Foreign Office telegrams. Crèches, job sharing etc can postpone the central problem, but cannot solve it.

By contrast, one of the great attractions of the Service is that there is so much to share with your wife – the highs to be enjoyed, the lows to be endured and the humorous moments to be savoured together. I know that I could not have done it without my wife; indeed, it is hard to express my debt to her.

I conclude with a puff for the Public Service. My wife and I have been brought up to it and are deeply committed to it. The idea promoted by private sector consultants that you can 'drive your own career' is simply absurd. The sense of purpose and the satisfaction of public service cannot be matched by the pursuit of a personal agenda, still less of personal gain.

So I leave the Service well content but I echo Sir Francis Walsingham: 'Would that I had served my God as I have served my Queen.' It is to that which I shall turn my attention in such years as He may grant me.

GREEN

1. *Desert Fox*: 1998 bombing campaign by Britain and America against Iraq for refusing to allow in weapons inspectors, in defiance of United Nations Security Council resolutions. The four-day attack with cruise missiles and aerial bombing destroyed what little military infrastructure Saddam Hussein had managed to rebuild since the end of the first Gulf War. Saudi Arabia opposed the campaign and refused to let America launch air strikes from its bases.

∾

'Departing from international humanitarian law even just a little is like being just a little bit pregnant'

DAME GLYNNE EVANS, HM AMBASSADOR
TO PORTUGAL, 2004

In 2004, fifty-two former British diplomats signed a letter to The Times *criticizing British policy in the Middle East. While stopping short of condemning the invasion of Iraq outright, the letter was unstinting in its attack on the coalition's tactics, calling its belief that a democratic society could be imposed upon Iraq 'naive', and its occupation strategy 'doomed to failure'.*

Many serving diplomats also had serious reservations. Elizabeth Wilmshurst, a senior Foreign Office lawyer, resigned two days before the invasion, believing the war was illegal. Others found different ways to express their discontent. In her valedictory Dame Glynne Evans makes an elegant case for sticking to international law; even in times of crisis, and however strong the pressure from allies to backslide. The case is made softly, and it is voiced as a warning, rather than direct criticism.

As well as spells in Spanish-speaking countries Glynne Evans had great experience in multilateral bodies. Postings in Brussels and on secondment to the United Nations in New York gave her expertise in international peacekeeping and conflict diplomacy. Her comments on international humanitarian law carried weight.

Evans's despatch was addressed, as is usual, to the Foreign Secretary. This was Jack Straw. Mr Straw had been Home Secretary, and Evans ambassador to Chile, when the former Chilean dictator Augusto Pinochet was arrested in London on an extradition warrant for crimes against humanity. Straw eventually ordered Pinochet's release on medical grounds before a trial could begin, a decision which Evans clearly supported.

En route to the door . . .

I told the BBC team on *True Brits* that I joined the FCO on the maverick quota. I am sure I would not get through the doors today. I have found the Foreign Office over the years fascinating, and also pompous and infuriating. And successive line managers have found me infuriating, unbiddable and much more besides, never mind the state of my desk. I had a most unpromising start. I am grateful to the Foreign Office for keeping me on the books and allowing me space. I loved working for the British Government and promoting British interests overseas on behalf of all departments; ... [but] I have always preferred the long hours in London and working with Ministers to any overseas post, and my 5 and a half years in ECD(E)[1] and six years in UND[2] were highlights, which gave much scope for both new approaches to old problems and creativity with the new challenges. I was lucky in my bosses who gave me latitude and top cover for risky approaches, sometimes *ex post facto*, from launching the Sarajevo airlift over a weekend to spending one August devising the gloriously technical mutual Advance Implementation of EC Rights between Spain and Gibraltar, annexed to the Spanish Accession Treaty that oiled the Lisbon agreement and opened the frontier. That said, the detention of Pinochet made life in Chile unusually interesting and not only in the sense of the old Chinese curse. It was rare to be at the centre of so major a historical shift and I have never received quite so many death threats. And the European football championship in Lisbon was a once-in-a-lifetime event for us all and a fantastic note on which to exit.

I have spent most of my career on multilateral work. We have always made a point of standing by international law and as Permanent Members of the Security Council, have been able to consider ourselves custodians of good international behaviour. Departing from international humanitarian law even just a little is like being just a little bit pregnant. You, sir, know that well from the Pinochet case when you stood by principle and the rule of law. The ICRC[3] historically have regarded us as sound custodians and practitioners of IHL.[4] In 1990 they told me that the UK MOD-FCO presentation on preparations for the First Gulf War was so exemplary they could have wished for a video; they wished others followed our example. In my time, I have had stand up and knock down battles with the Americans over IHL, and lived to win the battle and tell the tale, even with John Bolton.[5] The Americans may hate our legalism, but that is not to say they are right and we are wrong. I believe we need to fight back, and hard, for our principles. In the same way, we need to sell ourselves and the largely unsung work we do much more aggressively in Whitehall and to the public as part of the non-stop battle for resources. We should not be 'gentlemen' any more, but warriors (and amazons).

The London Business School have always been fascinated to find from their assessments that senior members of the Diplomatic Service do not work for financial reward, we work for the fun of it and for recognition that we are valued (we hope) and that sometimes we can contribute to the course of history . . . I have long argued for the FCO to have a serious social outreach programme as a means of overcoming our image. I hope it may yet happen. I have been privileged to serve and work with so many talented and tolerant colleagues. But to stand by my principles, I shall now cultivate my garden with a new career as a volunteer social worker and see where that leads.

EVANS

1. *ECD(E)*: European Community Department (External).
2. *UND*: United Nations Department (in the FCO).
3. *ICRC*: International Committee of the Red Cross.
4. *IHL*: International Humanitarian Law.

5. *John Bolton*: Combative US representative to the United Nations (2005–6); the neocon's neocon. Bolton's appointment hearing in Congress was dominated by his visceral opposition to the UN, summed up in a widely circulated video from 1994 showcasing his views on its inefficiency: 'The Secretariat Building in New York has 38 stories. If you lost ten stories today, it wouldn't make a bit of difference.' Bolton's appointment was never confirmed by the US Senate.

~

'Bullshit bingo'

SIR IVOR ROBERTS, HM AMBASSADOR
TO ITALY, SEPTEMBER 2006

The last valedictory to be circulated in the traditional manner, and arguably the last straw that broke ministers' and mandarins' tolerance of the tradition, we reproduce this almost in extenso. *Hours after Sir Ivor Roberts's telegram was sent, ambassadors were told that the practice of distributing valedictories widely around the Service was to be discontinued. Someone had thrown a serious wobbly.*

Roberts had sent his to all diplomatic posts; some 4,000 people. The advent of email meant valedictories no longer remained 'in the family' and the question was not whether, but when, it would reach the outside world via a leak. It was in fact six months after Roberts left Rome that the Independent's *Jerusalem correspondent got hold of a copy, writing it up as a 'devastating attack on Blair's "bullshit bingo" management culture of diplomacy'. The article made much of a previous remark by Roberts in 2004 (spoken in private, but also leaked) that US President George W. Bush was 'Al Qaeda's best recruiting sergeant'. A strain of anti-neocon opinion is certainly apparent in Roberts's despatch.*

Like many of his colleagues, Roberts regrets the ban on valedictories: 'It seemed to me that the accumulated wisdom of someone who has served for almost 40 years, in my case, in diplomacy ought to be shared as widely as possible, and not limited to a handful of people in London who might or might not have a particular axe to grind in burying that criticism or those reflections if they were felt to be politically inconvenient.'

Roberts is now President of Trinity College, Oxford, and the author of Satow's Guide to Diplomacy *– a handbook which teaches diplomats how to behave.*

Atque Vale

I return full circle to the university I left in 1968, being, I'm told, the last person to retire under the 60 rule.[1] If I'd been born a week later, I'd be under the wire. But after 38 years in harness, it's time to shuffle off in any case. I have no regrets nor complaints at the postings I've had. I'm particularly grateful to have had the opportunity of heading three Missions in Belgrade, Dublin and Rome even if it has brought me into some outlandishly disreputable company over the last twelve years. Negotiating with war criminals in the Balkans (indeed nearly everyone I dealt with is now either dead – several suicides – in prison or on the run), surrendering my immunity to give evidence in a Dublin court against the head of the Real IRA (fortunately he got twenty years) . . .

The Foreign Office I leave is perforce very different from the one I entered in 1968. And most changes have been for the better, particularly those long-overdue reforms on the status and parity of women. Over hierarchical, too deferential, rigid regulations where women had to offer their resignation on marriage, as did those of us who married non-Brits. But the culture of change has reached Cultural

Revolution proportions with no opportunity for new working methods to put down roots. Three recent criticisms of the FCO are disturbing. Chris Patten mused that it was 'sad to see experienced diplomats trained to draft brief and lucid telegrams ... terrorized into filling in questionnaires from management consultants by the yard ... and expected under Orwellian pressure to evince enthusiasm for this work'. The former foreign policy adviser to John Major, Rodric Braithwaite, claims that No. 10 has reduced the Foreign Office to a 'demoralised cipher' while a recent *Independent* editorial asked 'What is the Foreign Office for?'. Tempting as it is to brush aside such comments as unconstructive, perhaps we need to ask whether they have a point? Can it be that in wading through the plethora of business plans, capability reviews, skills audits, zero-based reviews and other excrescences of the management age, we have indeed forgotten what diplomacy is all about? Why have we failed so signally to explain to the likes of the Cabinet Secretary that well-conducted diplomacy cannot properly be measured because diplomatic successes are more often than not elusive or ephemeral? The diplomat is condemned to a Sisyphean task in which, as (s)he attempts to grapple with one conflict, another breaks out. We manage or contain disputes; very rarely do we deliver a quantifiable solution. Indeed we should be sceptical of 'permanent' solutions or models: think democracy in the Middle East or war on terror. Diplomacy is the classic example of the Spanish proverb, 'Traveller, there are no roads. Roads are made by walking.' We need to keep flexible and innovative and be less worried about strategic priorities which may need to be displaced at short notice or added to with no commensurate additional resources. Priorities and objectives have their place, clearly. But an excess of them smacks of a command economy with its long and inglorious pedigree. Ordered to come up with a business plan by Stalin in 1929, Commissar Maxim Litvinov refused. 'The Commissariat for Foreign Affairs cannot, unfortunately, put forward a five-year plan of work. We have to deal with a number of factors that are scarcely subject to calculation, with a number of elements outside our control . . . International affairs are composed of those of a large number of countries, built on different lines from our Union, pursuing other aims than ours, and using other means to achieve those aims than we allow.' Rather prissy and fastidious coming from the pen of Comrade Litvinov but the point is valid. I suggest a variant of it be used on the Treasury . . .

. . . [C]hange management is a means not an end. Our prime purpose should remain objective, trenchant foreign policy advice. We used to be better at this. Overloading the successor to the Planning Staff with the responsibility for the process of change management seems to me a serious mistake. DSI[2] should be writing incisive think pieces such as 'Iraq. How did we get into this mess and how to extricate ourselves'. Or 'Why are we so hated in the Middle East and what we should do about it'. Or 'Balkan map-making. Time for a new Congress of Berlin?' It's been an excellent initiative to bring together senior Ambassadors from around the world twice a year but it would make better sense even if occasionally uncomfortable for the home team if we were allowed to debate foreign policy rather than corporate governance.

Too much of the change management agenda is written in Wall Street management-speak which is already tired and discredited by the time it is introduced. Synergies, vfm, best practice, benchmarking, silo-working, roll-out, stakeholder, empower, push-back and deliver the agenda, fit for purpose are all prime candidates for a game of bullshit bingo, a substitute for clarity and succinctness. A personal aversion is the Utopian mission statement (so 1980s) which should be dispensed with rather than affronting me every morning on my Firecrest screen and even appearing on my pay slip! I'm not suggesting a statement along the lines of Thucydides' Melian dialogue 'The strong do what they can; the weak suffer what they must' – an obvious neo-con nostrum. But if we have to have one of these statements to get our CSR[3] settlement, let's make it either more realistic and sharper about promoting our interests or put it in the fully-fledged, caring department of looking after our citizens in a dangerous world. 'We'll BE there for you.' Of far greater use would be the old-style individual despatch to Ambassadors departing for their post. Less than a side would do but it should be endorsed/written by a Minister. Jonathan Powell's[4] reported instruction to Christopher Meyer conveys the brevity if not the flavour.

As Chris Patten adumbrated, the bane of the FCO in recent years has been the explosion of use of consultants, many of whose recommendations (I'm talking specifically of Collinson Grant) do little more than reverse the recommendations of the previous consultants (Coopers and Lybrand) fifteen years ago. A more cynical observer than me might think they were all in collusion at the FCO's expense.

1. *the 60 rule*: Until quite recently diplomats had to retire on their sixtieth birthday. The rule was less a cushy benefit, more of an acknowledgement that extended overseas service could take its toll. The 60 rule opened the door to many successful second careers after retirement. It also allowed new blood to come through.

2. *DSI*: Directorate for Strategy and Innovation.

3. *CSR*: Comprehensive Spending Review.

4. *Jonathan Powell*: Chief of Staff to Tony Blair. Powell's reported instruction in 1997 to Christopher Meyer, who had just been appointed ambassador in Washington: 'We want you to get up the arse of the White House and stay there.'

3. Cold Warriors

As many of these valedictories suggest, diplomatic life behind the Iron Curtain was a strange affair. Alison Bailes, who retired in 2002 as ambassador in Helsinki, wrote in a recent collection of essays that service as a NATO diplomat in a hostile Communist state and the surveillance and suspicion that entailed did have some unexpected upsides:

> ... [S]ome diplomats and especially their families found the combination of minimal privacy and permanent vigilance much harder to bear, while all of us were marked by the need constantly to question the genuineness and motives of any local contact who behaved in a half-decent way towards us. On the other hand, I do not think I have ever felt physically safer than in my years in Hungary (1970–74) when I travelled alone in the remotest parts of the country and never thought twice about picking up hitchhikers in the hope of some revealing grass-roots gossip. The new generation of diplomats will never experience this particular combination of physical ease and a homely environment with a no-holds barred ideological threat.
> (*The Foreign Office and British Diplomacy in the Twentieth Century*, ed. Gaynor Johnson)

In this chapter's extracts we encounter a very grave tone indeed. Directly or indirectly, they concern what was believed to be a threat to the whole future (and the phrase was used seriously) of 'Western civilization as we know it'. The threat came from the Communist bloc.

Margaret Thatcher, in her 'Iron Lady' phase in Opposition when I worked for her, seriously misjudged the Foreign Office (under a Labour government) as a nest of pinkos inhabited by a naive belief in the good faith of the USSR. The opposite was true. I remember well the prevailing ethos in King Charles Street (the FCO's Whitehall home) when I had been there, before working for Mrs T: it was an ethos of unrelenting hostility, wariness and scepticism towards the entire Communist bloc, but particularly East Germany and the Soviet Union; fear of its creep in Asia and in Europe (especially Italy); coupled with a certain negativity as to what, beyond containment and abiding mistrust, the West could actually do. There was a compelling sense of the constraints upon HMG itself.

What, however, none of us – neither the sceptical defeatists nor the cold warriors (and the Office contained both) – appeared to be institutionally aware of, was the incompetence and economic failure of the Eastern bloc as a whole. Communism was regarded as having produced formidable governments; the growing failure of Communist economics to sustain Communist politics was by many – particularly (perversely) free-marketeers – widely overlooked.

In retrospect this surprises me – as, when the Berlin Wall fell, the speed and finality surprised most of the West. A hawkish Western media had assured us that Communism was on the march. Perhaps British ambassadors behind the secure walls of the diplomatic compounds in Moscow, Peking or Bucharest were not aware of the economic and bureaucratic basket cases that their host nations had become, but did our intelligence services offer no report?

However, the first of these despatches, from Sir John Killick in Moscow, does give some hint of recognition of incapacity, as opposed to malevolence.

∼

Russia

'Much too good for its inhabitants'

SIR JOHN KILLICK, HM AMBASSADOR TO
THE SOVIET UNION, OCTOBER 1973

(CONFIDENTIAL)

Moscow,
29 October, 1973.

Sir,

Two years in the Soviet Union have given me a bare
minimum of confidence to embark on some first
impressions! Even at this stage, the impenetrable nature, not
only of this very strange society but of its people, makes me
hesitant to come to any firm conclusions.

Somebody must have said it before, but I think the basic
feeling with which I leave is that the Russian Revolution has
not yet taken place. For one autocracy has been substituted
another, and although the faces of the accompanying
aristocracy have changed, their lifestyle and general attitude of
unconcern and even contempt for the interests, feelings and
concerns of the people often seems very much the same. The
established Church, with its Saints in the mausoleum on Red
Square and in the Kremlin Wall, has failed badly in its attempt
to provide a spiritual alternative to the Orthodox Church as
the opium of the people, and its liturgy carries less and less
conviction; but its role is intended to be much the same . . .
Below the upper crust aristocracy of the Party, the various
ranks of the *chin*[1] throughout the lower level Party Structure
continue to provide much the same avenue to respectability as
they did under the Tsars. They are also peopled by much the
same characters from the pages of Gogol or Chekhov. The

uniforms are lacking, but the decorations are not. The secret police and Siberia play an unchanged role, save only that so far as I know, the *arestanti* no longer have to walk all the way. Finally, and at the lowest level of all, the serfs, now essentially the property of the Soviet State, continue to toil on much as they always did – without much incentive to effort and on the basis that it is best to do the minimum compatible with avoiding a beating; the minimum plus five per cent positively curries favour and may even lead to advancement. The industrialisation of the country does not seem yet to have made much difference to their essentially Russo-Slavonic attitudes. I feel that Tolstoy would be as exasperated to-day as he was with his peasantry 120 years ago . . . The masses . . . remain largely inert on a diet of bread and very boring circuses (both literally and metaphorically) . . .

Lord Trevelyan, in his latest book, argues that an Ambassador must do his utmost to like and take a genuine interest in the country in which he is living and its people. I hope I am not inadequate by his standards. My interest in both has been keenly whetted. My liking for the country is real; but I think it is much too good for its inhabitants, whom I do not have it in my heart really to like. Having lived in the countries of both Super Powers, I find many similarities between them – a tremendous 'Victorianism' (for want of a better word) in different ways in both internal attitudes and foreign policies; in the case of the former a marked conservatism and of the latter a sense of 'manifest destiny'. Yet there is one great difference – Americans want and need to be liked, and respond immediately to a foreigner who fills Lord Trevelyan's bill; Russians have no such need, and indeed are suspicious and even contemptuous of those who court them too eagerly. They want respect in all its forms, and in turn respect those who insist on the same treatment. I respect them and even admire them in many ways.

On the fly-leaf of his well-known (but not really very profound) book about Russia in his day, the Marquis de Custine quotes the advice of Vladimir Monomakh to his sons, 800 years ago: 'Above all, respect foreigners, and if you cannot heap presents on them, at least be prodigal with marks of goodwill, because on the manner in which they are treated in a country will depend what they say of it – good or ill – in their own.' In saying that I have not exactly been overwhelmed with goodwill, I am not thinking of the superficial manifestations to which some foreign representatives are treated as a matter of policy by the Soviet Government or, on instructions, by well-known front organisations like the Friendship Societies, the Supreme Soviet, the All-Union Council of Trade Unions or (sometimes) Intourist and the foreign currency shops. I have in mind such fundamentally more revealing things as the blank stare and total absence of helpfulness usually met with in any Soviet shop or office and the total lack of the more elementary courtesies and consideration encountered in any public place. I am bound to admit that all this does have the merit that it is non-discriminatory – they are no less bloody to each other! Nor am I under the illusion that the lot of the foreign visitor to Britain – even if he speaks some English – is ideal! Possibly one of the troubles in Anglo-Soviet relations is that we do at bottom have a certain amount in common. At all events, I look forward to pursuing the subject with Lord Trevelyan.

In conclusion, two reminiscences. First, of a quotation from Chekhov on a wooden board in a flower bed in the garden at Melikhovo, where he once lived and wrote. It reads 'If each one of us, on his own piece of land, would do everything he could, how lovely our land would be.' An exhortation which would not be there if it did not have official approval. Yet the 'If . . .' is also still there, and the 'own piece of land' has been taken away. Second, a treasured memory of the delighted and helpless laughter at lunch of a Soviet factory management, whose director had been expressing some pretty forthright criticism of Soviet bureaucracy, both Ministerial and Party. A rather pawky Scottish engineer, working there under contract on the installation and commissioning of some British machinery, remarked dryly that it reminded him of the old saying 'The higher a monkey gets up a tree, the more you see of his behind!' He did not in fact say 'behind' but it all came out in the wash of the translation. There's always some hope for those who can laugh at themselves, and Russians certainly can; but they're a long way from taking the mickey freely out of their Royal Family and their established Church.

   This valedictory is written without benefit of any consultation with my colleagues here, but I believe such an essay should be of a personal nature. They may well disagree with much of it; with more experience, I might come to declare some of it 'inoperative' myself. I hope they will freely send any comments they have to the Deputy Under-Secretary supervising the East European and Soviet Department, who faithfully guarantees them immunity from prosecution.

I have, etc.,

J. E. KILLICK.

1. *chin*: A grading system introduced by Peter the Great in 1722 dividing the upper echelons of Russian society into 14 classes, or *chins*.

～

> '*Russians have many attractive qualities but they are and always have been natural bullies*'

SIR BRYAN CARTLEDGE, HM AMBASSADOR TO
THE SOVIET UNION, AUGUST 1988

The perils of forecasting! In this valedictory, Sir Bryan predicts the survival of Communism in Russia into – perhaps – the twenty-first century. Fifteen months after it was written the Berlin Wall came down. Events snowballed with incredible speed, outpacing the predictive powers not just of HM Ambassador in Moscow but of virtually every other foreign policy expert in the West. The timescale for lasting change in Russia was not twenty years, nor 'a generation'. The Soviet Union had, as it turned out, just over three years left to run.

But one cannot help feeling that Cartledge has been proved more accurate than a mere calendar of events might suggest. He badly miscalculates the timing of the tipping point at which Soviet political institutions will collapse but he forecasts, even more emphatically than his successor Rodric Braithwaite (see the next despatch), the innate resistance of the national culture and mindset to bottom-up, grass-roots reform.

Mikhail Gorbachev's policy of perestroika ('reform') may have yielded a 'virtual absence of tangible results' by August 1988, but it was a slow-burning fuse. The addition of glasnost ('openness') – the birth of which Cartledge records here as the regime's 'political coming of age' – provided the spark. Gorbachev's political reforms, which gathered pace once he assumed the Presidency in 1990, were designed to weaken the ossifying control of the Communist Party over government, but in doing so they fatally weakened its ability to keep the Soviet Union together. A string of breakaway states asserted their sovereignty the following year. Freedom of expression –

a product of glasnost – *gave life to independence movements in the Baltic states, which quickly spread to inner Soviet satellites like Georgia and Ukraine. The Soviet Union was eventually dissolved on Boxing Day, 1991.*

Cartledge was entirely right in drawing from Soviet history the lesson that reform at the centre leads to trouble on the periphery. And he might well have been correct in predicting slow-going for Gorbachev's reforms within Russia, had the track along which they were pushed been solely internal. But in the event Communism in Russia was overthrown partly from the outside. And while it was indeed 'explosive', the interaction between change at the centre, war at the periphery and satellites jostling for independence actually conspired to accelerate reform rather than put a brake on it.

SOVIET DEPARTMENT: GENERAL DISTRIBUTION

Her Majesty's Ambassador at Moscow to the Secretary of State for Foreign and Commonwealth Affairs.

A LAST LOOK AT PERESTROIKA

BRITISH EMBASSY
MOSCOW
8 August 1988

Sir,

My impending departure from the Soviet Union, for the last time as a government servant, naturally tempts me to draw broad conclusions from my experience of dealing with this country over a quarter of a century and particularly from the eight years which I have spent in its capital. Before the yawns begin, I hasten to assure you that I shall resist the temptation. I am leaving the Soviet Union at such a critical point in its history that the best use of my final despatch would, I believe, be to provide a snapshot of the Soviet political scene at the moment of my exit, which happens immediately to follow a momentous Party Conference and a crucially important Central Committee Plenum.[1] Perestroika is about to enter a new phase: what are its prospects? . . .

The virtual absence of tangible results from three years of attempted perestroika was not, perhaps, surprising given the scale of the problems which Gorbachev faced . . . The 'Law on Cooperatives', approved by the Supreme Soviet[2] in May, represents a major attempt to revitalise Soviet agriculture by legitimising and encouraging independent activity by small teams of farm workers. The new emphasis on political reform, reflected in the agenda ('theses') for the 19th Party Conference stemmed from Gorbachev's growing recognition of the strength of the forces in Party and government, at all levels, which have a vested interest in resisting change . . .

Of the Conference itself, a frequent comment by participants and Soviet spectators alike is that they still cannot believe that it really happened. It left few taboos untoppled, the main exceptions being the sanctity of Lenin and of the KGB. The Conference marked, I believe, the Soviet Union's political coming of age – a qualitative change in its political life. More immediately, some of the unscripted interventions from the Conference floor – especially those which exposed the shortcomings of Soviet daily life – appear to have completed the progressive refinement of Gorbachev's objectives and priorities . . .

It is ironic, and illustrative of the enduring gulf between

ruler and ruled in this country, that it apparently took a Party Conference and a more recent factory visit to make Gorbachev aware of that central feature of Soviet daily life, the queue. The complaint of a female worker that she spent two or three hours daily queuing in shops was apparently a revelation to the General Secretary – who then demonstrated that his education still has some way to go by adding: 'And this, comrades, was in Moscow, where you can buy anything.' Tell that to the Muscovites, whose larders have been particularly bare this summer.

Gorbachev's acquaintance with Soviet reality may be belated, and still incomplete, but at least he now has his sights trained on the right targets. He has recognised the limitations of the traditional Russian phenomenon of revolution from above . . . This is the first leadership to show constructive concern for the welfare of the Soviet people rather than treating it simply as a dumb instrument for the achievement of national and Party objectives. It is also, of course, the first leadership to question the canons of classical Soviet communism and tacitly to admit the failure of the Soviet system as it has developed over the past sixty years. In an ideal world, these political virtues would produce early results and create the prospect of a more prosperous and more democratic Soviet society this century. I fear, however, that the legacy of the past sixty years will not be cast off so easily.

Gorbachev's plan for political reform already bears evidence of the difficulty of persuading a ruling party to give up some of the powers which it has gathered and consolidated over the years. The theory is to transfer the day-to-day business of government and local administration to the Soviets,[3] elected by and accountable to the whole people: while the Party, self-selected and electing its own elite, resumes the broader guiding, inspirational role which Lenin originally had in mind for it, sloughing off the executive functions which have accreted to it. But any bureaucrat knows that it is precisely in the day-to-day execution – or perhaps more importantly non-execution of policy that real power lies. The Party's reluctance to relinquish these levers is likely to impose a substantial brake on the reform process. Local Party First Secretaries who are (as is planned) elected to be Chairmen of their local Soviets will not easily become obedient, accountable servants of the people. Officials from the dissolved economic and other functional departments of Party Committees will, in the euphemism of the relevant Revolution of the recent Plenum, be deployed in 'strengthening the apparatus of the Soviets of Peoples Deputies': in other words, they will move their desks across the road. In so heavily conditioned a society, the habits of authority and obedience will continue to die hard. In Soviets, ministries, factories and farms the Party man or woman will continue to call the shots for some time to come; and will remain, therefore, in a position to frustrate any changes which could threaten the power and privilege which attracted them to the Party in the first place. At the very top, if the General Secretary does become President of the Supreme Soviet, the Politburo will be concerned to ensure that the elected state body does not get ideas above its station and that their man keeps it in order. If he fails to do so or, worse, tries to use the Supreme Soviet to impose his will on a divided Politburo, the fate of Khrushchev[4] will await him.

Gorbachev's campaign to create incentives to better economic performance by improving the lot of the Soviet consumer also faces inherited obstacles. The 'Law on

Cooperatives' and the promised law to protect leaseholders cannot in themselves generate the activity which they are designed to encourage. The human material is unpromising: two Soviet generations have been brought up to eschew risk, suspect individual initiative and despise profit. A family or small group which wishes to farm a cooperative or to lease land together with the wherewithal to cultivate it – and to work long hours to make their enterprise profitable – is all too likely to encounter obstruction and hostility from their neighbours and their local Soviet. If they persevere and create a going concern, their success will be the target for the malice and envy of those to whom equal misery has always been a higher good than unequal happiness. If any intrepid cooperator or leaseholder overcomes these obstacles he still has to contend with the same poverty of infrastructure as his less efficient state-owned competitors – poor or non-existent roads and communications, inadequate storage, primitive distribution arrangements: and, at the end of the line, a customer whose income – especially if fixed – is geared to the tradition of low quality at low prices and who regards a premium for good quality as evidence of immoral rapacity. The Praesidium[5] of the Supreme Soviet and the Council of Ministers[6] have just, in an encouragingly enlightened move, rescinded the tax law introduced last March which threatened, and may well have been designed to, strangle the renascent cooperative movement at birth. But those operating outside the state system are likely – whether from greed or as a prudent hedge against the risks they run in uncharted waters – to over-charge until Soviet society has learned to accept the realities of market economics.

I do not believe that any of these difficulties, political or economic, are permanent or insuperable. The Party

Conference demonstrated the extraordinary degree to which the capacity for political thought and debate has survived sixty years of repression and anaesthesia under Stalin and his successors. I would expect a new political generation to accept the new political structure which Gorbachev has mapped out – including the modified role of the Party – to exploit the enhanced role of the Soviets and even, perhaps, to tolerate a degree of licensed opposition . . . In the economy, too, I believe that a healthy degree of pluralism will come to be accepted: even Abalkin, the eminent economist who was castigated at the Party Conference for his pessimism (ie for telling the truth) about perestroika's failure so far to produce results, forecast in a recent interview that by 1995 cooperatives would account for 10–12% of turnover in goods and services and for 15–18% by 2005. This, quite apart from a possibly equivalent growth in leaseholding and individual economic activity, could solve the problem of the supply of food and consumer goods to a sufficient extent to fuel the regeneration of the economy as a whole. The services sector is likely to take the lead and to set the example.

This prognosis is nevertheless based on a timescale of twenty years, perhaps of a generation. I do not believe that Gorbachev and his allies can bring about a moral, social, psychological, political and economic revolution in the Soviet Union more quickly than that. The length of time over which he and his policies will be at risk from random extraneous factors, before they have been able to produce results, is therefore uncomfortably long. The re-invigoration of a moribund, stagnant society – such as this still was when I returned to it three years ago – can release inconvenient forces with unpredictable consequences: I have just commented on one of them, in my despatch of 2 August on the nationalities problem. The radicals can become impatient, the conservatives nervous and vengeful. The traditional Russian fear of anarchy remains potent. The process of change in the Soviet Union and that of change – or the lack of it – in Eastern Europe could interact explosively: in Russian as well as Soviet history, reform at the centre of the empire has always led to trouble on the periphery. An international crisis endangering Soviet interests could arrest the process of change in this country overnight. Gorbachev himself will, under his own new rules, be obliged to retire in 1999 – some time before, in my view, his reforms will have been able to take root and produce results: his eventual successor is, in every sense, an unknown and uncertain quantity. Risks, therefore, abound . . .

Short of initiating a holocaust, there is nothing the West can do to prevent the Soviet Union from realising, at last, its proper human and material potential. As I have suggested, it will in any case take some considerable time to do so. The long period of internal change will generate numerous domestic problems to preoccupy the Soviet leadership and will produce a more complex society requiring more sophisticated political management than hitherto. The years ahead will nevertheless pose problems for the West. The progressive diminution, which seems likely, of the 'Soviet threat' in its classic form will make Western defence expenditure harder to sustain: and the new generation of Soviet policy makers is much less likely than its predecessors to make the contributions to Western cohesion which the latter provided in Berlin, Korea, Hungary, Czechoslovakia and Afghanistan . . .

In facing up to these novel perspectives the West can only, I believe, cleave fast to two basic truths which no amount of perestroika is likely to change. The first is that the Soviet Union has permanent interests dictated largely by geography, including the establishment of a predominant political influence in Western and Southern Europe, which run directly counter to Western interests. The second is that even if Soviet political society and the Soviet economy undergo radical change during the next twenty years, the Russian character will not. Russians have many attractive qualities but they are and always have been natural bullies. They despise weakness and rarely resist the temptation to abuse strength. Along with his intelligence and charm, there is plenty of evidence that Gorbachev possesses these attributes in full measure. Taken together, these two propositions argue that, however great the political difficulty of doing so during the long period of perestroika, the West must somehow maintain its capacity to deter the Soviet Union from throwing its weight about when it has more economic and political, as well as military, weight to throw.

Envoi

My secretary warns me that I have already exceeded my allotment of column inches for a farewell despatch. I hope that I may be allowed a degree of licence if, in return, I spare you my views on Britain's place in the world, the British economy, the future of the Diplomatic Service, our working conditions and other traditional ingredients of valedictories. It has been a privilege to serve in the Soviet Union during three of the most remarkable years of its history: I can imagine no more rewarding conclusion to a diplomatic career. I am happy that our bilateral relationship with this country has improved to an extent which would have been inconceivable at the nadir of the expulsions crisis[7] almost exactly three years ago – a recollection which prompts the thought that the ultimate touchstone of perestroika will be the dismantlement of the KGB as an instrument of subversion and repression. I owe a particular debt of gratitude to the staff at this Embassy, now widely dispersed, whose good humour and resilience saw us through those difficult days. But I also record my thanks to all those members of the Service and their wives with whom I have had the good fortune to serve in Moscow and who have so effectively maintained the best traditions and high standards of this Embassy.

I am sending copies of this despatch to HM Ambassadors in Eastern European capitals, Washington, Bonn, Paris, Peking, Tokyo, Helsinki and Ulan Bator; and to HM Permanent Representatives to NATO (Brussels) and the United Nations (New York).

I am, Sir,
Yours faithfully

Bryan Cartledge

1. *Central Committee Plenum*: A meeting of the Central Committee of the Communist Party. The Central Committee elected both the Politburo and the General Secretary (Party leader).
2. *Supreme Soviet*: USSR parliament.
3. *Soviets*: Local workers' council.
4. *fate of Khrushchev*: Khrushchev denounced Stalin's reign of terror, introduced reforms so that fewer dissidents were prosecuted for political crimes, and let more ordinary Soviets travel outside the USSR. In 1964 he was forced to resign in a bloodless putsch led by Brezhnev, his successor. Khrushchev was allowed to go peacefully into retirement, unlike some previously deposed Russian leaders.
5. *Praesidium*: The permanent, standing staff of the Supreme Soviet.

6. *Council of Ministers*: Cabinet.

7. *expulsions crisis*: Tit-for-tat expulsions in 1985 of Russian and British diplomats, precipitated by a hard-line consensus between the FCO and Number 10 in Britain, leading to twenty-five expulsions by London, then twenty-five by Moscow (and then another six by both sides), which followed the defection of KGB agent Oleg Gordievsky to the West.

～

'The Bolshevik horrors were a crude and brutal satire on the Russian political tradition, not a fundamental departure from it'

SIR RODRIC BRAITHWAITE, HM AMBASSADOR
IN MOSCOW, MAY 1992

A big hitter, Sir Rodric became foreign policy adviser to John Major after leaving Moscow, and went on to chair the Joint Intelligence Committee. This masterly and beautifully drafted despatch, one of the finest we have come across, and which we reprint in extenso, *is fascinating in its diagnosis of the Russian condition. The footnotes here appear as they do in the original.*

Arriving in 1988, Braithwaite presented his credentials to the Soviet Union. It was from the Russian Federation that he took his leave four years later. Literally speaking, his immediate predecessor as British Ambassador to Russia was indeed an envoy to the Court of Tsar Nicholas II. In practice Braithwaite actually had the ambassadorial baton passed to him in Moscow by Sir Bryan Cartledge, whose valedictory features above. Both Cartledge and Braithwaite make forecasts in their last despatches about the demise of Communism and the prospects for democratic rule. In this, Braithwaite was apparently the luckier (but see the note in the foreword to

Cartledge) in that when his time came the direction of travel was clearly signposted, if not quite certain. In 1992 the old certainties in Russia had been swept away. The economy was reeling from the side effects of a transition through 'shock therapy' to capitalism. Standing on a tank the previous year Boris Yeltsin had already faced down one final attempt by Communist hardliners to turn back the clock. After Braithwaite left Moscow tanks rolled on to the political scene once again, shelling the Russian parliament in 1993 in a constitutional crisis the culmination of which saw Yeltsin safe in power for the rest of the decade. Sir Rodric makes clear that his prophecy is for the longer term; but it remains true that his optimism, if not discredited, has yet to be vindicated.

THE OBSESSION WITH RUSSIA
(Final Despatch of 17 May 1992)

'It is a matter of doubt whether the brutality of the people has made the prince a tyrant or whether the people themselves have become brutal and cruel through the tyranny of the prince'.
(Baron von Herberstein, Rerum Moscoviticarium Commentarii, 1549)

'A people passing rude, to vices vile inclinde . . .
In such a savage soile, where lawes do bear no sway,
But all is at the king his wille, to save or els to slay.'
(George Turbervile, Secretary at the British Embassy, Moscow 1568)

On Sunday, 11th October, 1552, the soldiers of Ivan the Terrible stormed the Tatar stronghold of Kazan: a spectacular victory after an arduous siege. Thus the Russians ended three centuries of domination by the Horde, and took their first step towards the creation of their landbased empire. By the end of the next century they had reached the Baltic and the Black Sea, and constructed cities across Siberia which are older than St Petersburg. Thus too the Russians began their halting return to the European civilisation from which they had been forcibly sundered when Baty Khan destroyed Kiev in 1240. The Tatars remained in sullen resentment, dreaming of the day when they too would be able to reassert their rights against an infidel and despised enemy. The problems which attend the collapse of the Soviet system were already set four and a half centuries ago.

With Ivan's victory Western European diplomats, traders, and technical advisers flocked to Russia in increasing numbers. Their judgements were universally harsh. They disliked the monotony of the landscape, the impassability of the roads, the ramshackle dirt of the towns, the morals of the women, the drunkenness and dishonesty of the men. But they agreed above all on the unacceptability, by the standards of civilised Europe, of the Russian political system: the secretiveness, incompetence, corruption and sycophancy of the officials of state; the instability of the law*; and the unbounded tyranny of the absolute ruler, his position sustained by an all-pervading political police and the liberal use of terror to atomise society and make it impossible for anyone, at any level, to combine against him.

These were not simply the prejudiced judgements of foreigners: they have been echoed by generations of Russian writers as well. Asia, the foreigners said. Many Russians agreed with them; and still do.

If one looks for an explanation, it lies no doubt in the impossible size of the country. To hold together a political

---

* Count Benkendorf, the Chief of the Russian Secret Police in the 1830s, once said: 'Laws are written for underlings, not for their bosses.'

system on the scale of a continent with the techniques of communication – physical, oral, administrative – which existed until the last few decades of the twentieth century may well have been impossible without the use of the methods of repression perfected by the Tsars and their successors. The effect on Russian society was devastating. In the Russian police state no independent political activity was possible, no unorthodox expression of view was permitted, and the penalties for both were horrific. No-one dared trust his neighbour, no-one dared cross a superior, no-one risked speaking to a foreigner. Delation and betrayal flourished.

And the great Russian lie was borne, initially as an essential instrument of self-preservation: to tell the truth was as likely as not to be fatal, in the most literal sense. But it goes much beyond that. All those who have dealt with the Russians over the centuries have commented on their indifference to the truth. The lie in Russia has indeed gone far beyond its original purpose and has become an art form. Russians lie when they feel they need to, as the Russian military lied to the West and to Shevardnadze about the purpose of the Krasnoyarsk radar.[1] But they also lie without reason, by some inner compulsion, even when they know that their listener knows that they are lying. The Russians have a word for it – 'vranyo' – which in their usage has acquired almost benign overtones. The latest example I have come across occurs in hotels frequented by foreigners: the notice in five languages on the lavatory: 'Disinfected for your comfort and safety'. Every Russian knows that this cannot be true. Only the most naive of foreigners would think any different. Yet in a great country, you disinfect the lavatory seats. So the notice has to go up.

By the turn of this century, Russia was at last beginning to shed these traditions. The Russian economy was growing faster than the American. A class of genuine Russian capitalists was beginning to emerge. Farmers were being encouraged to displace their incompetent peasant brothers. A liberal legal and political system was beginning to strike tentative roots . . .

It is barely surprising, though we may now choose to forget it, that the fall of the monarchy in February 1917 was widely, and perhaps rightly, welcomed in liberal circles in the West and in Russia as well. The Bolshevik horrors which followed were a crude and brutal satire on the Russian political tradition, not a fundamental departure from it. No wonder George Kennan, another acutely perceptive observer*, wrote in 1944 as the Red Army was sweeping victoriously across Europe, of 'the suspicion . . . latent in every Russian soul, that the term 'Russia' does not really signify a national society destined to know power and majesty, but only a vast unconquerable expanse of misery, poverty, inefficiency, and mud'.

Nearly fifty years after Kennan, that is still what most Russians fear. Yet my tentative thesis is that the last decade marks a qualitative change in the underlying thrust of Russian history. It is a large claim, which I cannot substantiate in the space of a despatch, or even perhaps of a book. But as one contemplates the present political and economic chaos, there are two questions which one needs to ask. Can Russia survive as a great nation? Can it become a modern and prosperous liberal democratic state?

To the first question the answer is unequivocal. The Russian state has survived assault, invasion, sometimes centuries of domination by Tatars, Poles, Swedes, Frenchmen, Germans.

* Kennan, the American diplomat and scholar, was briefly US Ambassador in Moscow in the early 1950s, but was expelled for a disobliging remark about the Stalinist system.

Its cities have been repeatedly destroyed, its governments dispersed. Yet the toughness and patriotism of the people have always prevailed. For the Russian people do have the strongest sense of the state, of the rightness of Russian glory. This sense is poles apart from the English genius for building state institutions, at which the Russians have always proved themselves incompetent. But not a single Russian that I have met, whether dissident country priest or Siberian provincial governor, is prepared to accept in his heart that Russia will shrink back to the size of Ivan the Terrible's Muscovy. Last summer before the putsch a prominent liberal told me, with the greatest passion, that Russia could afford to do without the Balts, the Caucasians, the Central Asians, or even the Ukrainians. But if the Tatars thought they could reverse the verdict of 1552 he for one would be prepared to send in the tanks.

There is of course no likelihood that Russia will become a model democracy on Nordic lines. And Russian history from the time of Catherine the Great (I do not count Peter, who was a tyrant almost as bloody as Ivan or Stalin) is littered with failed attempts at reform. Yet today real political change is occurring, and has already gone far further than I or anyone else would have believed possible when I returned to Moscow in September 1988. At that time there were those in the West who still believed that the Gorbachev reforms were deliberate disinformation, or at least a pause to regroup in the Soviet Union's secular advance under the banner of Communism. What has happened since then is that the political conditions described by . . . countless writers on the Soviet period, no longer apply. Since September 1988 we have seen the first parliamentary election with universal suffrage in Russian history. We have seen the Russian people choose their own leader, also for the first time in their history. We have seen a Russian leader ousted peacefully (though not quite by due process) and allowed to retire gracefully. We have seen the centuries old Russian empire crumble with – so far at least – less blood shed than at Amritsar[2] and during the partition of India. And we have seen Communism – the menace to prevent which we once thought it would be worth blowing up the whole world – disappear in a puff, leaving a mere miasma behind.

There is a famous stage direction at the end of Pushkin's *Boris Godunov*: 'The people are silent.' In the last four years the Russian people have not been silent. Time and again, supported by an increasingly free press, they went onto the streets to demonstrate their rejection of the age-old Russian lie, their abhorrence of the Communist regime, and their support for the chance at freedom which Gorbachev gave them. Such massive displays of civic responsibility and political maturity are unprecedented in the dismal tale of Russian history, in which long ages of political repression have been mitigated only by vicious outbreaks of mob violence. Sceptics argue that only a tiny proportion of the Russian people were involved on the Moscow barricades last August: as if the great democratic revolutions of 1688 and 1776 – so far the only successful revolutions in history – were made by the whole of the English and American peoples. The truth in my view is that we are witnessing a qualitative change in the nature of Russian politics, of a kind which occurs very rarely in the history of any nation; and that this is an event of the greatest importance for the whole world, as well as for the Russian people themselves. The political, constitutional, economic, imperial, and other difficulties have been reported almost ad nauseam by this post and will take decades if not generations to overcome. But I do not think it is an act of mindless optimism to look forward to a future in which

Russia has developed its own form of democracy, no doubt imperfect unlike those which have sprung up elsewhere, but still a vast improvement on what has gone before.

Which leaves a question begged. When they contemplate their disastrous history and the chaos which now surrounds them, few Russians can understand why they remain so passionately attached to the country which has treated themselves so harshly. It is an intensity of passion which few other patriotic peoples can match. Even more remarkable is the impact which Russia exercises on the minds of foreigners . . . George Kennan, businessmen, journalists, and even members of this Embassy (though not Mr Turbervile) – who have become obsessed with this immense, shambling, muddy, disorganised, and ferocious country.

It is not at first sight the physical look of the place, a boundless plain on which even the oldest cities sit precariously like nomadic encampments. Nor is it the art, the literature and the music, which are among the glories of European culture.* Nor is it even the marvellous Russian language, in the view of one of our friends the only thing the Russians have produced whose value is beyond all doubt. All these exercise a fascination which is easier to experience than to explain. But in the end it is the people themselves who constitute the riches of the country. This judgement is none the less true for being wholly unoriginal. Political oppression, the atomisation of society, and generations of poverty have forced the Russian

* The argument about whether Russia is European or Asian will no doubt rage for ever. The Russians themselves cannot decide. But Russia is part of Christendom, an integral part of European history, and the great Russian novelists are read by all educated Englishmen, most of whom have never read a page of Goethe, Dante, or Racine; and have no idea whether or not there is such a thing as the great Indian, Japanese or Chinese novel. Russia is a problem to the rest of us, not because it is insufficiently

people back on one another. Only in small groups have they been able to muster enough trust to guard against the informer. Only in their kitchens have they felt free to talk – endlessly, ineffectively, and beguilingly – about the problems of life and the universe which their political system has never allowed them to tackle direct. Because they are so vulnerable, human relationships in Russia have an intensity which they lack in the more orderly West. Foreigners can be admitted at least in part to these relationships: Russians are embarrassingly generous with their time and their few possessions, in a way which is wholly uncharacteristic in the West. We would not dream of sharing our last piece of sausage with a guest, not least because either of us could just slip down to the supermarket for another. It is the lack of these things which all Russians notice as soon as they go abroad, and which makes exile so hard for them to bear.

Above all, Russia is an epic country, not only in its size but in its moral quality. Because it is a land where the lie has been erected into a principle of conduct, concepts such as Truth, Honour, Loyalty, Courage have a real meaning for the most ordinary of people, who are continually having to make the kind of choices which Englishmen have not had to make since our Civil War three hundred years ago. To us these big words are an embarrassment. For Russians they are an inescapable part of everyday life. Because Russia has always been a land of villains, it is also a land of heroes and saints. Without Stalin, there could have been no Solzhenitsyn and no Sakharov.[3]

European, but because it is insufficiently small: it stretches across eleven time zones, and the larger part of its territory – though a minority of its people – looks to the Pacific and Asia. This affects attitudes and politics, but does not affect the essentially European nature of Russian civilisation.

My immediate predecessor as Ambassador to Russia, George Buchanan, left Petrograd in January 1918 exhausted after eight grinding years of war and revolution. He wrote in his diary: 'Our last day in Petrograd! – and yet, in spite of all that we have gone through, we are sad at the thought. Why is it that Russia casts over all who know her such an indefinable mystic spell that, even when her wayward children have turned their capital into a pandemonium, we are sorry to leave it?'

Buchanan writes with the grating condescension of a British diplomat of the old school. But I recognise the sentiment. Russia is an addiction to which there is no sure antidote. [The despatch seems to end here.]

1. *Krasnoyarsk radar*: In 1989 Eduard Shevardnadze (Soviet Foreign Minister, and latterly President of Georgia) finally admitted the existence of a secret early warning radar system at Krasnoyarsk after years of complaints from Washington. In the spirit of *glasnost* Shevardnadze told the Soviet parliament the station was 'as big as an Egyptian pyramid' and 'directly and openly violated' the Anti-Ballistic Missile Treaty.

2. *Amritsar*: See p. 127.

3. *Sakharov*: The nuclear physicist Andrei Sakharov helped Stalin develop the hydrogen bomb. His later writings in favour of arms control and human rights won him the Nobel Peace Prize in 1975, which he was not allowed to leave Russia to collect.

∼

Czechoslovakia

'A symbol of hope in the midst of a dark nightmare life'

SIR DERWENT KERMODE, HM AMBASSADOR
TO CZECHOSLOVAKIA, JUNE 1955

In the field of foreign affairs it is important to know who one's real friends are. Here in Czechoslovakia that is not hard to know. Our friends are not the Government but the broad mass of the people. In the course of my two years in Czechoslovakia my wife and I have motored little short of 30,000 miles, on main roads and off the beaten track, through town and village, among woods and over rolling agricultural country, in industrial as well as rural areas; and everywhere we have gone we have flown the flag. As workers in the fields or streets have seen and recognised it their sad faces have lit up and they have waved to us or saluted as we passed, and children have excitedly shouted 'England!' And sometimes, when the car has been parked in a Prague street, men have come up and reverently touched and even kissed the flag. I have seen women's eyes fill with tears, tears both of memory and of longing, with our flag, like the flag of the United States, as a symbol of hope in the midst of a dark nightmare life.

~

> '*A pretty girl can walk through Prague at 2 a.m.*
> *with a bulging hand-bag with little fear of violence*'

RONALD SCRIVENER, HM AMBASSADOR
TO CZECHOSLOVAKIA, APRIL 1974

Very occasionally, despatches in the mid-Cold War period reflect a readiness to acknowledge the positive side of Communist life alongside the overwhelming negatives. Any such sentiments were stamped on hard within the Office. Scrivener's valedictory from Prague, making the rather mild claim that grasping materialism was pleasantly absent in Prague, is one such example. A less-than-impressed senior clerk sent it on up the bureaucratic chain with a note attached: 'Of course there is less "materialist vulgarity" in Prague than there is in New York or Paris or London ... It would be fairer to compare Prague with, say, Edinburgh ... It is a (perhaps regrettable) fact too that materialist vulgarity appeals strongly to many people. There would not be so much of it about if it did not.'

(CONFIDENTIAL)   *Prague,*
                                              17 April, 1974.

Sir,

On leaving this post I realise that my three years in Prague have been marked by a certain frigidity in Anglo-Czechoslovak affairs. There have been a number of reasons, all in one way or another reflecting the Czechoslovak Government's view that international relations are (to quote the Foreign Minister) 'not some diplomatic tea party but a platform of the class struggle' ...

To live alongside the present Czechoslovak social system

has been an interesting experience. There is much that Czechoslovakia can be proud of. The very largely effective conservation and restoration of its urban magnificences do not owe a lot to the absence of much personal choice in the matter of domicile. A pretty girl can walk through Prague at 2 a.m. with a bulging hand-bag with little fear of violence. The schoolchildren and university students work; they neither streak across their campuses nor mob their Vice-Chancellors, and I doubt if they would engage in such capers even if the consequences fell short of exclusion from a worthwhile career. Entertainment and the creative arts may be banal and unoriginal, but they do not peddle violence and smut. The drug problem exists, but on a barely perceptible scale.

As a young man in the Foreign Ministry put it to me, 'of course our system is a lousy one; but when I see the materialist vulgarity of New York and Paris and London I prefer it to yours'.

This is the brighter side of the Czechoslovak scene, reflecting not the merits of the present political system but rather the heritage of respect for law and custom, learning and craftsmanship without (because statehood was for so long denied to the Czechs) the profligacy and jingoism which went with national power and wealth in the heyday of the nation states.

But there is another and less attractive side: the intrigue, the backbiting and the corruption which accompanies rule by an apparatus enjoying power not by popular will but by its capacity, buttressed by the support of a Super Power, to lift up one person and cast down another. To find somewhere to live, to get the best education for one's children, to spend a holiday in Dubrovnik and to deploy one's talents in work or even in recreation means that someone has got to be squared. For some the squaring represents no problem, particularly if the process can be taken to the point of acquiring party membership. This self-perpetuating elite can build private country cottages, or even substantial private villas in the favoured Prague suburb of Barrandov, travel abroad with a generous allowance of foreign exchange, acquire a Government Tatra or an imported Saab, and be sure that their children will enjoy the best of the educational system. But for the vast majority of Czechoslovaks who have no marketable political or professional status the daily problem is how to square those who have. By informing; by gifts; by sycophancy. To get decent service in the shops the tip can range from a packet of 20 to a carton of cigarettes. For the doctor to look at one's daughter's tonsils, a bottle of Scotch. To join a (bear-led[1]) group on a package tour to Italy, several bottles, a carton or two, and friends in the right places. In the more perilous field of ideology the prices are higher. A misplaced political observation by someone of 'bourgeois' origins, a friendship with a known dissident, and goodbye to the office with the secretary and the potted plants, followed by a job stoking the boiler in a block of flats or as an hotel porter. Or the minimum pension – with a purchasing power of £2 per week.

As the supply of consumer goods and the availability of housing improves, so the need for economic fiddling should ease off. But there is no sign that the ideological climate is going to become more benevolent. Rather the reverse. It follows that Czechoslovak society is endangered by precisely those evils which the leadership ascribes to 'the West': the adulteration of human values, and class strife created by the existence of an unmeritorious elite.

Of these two aspects of the Czechoslovak condition

I believe that in time the good will oust the bad, firstly because there is in the Czech character a strong built-in sense of morality which goes back to the Hussites[2] and the Moravian Brothers,[3] secondly because the ideological poison is, fundamentally a foreign import. But for some time Czechoslovakia will continue to be two nations – not Czech and Slovak, but Ins and Outs; and Czechoslovakia will show two faces – the windy rhetoric and folkloric festivals for the foreign visitor, and the nocturnal telephone calls and aggressive tailing by the 'heavy mob' experienced by foreign residents whose Governments or media happen at the time to be in hot water with the Czechoslovak authorities. We should not allow this to repel us, for here is at bottom a worthy and productive community of people who for geopolitical reasons will always merit attention. Particularly I believe by us, for whom the Czechoslovak people have a regard out of all proportion to our very modest interest in them.

1. *bear-led*: Russian led.
2. *Hussites*: Early Protestant revolutionaries. In 1419 the Hussites rose up against King Wenceslas (who was not so good, after all) in the First Defenestration of Prague, throwing seven city leaders out of a Town Hall window on to pikes below. Their one-eyed leader, Zikka, defeated five Catholic crusader armies sent into Bohemia after him. After Zikka's death his followers stretched his skin over a drum so he could continue to lead them in battle. In short, an unsqueamish crowd.
3. *Moravian Brothers*: A Hussite religious movement.

~

Poland

'The country is living on a lie'

SIR NICHOLAS HENDERSON, HM AMBASSADOR
TO POLAND, APRIL 1972

CONFIDENTIAL

BRITISH EMBASSY
WARSAW
14 April 1972

The Right Honourable
Sir Alec Douglas-Home MP
etc etc etc

Sir:

POLAND: VALEDICTORY

Outstanding Impression

If you were to ask me to express in a sentence the most
important fact about Poland relevant to the UK (and
perhaps to other Western countries) that has impressed
itself on me after three years here, it would be this: that the
country is living on a lie and that it remains, after 25 years
of the present regime, marked by irreconcilable conflicts
and instability.

Poland is a state run on Communist lines, subject to
the dictates of Russia. But it is a nation more religious,
probably, than any other in Europe, Spain not excluded.
It is innately anti-Communist, fiercely patriotic and
independent, historically hostile towards the Russians and
attached spiritually and socially to the West. Unfashionable

though it is nowadays to look to national characteristics for underlying explanations of a country's behaviour, I do not think that one can escape doing so here. No geographical, political or constitutional definition is adequate to describe the essence and life-force of the 53 million Polish people.

Certain questions keep cropping up if you live for any length of time amongst the Poles under their present regime: have living conditions improved here since the war more than elsewhere in Europe; if not, is this due to the system; and, if so, is the system capable of improvement? I hope that answers to these questions will emerge in the course of the following very personal account which makes no pretensions to completeness.

Improvements in Daily Life

I am not here talking about conditions for the former upper or middle classes, or for members of the professions, or about artists or intellectuals – for all of whom Communism has brought degradation, dreariness and despair. I am discussing the daily life of the majority of the population.

For a Pole, to have the necessities of life is not something that can be taken for granted. Nowadays they are assured of essentials: employment; enough to eat; cheap accommodation; pensions; children's education; and health services . . .

The people are not deprived of their time-honoured right to make jokes, even in public, about living conditions and the system. The main political weekly, with the remarkably high circulation of a quarter of a million, has just published the following: 'They say there are three degrees of luxury in Poland: I. A car. II. A Villa (it does not exclude the first). III. Having your own opinion (it excludes the first and second).'

The system provides for paid holidays, special camps for children and, most vaunted of all, for extensive opportunities for higher education (according to published figures here 25% more students in relation to the population are undergoing higher education than in the UK).

How far the above material improvements could or would have occurred under another system is debatable. Certainly, much greater progress has been made in Western Europe since the war. But I think that there is little doubt that egalitarianism has been applied more sweepingly under Communism than elsewhere, and that the people of Poland themselves welcome what they consider to be their exceptional educational opportunities and the guarantee they have of work and a minimum wage. But having made this generalisation, I must qualify it by saying that the majority of Poles nevertheless rightly believe that living conditions are very much better in Western Europe than here, and that the economic system in the West seems capable of producing a bigger and better cake to be divided up.

Areas of Indifference
There are certain things that belong to the system, e.g. the lack of Press freedom, that most Poles probably do not mind about very much, largely because they have never known anything else; the same applies to the drabness inherent in Communism, as much of a blight today as 10 or 20 years ago, despite the improvement in material conditions (although to set against this it is necessary to mention the trouble taken by the State to restore and safeguard works of art). Perhaps for the same reason, nearly all Poles under 50, who constitute 78% of the population,

seem resigned to the verbosity and priggishness of all public pronouncements, something that stuns the visitor from the West . . .

There is little doubt that nearly all Poles resent bitterly the country's subjection to Moscow, even though it is discreetly conducted and Soviet troops are kept well out of sight. I do not think that it is always realised in the West how little is the rapport between the Poles and the Russians. This applies at all levels, except presumably at the summit of the Party, although even here there is little of the bonhomie that many people outside may think exists in the Soviet bloc. For instance I asked the ex-wife of the former Polish Prime Minister, who had been with him for 25 years when he held that office, whether, either here in Warsaw or in Moscow on visits, they and others in the higher ranks of the Party had seen much of the Russians socially and in private. Her answer was to laugh at the absurdity of the question and to ask me whether I knew that when she and the Prime Minister had been on visits to Moscow, they had always been subject to surveillance, and it had not been for their protection . . .

Corruption, Demoralisation and Boorishness

Not only does the system fail to deliver the goods but it is corrupt and the people are demoralised. The heavy sentence just passed on the former Deputy Minister of the Interior for participation in a racket in gold bars that is said to have utilised a car competing in the Monte Carlo Rally, is only the tip – a very Polish one – of a large iceberg. Despite the customary high moral tone of public announcements everyone knows the widespread wheeler-dealing that goes on. In the absence of either faith or incentive there is a go-slow on a national scale. A Polish weekly has described the malaise: 'Just as bad work is not a bad mark against anyone, so to carry out a job well does not earn a good mark. Promotion and dismissal are decided according to other criteria.' There are continual complaints from on high against the 'parasitism' and 'hooliganism' of the young. According to WHO statistics, Poland leads the world in alcoholism, and their own figures acknowledge that half a million Poles are absent from work each day due to drunkenness. Ten per cent of the population of productive age are estimated to be habitual alcoholics. Prostitution is also admitted to be a serious social problem.

Nor can I refrain from mentioning the boorishness that appears to be de rigueur whenever a Pole is set in a position of authority. There was a time when the Poles had a reputation for courtesy. But this is no longer so, partly, I think, because of the recent enormous influx of peasants to the towns where they appear quickly to adapt themselves to the lowest and commonest denominator of behaviour. It is also as though, according to some new biological law, Communism was breeding a special race of people with an acquired contempt for each other. The Poles remain, to be sure, half as boorish as the Russians, but this may be because they have been under Communism only half as long.

No visitor to the Polish People's Republic should enter a shop, restaurant or any public place, without expecting to meet discourtesy, or at best, almost theatrical indifference. I mention this here because I believe it illustrates one of the fundamental flaws of Communism as a philosophy for practical application. It presupposes man to be better than he is; more benign, less grasping. It assumes that he will live in harmony with and serve the community unselfishly regardless of personal gain, and that he will abjure all desire

DS 1/6

RECEIVED IN
ARCHIVES No.14
3 AUG 1967

Foreign Office and Whitehall Distribution

THAILAND
18 July, 1967
Section 1

GOODBYE TO THAILAND

Sir Anthony Rumbold to Mr. Brown. (Received 18 July)

SUMMARY

The Thais are as difficult to understand as other orientals. (Paragraph 1.)

The domination of Bangkok. (Paragraph 2.)

General contentment and lethargy. (Paragraph 3.)

The rigid structure of society and the rules which govern it. Unwillingness to assume responsibility and endemic corruption. (Paragraphs 4–6.)

The country is governed by a benevolent dictatorship without a dictator. A description of some of the leading personalities. (Paragraphs 7–11.)

If there are constitutional developments it will be because the Thais like to be thought up to date. (Paragraph 12.)

Boom conditions and prospects of indefinite economic progress. (Paragraph 13.)

Importance of not over-estimating the terrorist movement in the north-east. (Paragraph 14.)

The Thais are afraid of China and although they do not like to be dependent on foreigners they will tolerate the American presence as long as they feel that it keeps danger at a distance. If the Americans let go in Viet-Nam the Thais might change course. There is not likely to be a sudden revulsion against the Americans. (Paragraphs 15–16.)

Our stake in Thailand is the same as that of other West European countries. Our membership of SEATO makes no difference. Our export performance could be better. (Paragraph 17.)

The Thai tradition of sending children to England to be educated gives us a certain advantage. The best way we can help the Thais is in the field of education. (Paragraph 18.)

The pleasures of living in Thailand, the virtues of the Thais and a tribute to the Embassy staff. (Paragraphs 19–20.)

(No. 19. Confidential)
Sir,

Bangkok,
13 July, 1967.

I am on the point of leaving Bangkok after a stay of two and a half years and have the honour to set down some thoughts about Thailand which I hope may be of some interest to my successor. They are thoughts rather than convictions. There is a theory that the Thais are rather easier for Europeans to understand than are other oriental people. I do not believe this theory. It seems to me that Sino/Indian/Malay/Thai ways of thought are so alien to ours that analogies between events in South-East Asia and events in Europe are nearly always misleading, that forecasts based on such analogies are bound to be wrong, that the motives of Asians are impossible for us to estimate with any exactness, and that Thailand and the Thais offer no exception

20398—198   8030—46

A

---

1. 'The general level of intelligence of the Thais is rather low . . .' Sir Anthony Rumbold's withering parting shot from Bangkok was mistakenly given 'Q' distribution throughout the entire Commonwealth instead of the intended 'A' distribution (Canada, Australia, New Zealand). See pp. 72–5.

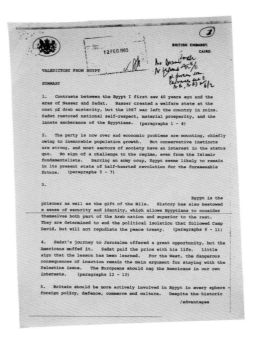

2. Sir Michael Weir, HM Ambassador to Egypt, 1985. Paragraph 3 of the summary has been partially obscured by the censors.

3. Lord Moran, High Commissioner to Canada, 1984. Moran's remarks on the parochialism of Ottawa politics and its back-scratching politicians still pack a punch. In 2009 the contents of this despatch briefly became a national talking point in Canada when it was revealed in our BBC Radio 4 series.

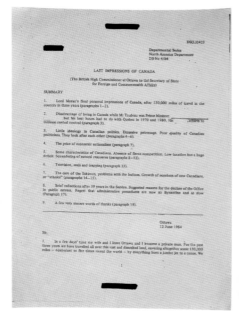

BRITISH EMBASSY
BONN

10 October 1997

The Rt Hon Robin Cook QC MP
Secretary of State for Foreign
and Commonwealth Affairs
Foreign and Commonwealth Office
LONDON
SW1A 2AH

Sir,

GERMANY: HELLO AND GOODBYE

1. As the shortest serving British Ambassador to Germany since the War, and probably ever, first and last impressions become one. I offer the Chief Clark a new concept in value for money: the combined first and farewell call.

2. My time falls into two distinct parts: before 1 May and after 1 May. Labour's massive win has transformed Britain's position in Germany for the better. The job is to turn this into a long-term increase in British influence.

3. Before 1 May Britain was in German eyes a tiresome irritant. Kohl felt personally offended by the last Government. In the EU we were a problem to be got round. Nobody was terribly interested in our views. Nobody wanted to admit that Britain knew something about restructuring and tackling unemployment that Germany did not.

4. For two months before the General Election I preached a constant message. There was an unsung solidity in British-German relations. There was a natural coincidence of interests across a wide range of issues. It was not possible to build a stable Europe without Britain.

5. The message fell on barren ground. Instead, three questions were repeatedly put to me: who would win the election; and if Labour did, would Britain's European policy change and would I be asked? My replies were on all counts suitably reserved.

6. The election result, in its decisiveness and drama, knocked the Germans' socks off. It has even to a degree destabilised German politics.

4. Into the modern era; Sir Christopher Meyer's valedictory despatch from Germany in 1997, released under the Freedom of Information Act. The Foreign Office refused to release Meyer's 2003 valedictory from Washington.

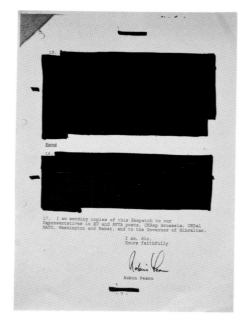

17. I am sending copies of this despatch to our Representatives in EU and EFTA posts, UKRep Brussels, UKDel NATO, Washington and Rabat, and to the Governor of Gibraltar.

I am, Sir,
Yours faithfully

Robin Fearn

5. Freedom of Information.

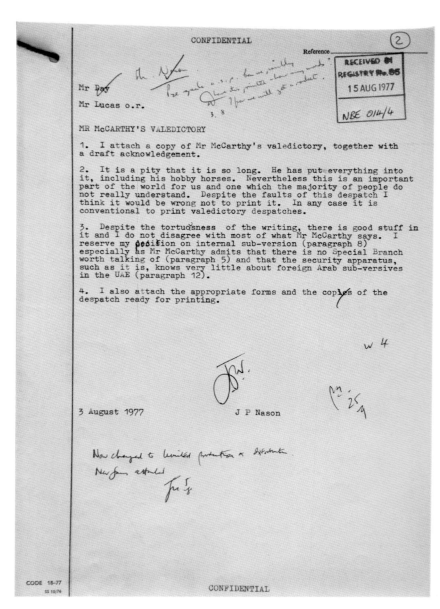

Mr Day

Mr Lucas o.r.

MR McCARTHY'S VALEDICTORY

1. I attach a copy of Mr McCarthy's valedictory, together with a draft acknowledgement.

2. It is a pity that it is so long. He has put everything into it, including his hobby horses. Nevertheless this is an important part of the world for us and one which the majority of people do not really understand. Despite the faults of this despatch I think it would be wrong not to print it. In any case it is conventional to print valedictory despatches.

3. Despite the tortuousness of the writing, there is good stuff in it and I do not disagree with most of what Mr McCarthy says. I reserve my position on internal sub-version (paragraph 8) especially as Mr McCarthy admits that there is no Special Branch worth talking of (paragraph 5) and that the security apparatus, such as it is, knows very little about foreign Arab sub-versives in the UAE (paragraph 12).

4. I also attach the appropriate forms and the copies of the despatch ready for printing.

w 4

3 August 1977   J P Nason

6. The sternest critics of an ambassador's prose were often his colleagues back in Whitehall. Clerks back at 'the centre' could be ruthless in pointing out the defects in a despatch. Despite their reservations this valedictory from the United Arab Emirates was grudgingly submitted for printing, in accordance with the tradition.

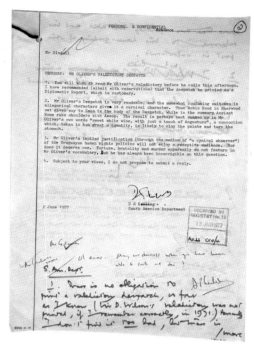

7. Literary criticism.
Extracts from Mr Oliver's
valedictory are on pp. 315–17.

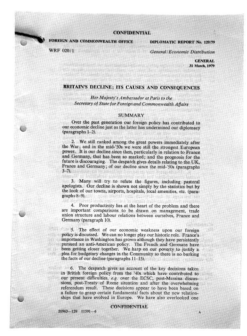

8. The Henderson despatch.

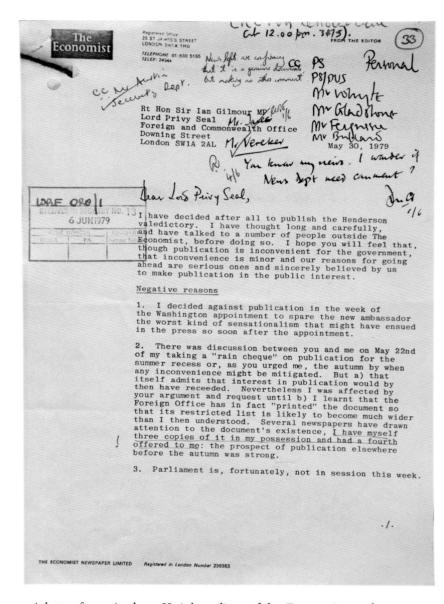

The Economist

Registered Office
25 ST JAMES'S STREET
LONDON SW1A 1HG

TELEPHONE 01-930 5155
TELEX: 24344

Cut 12.00 pm. 3675).

FROM THE EDITOR

(33)

*News Dept are confirming
that I is a genuine document.
but making no other comment*

CC PS **Personal**

*CC Mr Austin
Security Dept.*

PS/PUS
Mr Whyte
Mr Gladstone
Mr Ferguson
Mr Bullard

Rt Hon Sir Ian Gilmour MP
Lord Privy Seal *Mr Jakes*
Foreign and Commonwealth Office
Downing Street
London SW1A 2AL *Mr Vereker*

May 30, 1979

*R) You know my views. I wonder if
News Dept need comment?*

Jn G

Dear Lord Privy Seal,

LDBE 080 1

RECEIVED IN REGISTRY NO. 13
6 JUN 1979

I have decided after all to publish the Henderson
valedictory. I have thought long and carefully,
and have talked to a number of people outside The
Economist, before doing so. I hope you will feel that,
though publication is inconvenient for the government,
that inconvenience is minor and our reasons for going
ahead are serious ones and sincerely believed by us
to make publication in the public interest.

Negative reasons

1. I decided against publication in the week of
the Washington appointment to spare the new ambassador
the worst kind of sensationalism that might have ensued
in the press so soon after the appointment.

2. There was discussion between you and me on May 22nd
of my taking a "rain cheque" on publication for the
summer recess or, as you urged me, the autumn by when
any inconvenience might be mitigated. But a) that
itself admits that interest in publication would by
then have receeded. Nevertheless I was affected by
your argument and request until b) I learnt that the
Foreign Office has in fact "printed" the document so
that its restricted list is likely to become much wider
than I then understood. Several newspapers have drawn
attention to the document's existence, I have myself
three copies of it in my possession and had a fourth
offered to me: the prospect of publication elsewhere
before the autumn was strong.

3. Parliament is, fortunately, not in session this week.

./.

THE ECONOMIST NEWSPAPER LIMITED   Registered in London Number 236383

9. A letter from Andrew Knight, editor of the *Economist*, to the
government informing them that the magazine intended to publish
Nicholas Henderson's valedictory – having obtained not one but
three leaked copies.

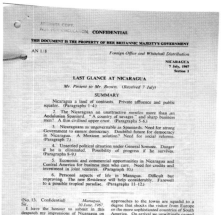

THIS DOCUMENT IS THE PROPERTY OF HER BRITANNIC MAJESTY'S GOVERNMENT

AN 1/8 *Foreign Office and Whitehall Distribution*

NICARAGUA
7 July, 1967
Section 1

LAST GLANCE AT NICARAGUA

Mr. Pinsent to Mr. Brown. (Received 7 July)

SUMMARY

Nicaragua a land of contrasts. Private affluence and public squalor. (Paragraphs 1-4.)

2. The Nicaraguan an unattractive *mestizo* more than an Andalusian Spaniard. "A country of savages" and sharp business men". A thin civilised upper crust. (Paragraphs 5-6.)

3. Nicaraguans as ungovernable as Spaniards. Need for strong Government to ensure democracy. Doubtful future for democracy in Nicaragua. A Mexican solution? Need for social reforms. (Paragraph 7.)

4. Unsettled political situation under General Somoza. Danger if he is eliminated. Possibility of progress if he survives. (Paragraphs 8-9.)

5. Economic and commercial opportunities in Nicaragua and Central America for business men who care. Need for credits and investment in joint ventures. (Paragraph 10.)

6. Personal aspects of life in Managua. Difficult but improving. The new Residence will help considerably. Farewell to a possible tropical paradise. (Paragraphs 11-12.)

(No. 13. Confidential)   Managua,
Sir,   10 June, 1967.
I have the honour to submit in this despatch my impressions of Nicaragua on leaving the country. I regret that there was not time to complete it before I left, owing to the political and social turmoil of the last few weeks, ending with the inauguration of the new President just before my departure.

2. I did not submit a report on my first impressions of Nicaragua after my arrival at the end of 1963, mainly because I did not wish to burden your predecessor with unnecessary paper; and partly also because my first impressions would probably have been too unfavourable to print. In this report therefore I will try to give a balanced view of the country and people as seen on departure.

3. The first thing that strikes one about Nicaragua is that it is a land of contrasts. It is a most beautiful country providing many magnificent prospects; but the

approaches to the towns are squalid to a degree that shocks the visitor from Europe or the more sophisticated countries of South America. On arrival we unwittingly caused some offence by enquiring the name of the first village we passed through on leaving the airport, which turned out to be the capital city of Managua. The present Embassy residence on its windy cliff edge looking towards Lake Managua has, if little else, perhaps the finest prospect of all Managua; it happens also to be on the high road to Costa Rica.

4. These contrasts go right through Nicaraguan life. If ever there was a country where the private affluence of the few is flaunted in face of the public squalor of the many, it is Nicaragua. It is distressing that still to-day after thirty years of *Somocismo*, which has undoubtedly brought stability and prosperity to the country as a whole, the conditions of living for the vast majority of Nicaraguans are little less than sordid: over half the population have

CONFIDENTIAL

2039B—187 8630—35

A

10. Roger Pinsent,
HM Ambassador to
Nicaragua, 1967.

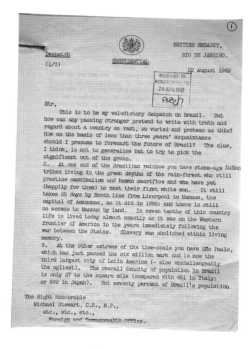

BRITISH EMBASSY,
RIO DE JANEIRO.

Despatch   CONFIDENTIAL
(1/3)

22 August 1969

RECEIVED IN
REGISTRY No. 12
26 AUG 1969
AL 6/7

Sir,
        This is to be my valedictory despatch on Brazil. But how on the basis of less than three years' acquaintance should I presume to forecast the future of Brazil? The clue, I think, is not to generalise but to try to pick the significant out of the gross.

2.   At one end of the Brazilian rainbow you have stone-age Indian tribes living in the green depths of the rain-forest who still practise cannibalism and human sacrifice and who have yet (happily for them) to meet their first white man. It still takes 25 days by Booth Line from Liverpool to Manaus, the capital of Amazonas, as it did in 1890; and there is still no access to Manaus by land. In seven tenths of this country life is lived today almost exactly as it was on the Western frontier of America in the years immediately following the war between the States. Slavery was abolished within living memory.

3.   At the other extreme of the time-scale you have São Paulo, which has just passed the six million mark and is now the third largest city of Latin America (- also unchallengeably the ugliest). The overall density of population in Brazil is only 27 to the square mile (compared with 461 in Italy: or 689 in Japan). But seventy percent of Brazil's population

The Right Honourable
Michael Stewart, C.H., M.P.,
    etc., etc., etc.,
    Foreign and Commonwealth Office.

11. Sir John Russell, HM
Ambassador to Brazil, 1969.

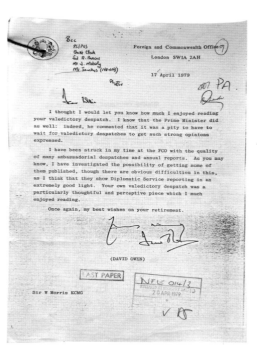

Foreign and Commonwealth Office

London SWIA 2AH

17 April 1979

I thought I would let you know how much I enjoyed reading your valedictory despatch. I know that the Prime Minister did as well: indeed, he commented that it was a pity to have to wait for valedictory despatches to get such strong opinions expressed.

I have been struck in my time at the FCO with the quality of many ambassadorial despatches and annual reports. As you may know, I have investigated the possibility of getting some of them published, though there are obvious difficulties in this, as I think that they show Diplomatic Service reporting in an extremely good light. Your own valedictory despatch was a particularly thoughtful and perceptive piece which I much enjoyed reading.

Once again, my best wishes on your retirement.

(DAVID OWEN)

LAST PAPER

NFL 014/3
20 APR 1979

Sir W Morris KCMG

12. A letter from the Foreign Secretary to Willie Morris, an accomplished Arabist, on his retirement from Cairo. Morris's earlier valedictory from Riyadh is on pp. 228–30. We are happy to grant David Owen his wish (thirty years on) to see some despatches published.

PAGE 3

13. Freedom of Information.

for personal property whilst treating public property as if it were his own . . .

As I suggested at the beginning of this despatch, I believe that the governing fact here is the contradiction inherent in Polish life. Discontent, already widespread, will not necessarily be reduced merely because conditions improve. Counter-revolution, like revolution, is the product of hope rather than despair. The Polish people are tough. They are determined to make a dynamic state out of their nation. One day, they are likely to succeed. But on the way there may well be further violent upheavals and there will certainly be long periods of torpor and frustration. There will not be stability.

~

China

'This is a country to which one should devote one's life or go away'

SIR JOHN ADDIS, HM AMBASSADOR
TO CHINA, JUNE 1974

(CONFIDENTIAL)   *Peking,*
14 June, 1974.

Sir,

My first year in China, 1948, I wrote home in anguish 'This is a country to which one should devote one's life or go away.' I have done neither but kept on coming back and became that most unsatisfactory of things, a semi-specialist. But even semi-specialists on Communist China were rare in the 1950s and 1960s and were therefore of some use.

During the cold war years there were so many adverse

preconceptions about Communist China that those who knew a little were always on the defensive. Communism in China was held to be an alien system imposed by force on an unwilling population and therefore to be a state of affairs that could not endure. Chinese Communism was moreover widely believed to be necessarily expansive and aggressive, even to the extent of being likely to send regular armed forces across frontiers, and it was held that this was proved by a succession of demonstrative acts: Tibet, Korea, the Taiwan Straits, the Indian frontier. Arguments to the contrary were discounted as special pleading, and those who put them forward were viewed askance as 'pro-Chinese'.

This climate of opinion added to the difficulties, already enormous, of trying to reach an objective assessment of the meaning and progress of the Chinese revolution under the leadership of Mao and the Communist Party. Everything here is so different from anything that we are used to in the West. All the values are different. The collective, both horizontally (*qua* membership of a group) and vertically (in the concatenation of generations) has always mattered more than the individual. It would not be true to say that ideology has taken the place of religion, because the Chinese in general have no need for religion. Individual salvation is an alien idea: the only hereafter is communal. Thus Communist doctrine has in many respects fitted easily on to the pre-existing thought processes and social structure. The guidance from the Centre passes down through the pyramidal structure of the Party and has a binding force on the individual. The Chinese traditionally have a talent for conforming to whatever is required of them by the established authority, while retaining an inner integrity. To anyone living in China for any length of time the most astonishing feature of the regime is that it works, in a country so vast, so populous and so disparate.

The achievements of a quarter century of Communist rule in China are very substantial. Out of chaos order has been established, and there is a sufficiency for all. Perhaps the greatest benefit has been the achievement of social security. Never before in China, certainly not since the 18th century, have so many people been able to look with so much confidence and with so little fear to the future. Everyone has a job and a wage and a place in society, women as well as men. Nurseries, kindergartens, universal education, a co-operative medical service, pensions, and old people's homes are being introduced. There is a rising standard of living, in housing and consumer goods; and over the years I have observed with amusement the escalation of status symbols – first fountain pens, then leather shoes, followed by bicycles, wrist watches, transistor radios and now cameras, with television round the corner. The improvement is for the general public at large. It is one of the many features of the system that marks the difference from our own that there is no incentive for individual advancement: on the contrary, it is safer for the individual to stay with the mass. The total achievement must be greeted with wonder and respect by Western society: stable prices, a fixed currency, expanding production, rising living standards, total employment, freedom from organised crime, no drug problem and sexual activity for the most part confined to the marital bond.

Of course a heavy price has been paid. The achievement has cost unremitting toil. There has been a never ceasing pressure through the collective on the individual and a heavy subordination of the individual will and judgment to the collective. The strain on the intellectuals is severe and constant. The principle of democratic centralism, while permitting and even encouraging some debate before decisions are taken, requires acceptance as doctrine of the line laid down at the higher level. For us it would be an impossible sacrifice of liberty. For China, in its misery and despair, it has been an acceptable price to pay for livelihood and security for the family and for future generations.

~

'In the socialist state it is the past that is unpredictable'

SIR PERCY CRADOCK, HM AMBASSADOR
TO CHINA, DECEMBER 1983

See also p. 323.

I shall be leaving Peking in a few days' time after five and a half years here. Not a cycle of Cathay perhaps; nevertheless, a good stretch ... It is a truism, but a necessary one to begin with, that China has changed immensely since I came here in the summer of 1978. Mao was then already dead and embalmed it is true, but his shadow still hung heavily over the land. His successor, that undistinguished and slightly sinister figure, Hua Guofeng, propped his position on a probably apocryphal conversation with Mao in which the latter was supposed to have said 'With you in charge I am at ease'; and pictures representing the occasion, with Mao in his study resting his hand benevolently on Hua's knee as he conferred the dubious credentials, were at one time universally displayed. Now Hua, though still a Central Committee member, is no longer seen. Deng Xiaoping, whose second return to power came at the Party plenum in December 1978, has ruled China ever since. Mao has been cut down to size; responsibility for the national catastrophe of the Cultural Revolution has been formally laid at his door. Mao's victims have been rehabilitated, headed by Liu Shaoqi, the former President, and Liu's widow, Wang Guangmei, whom I remember paraded in obloquy and derision before Red Guard rallies in 1967, adorned with a necklace of ping-pong balls to represent her bourgeois pearls, is now a great lady, anxiously deferred to wherever she appears. So time brings in its revenges. In the socialist state it is the past that is unpredictable.

<hr>

'They hawk and spit, and their lavatories are horrendous'

SIR ALAN DONALD, HM AMBASSADOR
TO CHINA, APRIL 1991

Donald's diplomatic career saw him three times posted to Beijing, returning finally in 1988 as ambassador. Anglo-Chinese relations were dominated at the time by the issue of Hong Kong. Donald accompanied Margaret Thatcher on her historic visit to China in 1982, but the talks that followed soon foundered, with China rejecting British demands for a continued role in the administration of Hong Kong after the handover. After the British government eventually conceded the point the negotiations made headway, culminating in the 1984 Joint Declaration which, crucially, spared Hong Kong from socialism. Under the slogan 'one country, two systems', China promised to allow Hong Kong's market economy and basic way of life to continue for another 50 years after handover.

Relations continued to be tense however, particularly after what Donald refers to here as the 'horror of June 1989'. Several hundred Chinese died in what became known in the West as the Tiananmen Square massacre. On Hong Kong Island, the crackdown seemed to confirm the worst fears of the population, already edgy about absorption into their giant neighbour, and many decided to emigrate. But Britain had slammed the door shut, except to a few. Hong Kongers were British subjects but had no right to citizenship. One morning a few weeks later, after Singapore relaxed its residency requirements, 10,000 people queued in Hong Kong for application forms. By the time Britain surrendered the colony in July 1997 shortly before its 99-year lease expired, one million Hong Kong residents had emigrated.

BRITISH EMBASSY

PEKING

30 April 1991

The Rt Hon Douglas Hurd CBE MP
Secretary of State for Foreign and Commonwealth Affairs
London

Sir,

CHINA: VALEDICTORY DESPATCH

On the eve of retirement, I confess I am not psychologically ready to leave China. Much of my career has been involved with this complicated country. One does not 'enjoy' China in the way that I enjoyed Hong Kong, Indonesia or Paris. It can be frustratingly hard work here. The Chinese are xenophobic. Officialdom is stubborn and doltish. Since in China, the individual has no rights, his life being State property, the Chinese are often indifferent

to each other, and sometimes downright cruel. I doubt
if the mainland Chinese will ever learn to make a basin
plug that fits, or maintain a car properly. They hawk
and spit, and their lavatories are horrendous. Yet China
intrigues and in the end holds you like no other country.
Its archaeology and art treasures are incomparable. There
is a never ending fascination in the way its political
processes operate. The stoicism and good humour of
its long suffering people fill me with admiration. But it is
not easy for us in the West to understand China. It is,
from our Atlantic viewpoint, distant in time and culture.
In the British case, our past historical involvement
arouses Chinese suspicions and colours our own
interpretation of Chinese motives. On both sides, it does
not take much for old animosities to surface, as we found
in 1989. It is against this background, therefore, that I
would like to make some personal observations as I leave
China for the last time as a member of the Diplomatic
Service . . .

When I arrived as Ambassador in May 1988, it was a time
of great hope. Deng Xiaoping's decision to open to the
outside world was ten years old. Sino-British relations in the
wake of the 1984 Joint Declaration and The Queen's visit in
1986, were excellent. The 'hundred flowers' at last seemed to
be about to bloom. The horror of June 1989 was all the
greater as a result. Like many others, I had expected the
Communist Party to reassert control, but not with the
violence used on 4 June. That shocked many in the West,
who watched on their TV screens the destruction of what
the media called the 'pro-democracy' movement. But the
movement was far less deep-rooted than the Western media
imagined. In the cities, especially Peking, intellectuals,
students and some workers showed their frustration with

the old men who created 'New China', with corruption within the Party and with the appalling conditions in which many still have to live and work. The vast majority of the people of China remained unaffected. China in 1989 was not Eastern Europe . . .

As I leave, we are in the middle of an unresolved argument with the Chinese over the governance of Hong Kong in the last six years of British rule. We are right to insist that Hong Kong should have an effective and authoritative government until 1997, and Hong Kong's nervousness at Chinese interference is understandable . . . Our immediate objective is the removal of the suspicion in the minds of the Chinese leaders that we intend to leave the coffers bare as we leave Hong Kong. We must equally persuade Hong Kong of Chinese sincerity in accepting what we agreed in 1984 as the basis for the transfer of sovereignty. If we fail to achieve this elementary trust, we have no foundation on which to build the future. We must tackle the Chinese hard on the question of confidence in Hong Kong. We have allowed them to put the onus for maintaining confidence on us. Yet it is for the Chinese to do what must be done to keep up confidence in Hong Kong . . . The irony is that, whatever Governments do, international capital moves as it likes and as fast as it likes . . .

Those who will govern Hong Kong after 1997 need to have a clear idea of what China understands by a 'high degree of autonomy'. In talking of the future leadership of Hong Kong it seems to me that we have paid a steep price for not having much earlier created a seedbed in which a responsible Hong Kong Chinese political leadership could grow. By this I do not mean the appearance of Western type 'democracy', but the training up of potential leaders in something like the style of the Singaporeans. Hong Kong's prominent figures sometimes fail to understand that choices have to be made between unpalatable options. If they wish to be political leaders in the future they have to be responsible for persuading the public to recognise this. It often means the forfeit of short-term good in the interest of long-term gain. As I have said before, if we wish the policy of 'one country, two systems' to work, this requires Hong Kong people, and especially the Hong Kong media to act responsibly and restrain themselves from interfering in China's affairs. The difficulty is that our British liberal tradition believes in minimum restraint on what the Hong Kong press and Hong Kong local leaders may say and do. Yet prudence and commonsense will increasingly require them to exercise that self-control. As we get closer to 1997 the people of Hong Kong themselves will have to accept the responsibility for building their own future with their giant neighbour. Otherwise the Territory could well be only as 'autonomous' as Tibet.

~

Afghanistan

'This regime has failed because it could not adapt to the natural grain of the country'

KENNETH CROOK, HM AMBASSADOR TO
AFGHANISTAN, SEPTEMBER 1979

Crook took his leave from the embassy in Afghanistan just two months before the Soviets invaded. The regime he dealt with in Kabul was Communist, but it was an Afghan Communism, imposed following the 1978 Saur Revolution. The atheists in command of the People's Democratic Party of Afghanistan instituted a policy of shaving off men's beards and banned women from wearing the burkha. Twenty years later in Afghanistan the Taliban would, of course, reverse all that. There is surely poignancy, to Western eyes, in Crook's conclusion that Marxism was failing in Afghanistan because it ignored the strength of fundamentalist Islam.

The attempt to introduce the alien philosophy of Communism into an old and very reactionary society seems to me to have failed miserably. It was in any case an unnatural intrusion of a bad European politico/economic system into an Asian context. Some blame for its failure must rest on this regime, which contains a high proportion of very old-fashioned revolutionaries (the Left-wing version of Jehovah's Witnesses or devotees of the gospel according to St Marx?) whose ideas are based on one particular theory invented about a hundred years ago and whose minds have closed to any other ideas, especially modern ones. It seemed to me soon after the revolution that if the parent body were not to reject the new tissue completely, with the attendant risk that the patient might die in the process, there would be required extreme delicacy and finesse. This regime has shown all the delicacy and finesse of a bull in a china shop. The regime had quite a good chance of success if it had played its cards more skilfully. Had it, when it first came to power, shown any sign of recognising the need to adapt its Communist creed to local conditions, even making a concession here and there to local opinion, especially Islamic opinion, its situation today would have been very different. It could not do this, and will, I think, pay the price of its inability. It seems to me to have made every mistake in sight. Perhaps its stupidest was failure to introduce a touch of green into the national flag, to symbolise a synthesis between Communism and Islam. As it is, the national flag symbolises Communism and Russia. It does not symbolise Islam and Afghanistan at all.

This regime has failed because it could not adapt to the natural grain of the country. Perhaps inability to adapt is characteristic of the Russian version of Communism. Experts can tell. If so, Communists would do well to remember the brontosaurus which finished up on the scrapheap of history as a model that failed because it could not adapt. The first-hand experience we have gained in Afghanistan of Communism in a Third World country may be of benefit elsewhere. It has created in me a strong impression that however long they may be on theory, when Communists have to face a real situation involving real people they cannot cope. They throw back to their bible and repress ruthlessly anyone who does not believe in it. Throughout my 25 years off and on in this area, all of it post-Indian independence, I have thought that the area's first need was for a positive attitude by governments to the alleviation of backwardness and poverty. In a spirit of honest questioning I was even prepared to consider the possibility that Communism might, in spite of its reputation, in practice have something to offer. I am forced to conclude that it has nothing. It is seen in under-developed countries as a possible alternative politico-economic system. Our experience here suggests that it is a very bad one. It seems quite incapable of attracting any popular support. Indeed, it does not seem to feel the need of any. It depends for its survival on overwhelming force. It is full of the hate-filled propaganda of the past. It appears quite insensitive to the real wishes of the people. Communists are full of propaganda about the common man, but, all too evidently, care nothing for his real welfare.

～

Cuba

'A fundamentally decent and likeable people'

RICHARD SLATER, HM AMBASSADOR
TO CUBA, JANUARY 1970

(CONFIDENTIAL)   *Havana,*
                                                 12 January, 1970

Sir,

On re-reading my first impressions of Cuba preparatory to
recording my final ones, I feel that, like the Bourbons, I have
forgotten nothing and learnt nothing. The picture has
perhaps filled out; it has acquired no new dimensions.

An initial impression which I find least reason to change
concerns the quality of the Cuban people. Good-natured,
good-humoured, courteous and incorrigibly hospitable,
they bear no resemblance to the mental picture I had
formed before I came out. With one or two exceptions the
Cuban representatives I had met in London seemed to me
furtive and uncouth. Cuban National Day receptions were
squalid affairs; most of the guests seemed to have crawled
out from under stones. The aggressive guttersnipe language
used by Cuban representatives at international meetings
suggested a seething mass of complexes – and was moreover
depressingly reminiscent of Soviet diplomacy in its most
abusive phase. Such evidence of the Cuban character as had
come my way contained no hint of either dignity or charm.

Yet the Cubans possess both in a marked degree, and this
goes for the Government as well as the people. Indeed, to
draw a distinction between the two would at the present
stage be misleading. Though some of the privileges that

used to go with money are tending now to go with position, I do not think it can be said that a ruling caste has emerged. Leaving Fidel Castro aside, the people who run the country are typically Cuban, and if in some cases their dedication to the revolutionary cause has been too much for their sense of humour, they are still capable of civilized behaviour. Their embarrassment when their friendly instincts are required to yield to the dictates of policy is often painfully apparent.

The fact that the Cubans are a fundamentally decent and likeable people has in a way compensated for the unpleasantness of living in a closed society, isolated to a degree which can only be comprehended by those who have experienced it and where the officially accepted values have little in common with one's own. But it has also in other ways made the experience worse. For it is impossible to preserve a sense of detachment in the face of the privations and the encroachments on personal freedom which continue to afflict the Cubans. In this small country, where travel is virtually unrestricted, it is hard for a diplomat not to identify with the people; and my emotions have been engaged here in a way in which they were never engaged during my service in Moscow in the mid-fifties by the suffering of the vast amorphous mass of the Russian people, unknown and virtually unknowable.

4. Friendly Fire

The relative post-Second World War decline of the economy, prestige and living standards of the British was marked by low points during the Suez crisis in 1956; and, twenty years later, by the near-bankruptcy of the UK economy, as a British Chancellor went (as the cliché fast established itself) 'cap in hand' to the International Monetary Fund in 1976.

As Sir Nicholas Henderson puts it in his despatch, beneath: 'A representative abroad has a duty to draw the attention of the authorities at home to the realities of how we look.' Some of our most senior diplomats discharged this function unsparingly – at times, it seemed, almost with relish. Keith Hamylton Jones, who wrote his valedictory one month before Henderson, was unapologetic: 'It is one of the functions of Diplomatic Service officers, when abroad, to provide London with the dimension dubbed by Robert Burns the "pow'r to see ourséls as others see us".' If Henderson and others were right, the picture was unflattering.

~

'How poor and unproud the British have become'

SIR NICHOLAS HENDERSON, HM AMBASSADOR
TO FRANCE, MARCH 1979

Nicholas Henderson's valedictory charts in unforgettable prose the moment in 1979 when many people in Britain overcame a sense of denial and finally faced up to the severity of the economic sickness afflicting the nation. As a valedictory it is justly famous; uniquely, it also carries importance as a seminal document in British post-war history.

Its argument – even its title – was designed to provoke a reaction, amplified once it was leaked and published in the Economist *weeks after the election that brought Margaret Thatcher to power. The valedictory prompted the new Prime Minister to recall Henderson from retirement and appoint him ambassador in Washington, the most important job in the overseas service.*

Henderson was convinced that Britain's destiny lay within Europe, but as ambassador in Warsaw, Bonn and Paris he had witnessed successive British governments squander the opportunity to take a leadership role in the drive towards integration. His valedictory set out baldly the price he thought Britain had paid in lost economic growth as a result of sitting on the sidelines for almost thirty years while France and Germany grew rich.

'Nicko', as he was universally known throughout the Foreign Office, was tall and thin, extremely charming and something of a maverick, although his eccentricities were perhaps a little contrived – critics noted that the Henderson 'look' of ill-fitting collars and overhanging ties did not come cheap. A giant pedigree Dalmatian called Zorba accompanied him to postings on both sides of the Iron Curtain. The dog proved its worth in Warsaw, delivering a nasty bite to the embassy's Polish washerwoman who was rifling around for confidential papers: a warning to other servants not to play the spy. Henderson's valedictories from Germany and Poland are on pp. 34 and 182.

In 1979 Chris Patten was head of the Conservative Research Department (and Matthew Parris's boss). Patten remembers the Paris valedictory as providing 'evidence from the dock' for

a frightening proposition: that the British people 'risked seeing relative decline compared to our principal competitors
turning into absolute decline. [Henderson] was, I think, stating something which is still a problem – our difficulty of
accommodating ourselves to a role in Europe – as well as
arguing that we were falling behind European countries that
had been reduced to rubble in 1945. It was powerful stuff.'

Henderson's daughter, Alexandra, told us her father was
'extremely frustrated and furious about the way he felt Britain
was being run'. The valedictory, written days before his sixtieth
birthday and (he thought) retirement, was an attempt to get
through to his political masters 'once and for all . . . he felt
they had treated him with some contempt and weren't really
listening'.

Henderson's call for a new 'sense of national purpose'
would have been music to Margaret Thatcher's ears. Nevertheless it was surprising that she should pick Henderson,
a staunch pro-European, for the critical Washington job.
Alexandra Henderson says he was 'incredulous' upon being
offered it. The ambassador himself recalled that Thatcher
impressed him on the occasions they had met in Europe, even
though he disagreed with almost everything she said.

When the despatch arrived in Whitehall, officials record
that David Owen, the Labour Party Foreign Secretary, ordered
it to be suppressed 'so as to minimize the risk of its content,
or indeed its existence, becoming known'. Owen told us he
ordered his private secretary to track down the five or six
copies of the despatch known to exist and lock them away
in his office. But a week later he changed tack, allowing
the valedictory to be circulated in the usual manner, having
realized that printing and distribution would take several
weeks and that copies would not arrive until after the
election.

The official file containing this despatch was fully declassified for the first time in 2010. It includes a letter dated 30 May to Ian Gilmour, the Lord Privy Seal, from Andrew Knight, editor of the Economist, announcing that the magazine intended to publish, Henderson having by then taken up his post in Washington. The despatch was more of an embarrassment to the previous Labour government than to the newly arrived Tories, but Gilmour had still tried to persuade Knight not to publish, arguing that 'the taint of partisanship' might make Henderson less effective as ambassador. In the letter Knight disagrees:

> Wherever in Washington Sir Nicholas is not already regarded as somebody of note, to be listened to, it is precisely this kind of statement, forthright but subtle and so beautifully argued as it is, that will help make him so . . . I think it will be widely read in the places that count in Washington, and it will do him (and Britain, and your government for appointing him) nothing but good.

The letter also reveals that while Henderson himself had 'strongly discouraged' Knight from obtaining the document, now that the Economist had it he was 'not averse' to the substance of it being reprinted. Rejecting the government's pleas for delay, Knight reveals that not only did he have three copies of the despatch in his possession, he had been offered a fourth and could not risk a rival publication beating him to his scoop.

The source of the original leak has never been identified. But some in the Foreign Office believe it may have come from the very top. Patrick Wright, a former head of the Diplomatic Service, revealed in 2000 his firm belief that David Owen was a 'material agent' in passing the despatch on – something the former Foreign Secretary rejects as 'conspiracy theory'. There was no 'deliberate decision' to leak the document, Owen told us in a radio interview; 'I just guided its publication until after the election.' Owen delivered this line with a chuckle, which perhaps suggests there may have been a tiny grain of truth somewhere in Wright's claim. 'The little devil in me,' Owen recalled, 'may have said overall, let's have the debate, the sooner the better.' The file shows the Foreign Office was in fact considering eventually releasing a bowlderized version of the despatch to the public (one po-faced official suggested that in order to defend civil service neutrality 'the factual material in the despatch could be presented without the judgements', an approach which rather sweetly manages to miss the point entirely).

Plain-speaking of the sort exemplified in the Henderson despatch is a force for good in the world and it is pleasing to note that the principal characters profited from the controversy that ensued. In Washington Henderson's rumpled, urbane charm served HM Government well during the Falklands War, when the ambassador appeared almost nightly on the American television news to state Britain's case. Thanks in part to Henderson's good relations with officials in the Reagan administration, America maintained a neutral stance in public while privately furnishing Britain with critical intelligence, as well as more concrete assistance – fuel, ammunition and missiles – at the American base on Ascension Island.

Andrew Knight's career also entered the stratosphere. After the Economist he helped Conrad Black buy the Daily Telegraph, which Knight ran as chief executive before jumping ship again to become chairman of Rupert Murdoch's News International.

CONFIDENTIAL

Foreign and Commonwealth Office Diplomatic Report   No. 129/79
WRF 020/1   *General / Economic Distribution*

BRITAIN'S DECLINE; ITS CAUSES AND CONSEQUENCES

Her Majesty's Ambassador at Paris to the Secretary of State for Foreign and Commonwealth Affairs

(CONFIDENTIAL)   *Paris
31 March, 1979*

Sir,

Since Mr Ernest Bevin made his plea a generation ago for more coal to give weight to his foreign policy our economic decline has been such as to sap the foundations of our diplomacy. Conversely, I believe that, during the same period, much of our foreign policy has been such as to contribute to that decline. It is to the interaction of these delicts, spanning my time in the foreign service, that this valedictory despatch is devoted.

I

THE ACCOUNT OF OUR DECLINE

In the immediate aftermath of the war we continued to rank as one of the great powers, admittedly a long way behind the United States and the Soviet Union but nevertheless at the same table as them. A quarter of the world's population did after all still belong to the British Commonwealth and Empire. I myself was able to observe Churchill, Attlee and Bevin dealing on equal terms with Stalin and Truman at the Potsdam conference when no

German or Frenchman was present. With the eclipse of Empire, and the emergence of America and Russia, it was inevitable that we would lose comparative power and influence . . . But in the mid-1950s we were still the strongest European power militarily and economically. We were also well ahead of all continental countries in the development of atomic energy.

It is our decline since then in relation to our European partners that has been so marked, so that today we are not only no longer a world power, but we are not in the first rank even as a European one. Income per head in Britain is now, for the first time for over 300 years, below that in France. We are scarcely in the same economic league as the Germans or French. We talk of ourselves without shame as being one of the less prosperous countries of Europe. The prognosis for the foreseeable future is discouraging. If present trends continue we shall be overtaken in GDP per head by Italy and Spain well before the end of the century . . .

You only have to move about Western Europe nowadays to realise how poor and unproud the British have become in relation to their neighbours. It shows in the look of our towns, in our airports, in our hospitals and in local amenities; it is painfully apparent in much of our railway system, which until a generation ago was superior to the continental one. In France, for instance, it is evident in spending on household equipment and in the growth of second homes . . .

II

INTER-RELATION BETWEEN THE ECONOMY AND FOREIGN POLICY

... For more than a decade after 1945 we held back from joining in schemes of greater European unity; we were confident of our superior strength in relation to our European neighbours, and we did not think that anything would succeed without us. Then when the others showed that they were determined to go ahead on their own we found that we were unable to prevent them doing so or to shape what emerged in the way we wanted. For long we underestimated the economic prospects of our European neighbours and for even longer we overestimated our own strength and influence in relation to them.

The recent intensification in the Paris/Bonn relationship owes a good deal to our economic weakness, as to our a-European diplomacy. President Giscard is not really very interested in us at the moment and gives the impression that Anglo/French relations only feature in his mind when the annual summit comes along. It is sometimes said in London that if only we pursued our interests in Europe as ruthlessly as the French did we would have a scoring rate as high as theirs. This is another example of how we overestimate our influence and our nuisance value: we do not count in Europe like the French; the other countries of the community know that they can get along quite well – some say better – without us as they have done for years ...

I should also interject here that British representatives abroad naturally do their best to prevent too pessimistic a picture of our economy from gaining ground; and, indeed, there are important tasks of correction and proportion to be carried out. But the facts of our decline are too well known for us to be able to persuade foreign observers that there is really little wrong with our industrial scene. Indeed we harp on our poverty to justify our plea for budgetary changes in the community. In France we have come nowadays to be identified with malaise as closely as in the old days we were associated with success. In many public statements Britain is mentioned as a model not to follow if economic disaster is to be avoided. It is striking how, at French functions where a British representative is present and there is a need for some obliging observation about us to be made, speakers seem unable to find anything to refer to that has happened since 1940–45, a period which still indeed affords us a good deal of capital. The French press is full of articles about Britain's plight, not least depressing for their patronising search for favourable elements such as our language and our humour.

Foreign policy decisions

We had every Western European government ready to eat out of our hand in the immediate aftermath of war. For several years our prestige and influence were paramount and we could have stamped Europe as we wished. Jean Monnet and others on the continent had originally hoped to build a European economic union around the nucleus of a Franco/British union. It was the failure of the British to respond to this idea that led them to explore alternative approaches, in particular the idea of a coal and steel community based upon a Franco/German rather than a Franco/British axis. This was a turning-point in postwar history. The French were not very tactful in the way they confronted the British government with the proposals for the Schuman plan. But Monnet knew by 1950 that the

British government was not prepared to make the leap necessary to join the sort of organisation that he was thinking of, one that would achieve lasting Franco/German reconciliation and set Europe on a new course. He sensed that London did not really believe that the idea would come off, and that in any case their fears of supranationality would deter them. He was correct in his analysis.

But what is amazing looking back is the way in which the British government reached so important a decision. The full British cabinet never dealt with the question. Neither the prime minister, nor the foreign secretary (Mr Bevin was in hospital), nor the chancellor of the exchequer, nor the lord chancellor, were present at the ministerial meeting which took the decision against British participation in the European Coal and Steel Community (ECSC) . . . In 1950 the National Executive Committee of the Labour party declared: 'In every respect, except distance, we in Britain are closer to our kinsmen in Australia and New Zealand on the far side of the world than we are to Europe.' . . . [The Conservatives] fought just as shy of supranationality as did the Labour party. Referring to the ideal of European integration, Mr Anthony Eden said in January, 1952, 'This is something which we know, in our bones, we cannot do . . . For Britain's story and her interests lie beyond the Continent of Europe. Our thoughts move across the seas . . .' At the start of the European Coal and Steel Community the *Financial Times* described it as a 'cross between a frustrated cartel and a pipe dream' . . . When, after de Gaulle's vetoes and further knocking at the door we were eventually admitted to the community, our policy towards it did not smack of wholehearted commitment even after the overwhelming referendum . . .

III

THE FUTURE

Even the most pessimistic account of our decline contains grounds for hope. The fact that France and the Federal Republic of Germany have managed to achieve such progress in so relatively short a time shows what can be done if there is the necessary will and leadership. Anybody who remembers the state of affairs in those countries in the decade following the war and compares it with the present day must conclude that nothing in a country's future is inevitable and that everything depends upon the national purpose. So far as we are concerned, if the fault that we are underlings lies 'not in our stars but in ourselves', we are surely capable, unless our national character has undergone some profound metamorphosis, of resuming mastery of our fate. But a considerable jolt is going to be needed if a lasting attenuation of civic purpose and courage is to be averted. North Sea oil should provide the material impulse, just as coal did two centuries ago. There are human elements that favour us compared with others: our political stability and the absence of that tendency to explosion that could always afflict France.

It would be outside the scope of this valedictory despatch to try to chart the course that we might follow to turn around our present situation. Obviously there are no simple solutions and the difficulties are to be found as much in attitudes as in institutions. At the risk of oversimplification I should like to end with three conclusions based on the years I have spent at the end of my career in France and Germany and comparing their present situations with ours.

First, if we are to defend our interests in Europe there must be a change in the style of our policy towards it. This does not mean giving things up or failing to assert our rights and requirements. It does mean, however, behaving as though we were fully and irrevocably committed to Europe. We should be able to put at the service of the community the imagination, tolerance and commonsense that have formed our own national institutions. We could have ideas to contribute . . .

Secondly, viewed from abroad, it looks as though the facts of our present circumstances are not universally recognised in Britain. The British people do not give the impression that they are fully aware of how far Britain's economy has fallen behind that of our European neighbours or of the consequences of this upon living standards. Naturally people are conscious that they are better off now than 25 years ago but they may not know to what extent others in Europe have done much better or of the effects needed to reverse the trend. As Isaac Newton wrote, the important thing is 'to learn not to teach'. It may be our turn to learn from others, having been teachers for so long . . .

Finally, and as a corollary to this process of enlightenment, there would appear to be a need at the present time to do something to stimulate a sense of national purpose, of something akin to what has inspired the French and Germans over the past 25 years. No doubt the sort of patriotic language and flag waving of former times is inappropriate for us today. The revival of Germany has not owed anything to that kind of stimulus. But nevertheless the Germans have felt motivated by the dire need to rise from the ashes in 1945, and they have had to recover from their past politically too. Hence the dogged devotion to democracy that the Germans have shown since the war and the obligation that every one of them feels to make a contribution to economic, as well as political, recovery. Reaching out from their traditional Bismarckian policy of trying to balance East and West, the Germans have now identified their cause with commitment to the West.

The French on the other hand have found their national revival in a more traditional appeal to patriotism. They started at the bottom of the pit but it has not only been de Gaulle who has played on the need to overcome the country's sense of defeat and national humiliation. Giscard is no less ready to play on chauvinistic chords. In a speech that he made recently that lasted only eight minutes he used the word 'France' over 23 times and the word 'win' seven times. Yet, to those who have known the French people in earlier days, it is impossible to believe that they are necessarily readier to make sacrifices or to respond to patriotic appeals than their British counterparts.

Conclusion

These then are the words with which I would like to end my official career, and if it is said that they go beyond the limits of an Ambassador's normal responsibilities I would say that the fulfilment of these responsibilities is not possible in Western Europe in the present uncertain state of our economy and of our European policy.

A representative abroad has a duty to draw the attention of the authorities at home to the realities of how we look, just as he has an obligation to try to persuade the government and people of the country to which he is accredited that present difficulties must be kept in perspective. The tailored reporting from Berlin in the late '30s, and the encouragement it gave to the policy of appeasement is a study in scarlet for every postwar diplomat. Viewed from the continent our standing at the present time is low. But this is not for the first time in our history, and we can recover if the facts are known and faced and if the British people can be fired with a sense of national will such as others have found these past years. For the benefit of ourselves and of Europe let us then show the adaptability that has been the hallmark of our history – and do so now so that the warnings of this despatch may before long sound no more ominous than the recorded alarms of a wartime siren.

I am sending copies of this despatch to Her Majesty's Ambassadors at European Community Posts and Washington, and to the Permanent Representative on the North Atlantic Council, the UK Permanent Representatives to the European Communities and the UK Permanent Representative to OECD.

I am Sir

Yours faithfully

NICHOLAS HENDERSON.

~

'The all pervading snobbishness of English life . . . the basic idleness of British workers . . . and lazy managers'

RALPH SELBY, HM AMBASSADOR
TO NORWAY, MARCH 1975

Selby wrote two valedictories on leaving Oslo. The passage below comes from his more serious essay on bilateral relations with Norway. Extracts from his more wide-ranging, personal valedictory about life in the Diplomatic Service are on p. 305.

Generally speaking, the goodwill towards Britain, to which I referred in my first impressions despatch, remains intact.

There have been periods when I have had occasion to wonder whether it all amounted to anything very much in practice. After being here a while, one meets so many people, particularly in business life, who go through the rigmarole of saying that the Norwegians can never forget all that Britain did for Norway during the war, but then go on to say that while they would dearly love to buy British they cannot afford to do so, because deliveries are always late on account of strikes due principally to the all pervading snobbishness of English life; because the finish of British goods now leaves a lot to be desired owing to the basic idleness of British workers; and because lazy managers, who never get to work until two hours after their employees, cannot even be bothered to let their Norwegian partners know when they are going to be late with deliveries. One yard at Horten, which buys many British products, and is in fact very well satisfied with their quality, has even invented a special clause to be inserted in all contracts with British firms and with British firms only. This clause involves special penalties, not for being late with deliveries – for that is now expected when orders are placed in Britain – but for failing to give the Horten Yard adequate notice of the lateness when it is going to occur. Culprits who have delivered 90 per cent of an order on time seem, it is claimed, disposed to argue that it is a bit unfair for people to grumble about the late delivery of the remaining 10 per cent. They forget that the missing 10 per cent can effectively wreck a complicated production process. But judging from comments from other posts all round the world, this sort of criticism is no monopoly of Norway's . . .

～

'Someone in the Office once told me I was regarded as an "eccentric"'

KEITH HAMYLTON JONES, HM AMBASSADOR
TO COSTA RICA AND NICARAGUA,
FEBRUARY 1979

It is hard to avoid the conclusion that Mr Hamylton Jones had gone quietly bonkers during his sojourn in two Central American backwaters about which he hardly deigns to say anything at all. Instead he seems to have made an attempt to sum up the future of Britain and the meaning of life. That some 500 copies of this valedictory were sent around Whitehall (despite a concern recorded by the clerks that it might 'ruffle a few ministerial feathers') is more likely to suggest that everyone wanted to have a good giggle at a known eccentric than that the ambassador's thoughts were considered important. In the file, a covering note from J. Shakespeare in the Mexico and Caribbean Department reads:

> Mr Hamylton Jones, in his valedictory despatch, has lived up to the reputation given him by Personnel Department as an 'eccentric'. His despatch . . . gives an account of his philosophy on life, pointing out that the present mercenary and envious attitude in this country is not only an error but does not achieve the happiness which is the aim . . . It certainly demonstrates that members of the Service are not cast in a stereotyped mould.

The head of department concurred: 'Marvellous stuff, and some nonsense!'

Shakespeare's letter of thanks to the ambassador is a masterpiece of the alloying of candour with tact. It reads:

I much enjoyed reading your valedictory despatch as did our Third Room who were waiting expectantly for something a little different from the normal run of the mill report. Our expectations have been completely fulfilled and I fear life will be a little duller after your departure. I am submitting it up the Office to Ministers. I have no doubt it will be received with a variety of feelings . . .

FAREWELL TO COSTA RICA, NICARAGUA AND HER MAJESTY'S DIPLOMATIC SERVICE

Her Majesty's Ambassador at San José to the Secretary of State for Foreign and Commonwealth Affairs

(CONFIDENTIAL)   San José
                                                  27 February, 1979

Sir,

To draft, or not to draft, a farewell despatch? Indiscretion, whispering 'yes', has prevailed over discretion, shouting 'no!'. After all, if nothing else, parts of it may provide light relief for the overworked Third Room in Mexico and Caribbean Department. And better to send it in time, rather than too late, for a crushing reply.

I shall devote few paragraphs to Costa Rica, which, as a Private Secretary once snootily but accurately observed, is hardly the hub of the universe . . . Looking back after five years (at least a year too long, in a small tropical post) I am tempted . . . to describe the 'average' city-dwelling Costa Rican as 'charming, quite intelligent, profoundly self-satisfied, and almost wholly unreliable' . . . I asked my Head of Chancery, Jerry Warder, who has spent longer in Nicaragua than I, for a comparative list for the average

Nicaraguan, and he suggests 'warmer, dimmer, more lethargic, more tolerant of oppression from above and even more unreliable' . . . The two most obvious sources of difference are race and climate: in Nicaragua 75 per cent have a strong admixture of Indian blood; in Costa Rica (where most Indians were polished off by disease or the sword in the 16th and 17th centuries) 90 per cent are of pure Spanish or off-white mestizo stock; Nicaragua's capital lies at 180 feet between lake and ocean, but Costa Rica's at 4000 feet on a mountain plain . . .

The affairs of . . . UK dependent territories (e.g. the Cayman Islands, whose fishing-boats are periodically apprehended by the Nicaraguans) sometimes also impinge on this post, and perhaps this gives me an excuse for a farewell reference to a subject which occupied me throughout 1973 – *viz.* the future of the less politically and/ or economically viable territories. One day, particularly if current trends towards devolution continue, Northern Ireland may be given the choice between *(a)* continued union with England, Scotland and Wales *(b)* union with the Irish Republic *(c)* independence. If she chooses *(b)* or *(c),* and we accept her choice, we shall have to rename our country again. What better moment to propose a positive change to 'the United Kingdom of the Greater British Isles'? (It is high time we jettisoned 'Great Britain', a name which an increasing number of foreigners – and even British – misinterpret as a symbol of nostalgic chauvinism rather than as a straightforward geographico-historical reference to an island bigger than Brittany.) The new State could incorporate as full members (if they consented) all citizens of Hong Kong Island and the Kowloon Peninsula, of the Falkland Islands Dependencies (if not of the Islands too), of the British Virgin Islands, of British Antarctic Territory,

Ascension, St. Helena, Tristan da Cunha, Pitcairn, and perhaps even of Gibraltar and/or the Cayman Islands. (The days when the UN seriously cavilled at – e.g. France's like and continuing incorporation of Martinique, Guadeloupe, etc., are long past.) The price to be paid would be extension of representation in the British Parliament, and of British social security arrangements (by then drastically reformed – see next paragraph) to these five million odd people (worthier candidates, perhaps, than increasing numbers from India, Pakistan and Bangladesh?). The potential dividends would include preservation of valuable fishing and oil exploration zones, bases for nuclear submarines and satellite-tracking stations (if not our own, then leased to the US), second holiday homes for Britons within an area exempt from exchange controls, etc., etc.

On the economic side, this post endeavours to subserve the well-understood need to promote British exports (though one can hardly expect great things from underdeveloped countries with populations of little over two millions each). However it is of little use increasing exports if the money thus earned is either frittered away at home or, even worse, allocated to tasks which merely make those exports less competitive. It is one of the functions of Diplomatic Service officers, when abroad, to provide London with the dimension dubbed by Robert Burns the 'pow'r to see oursels as others see us'. A high proportion of the 'others' I meet, in Costa Rica (also a 'welfare state' of not negligible efficiency), consider we would be a happier and more effective society if, *inter alia*,

a) we revamped our social security system so that payments from the rest of us to the genuinely ill and needy continued, but payments to the merely idle and greedy ceased;

b) we revamped our labour legislation and procedures so as to provide positive incentives for co-operation and production at *all* levels in the industrial structure, as in the early Soviet Union (? perhaps a new division in the Honours List) plus negative safeguards against the non-fulfilment of contracts, as in West Germany.

In other Central American countries where I have been accredited some critics are inclined to add: if your legislators will not fulfil the will of the majority in respects such as these, are they not risking 'our' traditional solution – *viz.* that the armed forces, tired of clearing up other people's rubbish to have it pile up again, step in to clear up in a more drastic way?

This is a sensitive theme, but I cannot forbear developing it. Someone formerly in the Personnel Department once told me that I was regarded there as an 'eccentric'; but (perhaps in consequence) it is others whom I regard as eccentric when I look at the current economic situation in Britain. I joined the Foreign Service in 1949 with no resources save the exiguous residue of a £200 Second World War wound gratuity. Earlier that year (then a schoolmaster) I had sat down and listed my basic objectives in life: in the field of possessions, they included a country cottage and (already achieved) a bicycle. I resolved to acquire sufficient money to purchase and maintain this list of possessions (the cottage was in fact achieved in 1969). Success in this aim, I reasoned, would be one element – the *secondary* element – in 'happiness'. If I chanced to earn *more* money (so that for example I could – in Britain – afford a car as well as the bicycle) then this would be a *bonus*, to be accepted as agreeable (at any rate in those days before use of the 'breathalyser' indiscriminatingly on those accustomed and unaccustomed to strong drink), but certainly not an *essential* (to be pursued with desperation). Once the means to a certain basic quality of joy are achieved, this will not be markedly affected by quantitative accretions. And the *primary* element in 'happiness' – it went without saying – would be the joy to be derived from creative activity – making the most (within innate limitations) of one's individual potential. This was – and is – clearly a reward in itself, irrespective of the money it may earn. As Aristotle observed over 2,300 years ago, 'pleasure lies in the putting out of active energy by an organism in its natural state'; it 'perfects the act of working . . . like the bloom on a young cheek'; and 'happiness, the end comprehending all others' comes from 'the working, or energising, of what is best in each of us'. Once initial education and training is completed, the decision to lead a fully active and creative life ultimately depends on oneself, not on the State; and provided one earns enough money for one's basic needs, why should it bother one in the slightest if one's neighbour happens to be earning more?

All this has always seemed to me to be self-evident. Judging however from some contemporary speeches by British politicians (of all parties) and, *a pejori*, from programmes on British commercial television, a very different philosophy seems to be meekly accepted – even sometimes encouraged – as the yardstick for an increasing number of Britons today – a philosophy which (if rightly reported) rests on a number of glaring psychological fallacies. Two of these may be singled out:

a) the fallacy that one is *happier* when 'contributing *less* than one's maximum potential', or even 'doing nothing'. This may be true for short periods (everyone needs a rest occasionally) but (even allowing for the inevitable spread of automation) it is hardly the basis for a truly satisfying way of life (*pace* the poster which I saw in London in 1974 during the three-day week: 'Vote for Ted: four days in bed'). If it is really the case (as we read) that some British Leyland 'workers' (or, for that matter, City directors or civil servants) *prefer* to sit idly at home or in restaurants/canteens and draw either 'unemployment benefits' or 'compensation payments', rather than to put out maximum effort to do a job well (even if the only job for which nature has fitted them is a filthy and/or back-breaking one) then our society is betraying our stock, and condemning it to that elimination of the unfittest which (whatever temporary palliatives may avail) is evolution's ultimate law.

b) the fallacy that, even if there is conceded to be a more *positive* aspect to 'happiness', this can be equated *tout court* with the acquisition of 'more and more money' (as somehow an end in itself, to be pursued even after one has accumulated the little clutch of electricity-consuming machines which we have now been persuaded to regard as a 'basic need'). In fact, as we all know, but sometimes find it unfashionable to admit, though money *may* sometimes help achieve happiness, it by no means always does; indeed it often does the opposite, and corrodes it. To take an example, the personal friendships by which one has benefited, over the years in different lands, inside and outside the Service, have not been dependent on money: and if they *had* been, they would have less, not more, true value.

Americans (among whom I spent the New Year, visiting Drake's Bay in California) profess to envy us our 'quality of life'. One of the supposed elements in this is precisely a commonsense British realisation (implicit rather than explicit) that human qualitative 'values' are created basically by human instincts and satisfactions, bred into all of us genetically, and modified by racial or individual experience. It is *possible* (and for some purposes useful) to apply quantitative measurements (e.g. monetary ones) to most qualitative satisfactions (as an intersubjective standard of comparison); but this practice must not be allowed imperceptibly to slide into the unjustified assumption that it is the monetary values, as distinct from the psychological values, which are somehow the 'basic' ones. If we fall into this error (so tempting to 'economic advisers' when they stray beyond their proper field (a preserve into which I have respectfully avoided straying in this despatch) we shall end up by embracing those very features of the American way of life which more enlightened Americans are now rejecting as inadequate.

The materialistic and quantitative-blinkered disease has even affected, to some extent, our own professional sub-group. From being when I joined, a trio of 'Services', each with its own distinctive emphasis on 'duty', the unified Service has, since the Plowden Report[1] of 1964 (half-way through my service) seemed to put ever-increasing emphasis on 'rights', *imprimis* pecuniary ones. At risk of sounding insufferably priggish I must confess that (even if it has not saved my fellow taxpayers very much) I derive pleasure from knowing that:

a) I never drew a penny (to the best of my recollection) in 'boarding school allowances' or 'language allowances' (albeit a father and a linguist);

b) I am now voluntarily moving onto half-pay and no allowances (but, I hope, equally strenuous activity) at 55, thus permitting someone else to have his or her own Mission who might otherwise – at a time of 'structural' constrictions – not have done so, rather than seeking to assert a 'right' to another.

And, *a fortiori*, I welcomed the 'freezing' of higher salaries a few years ago: the previous increase had, I think, given me rather too much.

1. *Plowden Report*: The recommendations of the Plowden Committee on Representational Service Overseas – one of many cost-cutting reviews – saw the Foreign Office and the Commonwealth Relations Office, hitherto separate bodies, merged to form the modern FCO. Plowden also recommended that every Head of Mission should have commercial experience, after which, alongside the usual political work, ambassadors were increasingly obliged to accept the unglamorous role of cheerleader for British exports.

5. The Camel Corps

It would take a book of its own – and an immersion in the psyche of the British elite deeper than your editors' – to inquire into the fascination that Englishmen of a type well represented in the Diplomatic Service feel for Arabs and the Arab World. We could dwell on Lawrence of Arabia; we could quote the *Rubaiyat of Omar Khayyam*; we could cite Wilfred Thesiger. We could speculate on a latent fear of women and hankering for an all-male society felt by some whose education has been at boys' boarding schools. We could even darkly hint at suppressed anti-Semitism. But perhaps this is psychobabble; and be all that as it may, it is an observable fact that many British diplomats have been drawn, by more than the region's international importance, to the Middle East.

And (as mentioned in the Introduction to this book) joining what the Office affectionately called the Camel Corps has been the only respectable way in British Diplomacy of 'going native'. An Arabist, according to David Gore-Booth, would try to 'put himself into the mindset of the Arabs and not to become an Arab or behave like one but to be able to predict or judge how Arabs would react in certain circumstances'. But that, of course, is something of an Arabist speaking.

In the FCO they have been something of an elite – new entrants of Matthew Parris's generation heard it whispered of the brightest among them that they might be potential Arabists. This is not to deny, however, that other elements within Whitehall have looked askance at the Camel Corps, and insinuated that the Corps has skewed British foreign policy towards a collection of shifting, sometimes shifty, allies with unstable and undemocratic political systems and economies based on oil, foreign labour and bling.

But the Arabists, as you will read below, are unrepentant. Many of the signatories to the 2004 letter from fifty-two retired diplomats, in protest against British policy in Iraq, were core Corps members. The MECAS language school was the glue that binded them – school tie and all – and it's said that after its disbandment the Camel Corps were never so distinctive or acted and thought in such a coherent way. At least one academic has suggested that their inheritors in terms of a distinct tribe within the FCO may be diplomats serving in Europe and working in multilateral bodies – who run the risk of becoming institutionalized and infected with the 'organizational virus'.

It would be wrong, however, to suppose that the Arabist virus predisposes a diplomat to admire the society or the government of the Arab country where he is posted. The most conspicuous example of a valedictory from an ambassador who in some ways did so, Sir Andrew Green's from Saudi Arabia, is placed, for other reasons, in Chapter 2 ('Settling Scores'). Another Ambassador to Saudi Arabia, Sir James Craig (whose valedictory from Syria you will find below, and whose farewell despatch from Dubai is printed in Chapter 8, 'The Sun Sets on Empire'), presumably took a different view from Sir Andrew, as even the Freedom of Information Act has failed to prise his Riyadh despatch from the FCO's secret files. It was briefly infamous. Charles Crawford (Chapter 9, 'Envoi') has recounted the story to us for our BBC programme, and tells it in his blog:

I served as Resident Clerk and indeed lived in my own room in the Foreign Office for some two years (1985–6). My finest hour came very early one morning.

At around 23:30 hours I was called by an unhappy FCO News Department duty officer to say that the *Glasgow Herald* had told him in a gloating tone that they were running a copy of a Diplomatic Despatch by Sir James Craig, who had finished a distinguished career as HM Ambassador in Saudi Arabia. The point was that earlier that day an injunction had been issued in London against the *New Statesman* to block publication of this Confidential document, said to be full of trenchant, heartfelt and pertinent observations by Sir James on the general subject of 'Arabs'. So the *Glasgow Herald* had decided to publish this tract in Scotland, confidently expecting to side-step the English court's injunction.

I telephoned the then new FCO Permanent Under-Secretary Sir Patrick Wright at his home. I told him that from my barrister training I recalled something about a procedure involving an overnight duty judge who could issue urgent legal orders; maybe that might work in this case? Sir Patrick said, 'Do your best, my boy' (or words to that effect). I telephoned Sir James and alerted him. He decamped to a friend's flat to avoid the throng of journalists he (correctly) expected would gather at his house the following morning as the Despatch story broke big.

I then feverishly started trying to track down (with the help of the excellent Number 10 switchboard) numbers for senior English and Scottish Law officers, hoping to explain the problem and see what if anything might be done. This dragged on for a couple of hours. Eventually deep into the night the *Herald* were startled to receive a formal order from the Scottish courts forbidding printing the Despatch. The early editions had already been printed and carried the text, but later editions had to be changed. The key thing was that thanks to my telephoning which had triggered the Scottish court's intervention, the text could not be quoted.

Thus the issue fizzled out to official satisfaction. Freedom of the press had been ruthlessly crushed by the Establishment in general and by me in particular. Hoorah. UK/Saudi relations were not 'embarrassed' (this time at least). Phew.

If Sir Willie Morris's valedictory (with which we start) was deemed fit for release (under the '30-year rule', see Notes on the Material) one can only wonder what was contained in Sir James's despatch . . .

∽

Saudi Arabia

'The theatre of the absurd is never far away'

SIR WILLIE MORRIS, HM AMBASSADOR
TO SAUDI ARABIA, 1972

Morris served as envoy to Egypt, Ethiopia and then Saudi Arabia. Riyadh clearly had its frustrations, as his valedictory shows. The ambassador also became embroiled in the ever-thorny issue of commission payments paid by British defence firms to middlemen in arms deals. A 1970 despatch from Morris (parts of which are still censored) raised the 'obviously crucial' question of systemic corruption in the Kingdom. Bribery, he warned, was so widespread that it had the potential to incite a revolution against the House of Saud: 'Commercially and politically "the system" is at best an infernal nuisance, and it is politically explosive – a time bomb under the regime.' (There was in fact just such an uprising in 1979, but it was quickly crushed.)

In Riyadh, the good offices of HM Embassy were sometimes at cross-purposes with the UK government's Defence

Sales Organization, in its lack of scruples 'just another Levan-
tine business organization' according to Morris. Lord Gilmour,
who ran the DSO at the time, admitted in 2006: 'You either
got the business and bribed, or you didn't bribe and didn't get
the business . . . It's not something you emblazon or are par-
ticularly proud of. It just happens to be the terms of trade.'

Saudi Arabia is a political, economic and social oddity, and this has been a fascinating experience I would not have missed. As it recedes, it may seem less like time spent in real life than being shut up in a theatre where the repertoire consisted of extravagantly over-written and over-acted plays constantly repeating themselves. It is a great tragedy that, with all the world's needs, Providence should have concentrated so much of a vital resource and so much wealth in the hands of people who need it so little and are so socially irresponsible about the use of it. (But the results could be worse for us if the motivation were less crudely selfish, and pointed in the wrong direction.) What they do with the wealth is often comedy and sometimes farce; there are also legal, social and religious dramas, and the theatre of the absurd is never far away. A country where the Head of State has strong personal views about the iniquity of male sideburns and where the barbers are ordered to cut them to levels consistent with morality; where a probable murderess of foreign nationality escapes with a deportation order because the only alternative is decapitation – and is then prevented from leaving until she gets an exit visa; a dry country, where one can find a Minister incoherently drunk in his office before noon – who could fail to be diverted in such a country, or fail to develop claustrophobia from time to time, and want to get out of the theatre into a street of real people outside?

I have not developed an affection for Saudi Arabia of the

kind that I feel for every other country I have served in. I shall remember many things with great pleasure: too infrequent camping expeditions; escaping to Yemen; people, of course – some Saudis among them; and even the exhilaration (amid the exasperation) of exercising one's ingenuity to do business with people so difficult to do business with. But the Saudi Arabians generally (perhaps especially those from Nejd) share certain personal attributes which make them – shall I say? – less lovable than some other people. I have crossed the land frontiers with Jordan and Yemen at points remote from the Saudi population centres, and even there been struck by the violent contrast between the curt, unsmiling downright rude reception of Saudi guards and officials, and the friendly, welcoming Jordanian or Yemeni faces on the other side.

I think a number of elements have contributed to the self-centredness and arrogance which mark off the Saudis from the generality of Arabs, who are rightly considered to overdo courtesy and hospitality. There is the freedom from past foreign occupation and relative isolation . . . There is religion: true piety may be declining fast, but the Calvinistic sense of being God's elect that is characteristic of Wahhabism continues unabated. Then there is the recent practice of slavery, abolished only in 1962. In other under-developed countries, the presence of foreign experts can arouse feelings of resentment and shame. Not in Saudi Arabia: if you are a Saudi and have money to buy them, it is not more shameful to have Yemenis, Palestinians, Pakistanis, British or Americans to do your work for you than it was to buy black slaves. And this governs your relations with them: it is a superiority, not an inferiority, complex that the Saudis suffer from. Wealth is the last and it may be the most important element in this corruption of character which enables the Saudis to regard the rest of the world as existing for their convenience; to act with unstudied, unconscious indifference to the convenience of others or what others may think of them.

Officials of a Government working by this philosophy are more infected by the attitude than private citizens; but it is of course in the Royal Family that it is most concentrated. They are a family which includes many of considerable ability, strong personality, and even their own kind of charm: but I doubt if there are any among them, not even King Faisal himself, who have seriously questioned the inherent right of the Saud family to regard Saudi Arabia as a family business, or to regard the promotion of the interests of the family business as taking priority over everything else. The sheer effrontery is breathtaking of a prince who will keep on talking about rights and wrongs, when you know (and he probably knows that you know) that his cut may be 20 per cent of the contract price.

If Europeans and Americans, who can deal with the Saudis more or less at arm's length, can react coolly and calculatedly to these attitudes, this is not true of the Arab helots working here, nor of the Arabs outside, who have to listen to the Saudis mouthing sentiments about brotherhood and contrast this with the extent to which they are prepared to limit their own self-indulgence to help their brothers. It is hard to find other Arabs who have good words to say for the Saudis, and no wonder: few disinterested Arab tears will be shed if they get their come-uppance.

~

Iran

'I feel desperately sorry for the Shah'

SIR ANTHONY PARSONS, HM AMBASSADOR
TO IRAN, JANUARY 1979

Parsons served as Britain's permanent representative at the United Nations during the Falklands conflict where in 1982, against stiff opposition, he managed to rally the votes necessary for a resolution condemning the Argentine invasion. Margaret Thatcher showed her gratitude by inviting Parsons to be her personal adviser on foreign policy. In her autobiography she described him as a man of 'intelligence, toughness, style and elegance'.

Historians, however, will probably also remember Parsons for his failure to see, while Ambassador to Tehran, the writing on the wall for the Shah.

The Iranian revolution began in January 1978 with riots in the holy city of Qom, with religious leaders calling for Ayatollah Khomeini to be allowed to return from exile. Informing London of these events by telegram, Parsons wrote: 'I do not foresee any serious trouble in the near future. There will be ups and downs, but in the short term I think the Shah will not be forced to make any radical alterations to his policies and will be able to govern, as he is at present, without any genuinely dangerous opposition from any quarter.'

The ambassador had become friends with Mohammed Reza Pahlavi (the Shah) during his five years in Tehran. Britain had more than just goodwill invested in the relationship: by 1978 Iran had become a key Western ally in the Middle East, and a market for some £600 million of British exports. Were the Shah to be ousted from the Peacock Throne all this would be lost. Perhaps the weight of all that hung on the outcome clouded Parsons's perspective.

Yet in May, when the riots had reached Tehran, the ambassador was still optimistic for the regime, writing in a despatch: 'My honest opinion is that the Pahlavis, father and son, have a good chance and my guess is that they will make it.' In October, Parsons counselled continued support for the Shah, for fear that were Britain to be seen 're-insuring' with the opposition, support for the regime might crumble. A week after this advice reached Downing Street, a mob torched the British Embassy in Tehran.

Few observers expected the Shah, with his mighty army, to be toppled by the ragbag and disparate opposition that took to the streets in 1978. Nevertheless, the embassy's failure to see which way the wind was blowing was a grave and enduring embarrassment for the Foreign Office, and one which exerted a powerful hold on the memory of subsequent generations of diplomats sent to represent Britain in the Middle East (see, for instance, Sir Andrew Green's valedictory on p. 135).

In a book published in 1984 entitled The Pride and the Fall Parsons was to pick at this failure in detail, drawing on T. S. Eliot: 'We had the experience, but missed the meaning.' This mea culpa went too far according to David Owen, who reviewed the book for The Times. Parsons, wrote the former Foreign Secretary, 'takes too much blame on his own shoulders . . . The worst public servants are those who never risk a judgment, who always hedge their bets. The best pose the right questions but are also ready to give the wrong answers.' Owen himself had been criticized for attaching British foreign policy too strongly and for too long to our continuing good relations with the Pahlavi regime. Our allowing ourselves to gain a reputation within Iran of having opposed the revolution and propped up the Shah was one of the era's *more serious foreign policy blunders, whose consequences are still with us: it left us with no lines of sympathy or communication with his successors (a criticism Parsons half tries to answer here) – and is one of the reasons some Iranians continue to see us as perfidious and ill-disposed.*

Parsons's valedictory – written two days after the Shah fled Iran, never to return – was declassified for the first time in 2010.

BRITISH EMBASSY
TEHRAN
18 January 1979

The Rt Hon Dr David Owen MP
Secretary of State for Foreign and Commonwealth Affairs
London SW1

Sir,

IRAN – VALEDICTORY DESPATCH

Since the middle of the Second World War I have been fortunate enough to have been the eye-witness of many historic events in the Middle East. The two occurrences which will I believe remain most vividly in my memory are the occasions on which powerful regimes, backed by loyal and united Armed Forces, have been brought low by purely civilian action. The first occasion was the downfall of General Abboud's military regime in the Sudan in 1964 when many disparate elements of civilian opposition combined to bring about a national strike. A week later, the military government resigned in bewilderment. They were able to control the streets but they were unable to force people to work. The second occasion is of course that which I have lived through during recent months in Tehran. Again, disparate elements of opposition have combined and, through street violence and, even more effective, a nation wide series of strikes including the oil fields, have brought the proud and arrogant Pahlavi regime, that 'bastion of stability' in this area to its knees and beyond . . .

There is of course no such thing as stability as we understand it in the Middle East. In this region, there is no clear distinction between regimes and governments. If the people want to change the government, they have to change the regime and there is only one way to do this – force. Hence the continuation in power of a Middle Eastern regime/government depends largely on two factors, namely the loyalty of the Armed Forces combined with a certain level of acquiescence (popularity is too strong a word) on the part of the population, principally those who live in the capital and the main urban areas.

In the case of Iran, I was always convinced, rightly as events have proved, that the Shah had secured the former imperative, the loyalty of the Armed Forces. I was also inclined to believe that, despite obvious areas of discontent, he had a reasonable chance of retaining the acquiescence of the people to the extent that he could with some safety press ahead with the fulfilment of his modernising vision . . . In this respect I and, with no wish to extenuate, most other close observers of the Iranian scene, have been proved wrong. Why?

The short answer is that, although we rightly identified the areas of opposition, we underestimated the capacity and will of the various elements to unite and we under-estimated the weight and volume of hatred and resentment which had been welling up over the years during which the Shah had kept the country under that repressive political discipline which he regarded as essential if he were to have his hands free to make the decisions and to implement the policies which would make his Great Civilisation attainable during his lifetime . . .

I always thought and still do that, thanks mainly to the loyalty of the Armed Forces, the Shah could have survived until the chosen moment of handover to his son, say in the mid 1980s, provided that he maintained his dictatorial political system while at the same time delivering a reasonable amount of the goods to his people. I even thought that he had a sporting chance of liberalising the political system without losing his throne in the process, although the dangers were always recognisable. If he had not unrealistically accelerated the pace of development beyond all reasonable limits in 1974, if he had timed his liberalisation move better, and if his personal relationship with his people had been different, the forces of opposition to him might well have proved unable to bring him down. To take the last point first, the Shah was in an important sense in an oriental society the wrong man for the job. He is intelligent, dynamic, efficient and formidable. He would have made a first class senior civil servant or head of a public corporation in a western country. But he is fundamentally a rather awkward, withdrawn person, at his best with technocrats, westerners or cronies, at his worst with people en masse. His shyness and introversion inclined him, as his power grew, to withdraw into grandeur, to isolate himself from the cut and thrust of genuine discussion, to rely on second-hand information coming from people who, as he became more remote and autocratic, were increasingly inclined to tell him what he wanted to hear rather than unpalatable truths. His security screen, necessary enough in view of the many attempts on his life during his long reign, helped to consolidate this isolation from his people . . .

Many people have expressed surprise at the degree of cohesion and organisation shown by the opposition in mobilising such massive popular hostility to the Shah throughout the country, even in remote villages. This factor has surprised me less than the sheer volume of opposition which had built up. Iranians, like all Middle Easterners, are wonderful last minute improvisers. They need far less prior planning and staff work than we do in order to get things right on the night. It has always been a source of amazement to me how they can sit back and do nothing about, say, the arrangements for a State Visit until about 48 hours before it takes place and then produce a perfectly organised programme of events. To a great extent I believe that the opposition elements have been improvising in this way as events have developed, probably as surprised as any of us at the response to their campaign. Furthermore, Iranians are very 'clubby' people. There is a long tradition in the country of anjumans (clubs or societies), some secret some open, and every Iranian is a member of a 'dowreh' or circle which often transcends social class or function. This kind of social structure tends to produce a pretty effective national grapevine. Moreover, for centuries the mosque and the bazaar have possessed a superb country-wide network and have played a far greater part in the lives of all sectors of the population than has any government administration. The mosques and the bazaars run schools, hospitals, religious processions and ceremonies, charities, industries, farms etc., in fact almost the full range of state activity. There are mosques even in the smallest villages and bazaars even in the smallest towns. Their communications leave nothing to be desired, particularly in these modern times . . .

. . . The Shah and the Empress left Iran on 16 January,

ostensibly for a rest. But, having experienced the climate of massive hostility to the Shah of the past months and having witnessed the wild jubilation which persisted in the streets for hours after the news of his departure was broadcast, it is extremely difficult to imagine him ever being able to return. For the moment the Government has no authority. Khomeini rules the streets and the strikers . . . The economy is in ruins, all business and industrial activity has ceased, governmental administration and financial activity are paralysed, oil production is still below domestic demand and shortages of important commodities continue. The country is in short at a standstill and in a condition of near anarchy . . .

Having said all this, there may be some compensations in terms of the conduct of our relations, so long as the present relatively free atmosphere prevails. The Shah's regime may have been beneficial to our interests but dealing with it at close quarters was often distasteful and exacting. Arrogance, meretricious glitter, touchiness and pretentiousness were all characteristics of the regime which western diplomats found hard to stomach. Nor did we enjoy the spectacle of repression and corruption, of the ostentation of the nouveaux riches, of the yawning gap between glowing promise and inadequate performance. We were also hampered by the intense jealousy and suspicion, particularly towards the British, of the regime, which restricted to the minimum what would in other countries have been perfectly normal contacts with its moderate opponents. I always hated this strait-jacket but knew that I and my staff had to wear it. If we had broadened our contacts beyond a certain very discreet limit, the Shah would have known immediately, suspected British intrigue against him and our interests would have suffered. I hope very much that my successor will have a reasonably long period in which the Embassy can take full advantage of the present 'Prague Spring' to widen its contacts against the day when Iran may again be subjected to a dictatorial regime and the old restrictions be reimposed.

I leave Tehran with very mixed feelings. It is sad to leave a house where I have lived for a longer continuous period than anywhere since I was born, and a country, however repulsive its capital, perhaps more beautiful, more varied and more interesting than any other in which I have served. I would not have missed the dramatic and historic events of the past few months for anything, although I feel desperately sorry for the Shah. With all his faults, I have grown fond of him, particularly in his time of adversity. In spite of his fatal vacillations as the hour of crisis struck, he tried to the end to find a moderate political solution; he restrained his generals and did his best to minimise bloodshed, perhaps at the cost of his throne. For this he must be admired and the humiliation he must be suffering now after so many years of power and glory, immodestly flaunted, would excite sympathy in the hardest heart. I also feel deep anxiety for some of my friends of the past regime who are now in prison and may well suffer a cruel fate to make a Persian holiday.

$\sim$

Egypt

*'When the average Egyptian speaks of Arabs he does not
include himself, rather like the average Englishman
speaking of Europeans'*

SIR MICHAEL WEIR, HM AMBASSADOR
TO EGYPT, JANUARY 1985

Weir, a Scot, spent most of his diplomatic career in the Middle
East. He began in the 1950s as a political agent to the Trucial
States of the Persian Gulf, a diplomatic title which ceased to
exist once Britain withdrew from empire. In the 1950s, however, the political agent had sweeping, if ambiguous, powers
over societies which were in many ways more medieval than
modern; in Qatar, Weir's objectives included pushing the
Sheikh into outlawing slavery. (See also James Craig's remarkable telegram from Dubai on p. 325 for more in this line.)

British envoys in the Persian Gulf were often drawn into
disputes between local chieftains over land. A conversation
over one such affair during celebrations to mark the Queen's
coronation in 1953 was to test the ambassador's powers of
subtlety and mischief to the full. The Sheikh of Bahrain came
across a weary Winston Churchill sitting on some steps after a
banquet and, with Weir translating, asked his help in retaking
lands held by the Emir of Qatar. 'Tell him,' Churchill replied,
'that we try never to desert our friends.' This much Weir
dutifully relayed to the Sheikh. When Churchill added, after a
pause, 'Unless we have to', Weir tactfully left this out of his
translation.

Cairo was Weir's final post. He was sitting two rows behind
Sadat at a military parade when the President was assassinated in 1981. The Belgian envoy beside him was badly

wounded. Diving to the ground for cover, Weir found himself clinging on to the American Military Attaché's foot.

BRITISH EMBASSY,
CAIRO
28 January 1985
The Rt Hon Sir Geoffrey Howe Kt QC MP
Secretary of State for Foreign and Commonwealth Affairs
London sw1

Sir,

VALEDICTORY FROM EGYPT

Forty years after first seeing Egypt, on wartime passage to India, and after eight years total service within the country, it is time for a last retrospective. That timespan would cover most of the recorded history of the first country I served in, Qatar. For Egypt it is but an evening gone, as the hymn says. Considering that a great deal of what Herodotus had to say about Egypt remains valid today, it is difficult for the contemporary observer to find novel themes, though over the past six years I have seen some interesting variations on old ones.

When British veterans of the Second World War make a sentimental return visit, as many still do, to the city that offered the juiciest fleshpots of any theatre of war, they are apt to be shocked by the transformation Cairo has undergone. Instead of quiet tree-lined avenues, Parisian arcades, palatial villas, polo at the Gezira Club and green fields stretching to the Pyramids, they see a teeming megalopolis of 14 million souls, its streets and pavements choked with strident traffic, new skyscrapers mushrooming unplanned, magnificent Islamic monuments crumbling unmaintained, dirt and pollution abounding, most services on the point of breakdown, and the Pyramids overtaken by urban sprawl . . .

In social terms, the Egyptian upper class may have been destroyed but there is still a middle and a lower. The values of the former may be judged by the popularity of the British TV serial *Upstairs Downstairs* which was shown a year ago at peak viewing time seven days a week and repeated at least once, driving *Dallas* off the screen. For the millions of adult Egyptians for whom the nightly episode had absolute priority, it represented a nostalgic evocation of a society that still flourished in their life-time, though it had disappeared in England half a century before . . .

While there is as much bombast, self-congratulation and self-deception in the Egyptian media as in other Arab countries – indeed much more by volume, since the Egyptian media eclipse the others in scale and experience – it is offset by a priceless national gift of humour and humanity. I have not met any other Arabs who are capable of laughing at their own foibles; in Egypt making irreverent jokes about authority is a national sport.

They are also extraordinarily forgiving, both of individuals and of institutions. As far as Britain is concerned, Suez disappeared from the Egyptian political vocabulary years ago, long before it did in Britain – if it has. Despite the occasional assassination and *crime passionel* the Egyptians are not a violent people and abhor bloodletting; the fratricidal carnage of Hama could not have happened here. But there is no lack of moral integrity. Among the Egyptian intellectuals, creative writers, journalists, film producers, and scholars, who for generations have dominated the Arab cultural scene, there were many who went into voluntary exile or refused to write rather than submit to the censorship and 'guidance' of the Nasser and Sadat regimes.

Restrictions on free speech, which James Craig[1] deplores as an endemic feature of Arab society, are milder under Mubarak than at any time in living memory, and numerous independent writers are taking full advantage of the thaw. The trouble in Egypt is that there is too much speech and not enough action. Government ministers know, and are constantly reminded by the IMF, what remedies are needed for the country's problems, and I do not think that their failure to act stems solely from fear of riots or losing their jobs. There seems to be a deeper inhibition afflicting almost everyone in authority which amounts to an unwillingness or even perhaps an inability to take decisions. The instinctive preference is for procrastination; no deadline is ever final; and the decision when taken is usually to set up a committee. As with the Arabs, this could be the fault of either the educational system (which is all theory and no practice) or of Islam. But I think a more important factor may be Egypt's 5000 years' dependence on the annual Nile flood and a complex irrigation system that left no room for individual initiative. Successive generations of Egyptians have always tended to turn their rulers into Pharaohs and to refer every decision to the top. We are seeing this happen to President Mubarak now, under the relentless sycophancy of the government, media and the unchanging protocol that dictates that a circle of ministers and courtiers must accompany him everywhere he goes . . . He would prefer to share responsibility, and I believe he sincerely wishes the democratic experiment which he launched with last year's elections to succeed. While one must share his hopes, my guess is that the system will defeat him, and that his experiment will end up in little more than a proliferation of debating societies designed to obscure the fact that there is going to be no devolution of power . . .

. . . But the Pharaonic tradition has also given the Egyptians a sense of security and identity that allows them without shame to accept their incompetence, indecisiveness, lack of foresight, and public squalor as part of the natural order of things: the rest of the world can take it or leave it. My wife and I find that we can take it, for the sake of their compensating human qualities, and of the extraordinary historical, cultural and physical panorama the country offers. We have made more genuine friendships here than in any other post.

One should perhaps pose the question, as many have, whether the Egyptians are Arabs at all . . . The most telling evidence to the contrary, is that when the average Egyptian speaks of Arabs he does not include himself, rather like the average Englishman speaking of Europeans. One has to put up with constant commiseration from those Egyptians who flock to London each summer on the fact that the place is being ruined by 'the Arabs'. At a deeper level, however, and unlike the British, I believe most Egyptians feel that by virtue of language and religion they are part of the wider Arab nation, though by virtue of their ancient culture superior to the rest . . .

. . . In the arts we almost appear to be ashamed of our heritage. In my six years here the [British] Council – as distinct from its admirable local initiatives – has not mounted one major artistic event, although they were common in the darker days and Shakespeare is a guaranteed sell-out. In the country which preserves the remains, literary as well as monumental, of a greater diversity of civilisations (Pharaonic, Greek, Roman and Islamic) than exists anywhere else in the world, Britain is almost the only

Western nation of significance to have no institute of its own. In field archaeology a handful of dedicated British scholars keep alive the tradition of Flinders Petrie[2] on a dwindling grant from the British Academy, but only by enduring conditions of extreme austerity and enlisting the help of unpaid amateurs. On the official side we teeter constantly on the brink of a decision to close the Consulate-General in Alexandria, the third largest city in Africa and a major commercial centre, to save some £50,000 a year. At least we are not burning the Library, like earlier conviction Christians . . . But it will not efface the impression that we are becoming a nation of Philistines more preoccupied with pennies than with power, more interested in making quick profits from the oil sheikhdoms than in developing our assets and opportunities in a country of much greater size and influence.

One must not exaggerate. The Egyptians like most people are susceptible to flattery, and will respond to a renewed show of interest. Unfortunately, they have been spoiled in the years since Sadat became the darling of America by the attentions of world, especially Western, statesmen at the highest levels. While the United Kingdom has managed to keep up a good working relationship through ministerial and official visits, the fact that no British Prime Minister has ever been to Egypt, despite repeated invitations and acceptances over the past ten years and numerous presidential visits to the UK, is beginning to assume the proportions of an affront to Egyptian national pride. I apologise for harping yet again on this familiar topic but I believe that the omission has now become an impediment to better relations such that they can only gradually deteriorate unless it is soon remedied. I must end with the customary tribute to spouse and Service, empty gesture though it is to include a sentence or two of compliments in a despatch which will be read mainly by colleagues. In my case I have two wives to thank, both of whom have been a great support but the first of whom decided that diplomatic life was crippling to the spirit. The second had joined the Service before we met, and has no excuse. I am not therefore taking my leave in the same way as other valedictorians, and look forward to several further years' service below stairs while my wife pursues her career. Already I owe to her a deeper insight into Egyptian society than I could otherwise have hoped to achieve. She has amply confirmed, from the personal friendships she built up with a range of Egyptian women from the wives of two Presidents to Marxists jailbirds, the view I formed during the testing time of Nasser that, broadly speaking, Egyptian women are much stronger characters than their menfolk. Leaving aside Queen Hatshepsut and Cleopatra, the earliest Egyptian feminists were active before Mrs Pankhurst, and achieved equality in politics and education well before the 1952 revolution. Regrettably the current female generation is suffering from, and indeed embracing, the Islamic revivalists' view of women's personal status, and these hard-won gains risk being eroded. This could have more than purely social consequences, for it is self-evident that the only solution for Egypt's greatest problem, overpopulation, lies in the continuing spread of enlightenment among its women.

To the Service I feel almost nothing but gratitude for 34 years of satisfying work and congenial companionship. For action and excitement there has been nothing to match the early, pre-oil, days in those one-man posts in the Gulf where the untrained equivalent of a District Commissioner found himself not only presiding judge, boundary demarcator, oil

concession negotiator and manumitter of slaves, but also
called upon to mobilise military resistance to the Saudi
invader – all unencumbered by cypher communications
bringing instructions or demanding reports. We made and
unmade a few Rulers too in our time, and it was gratifying
to note during a visit to the Gulf earlier this month that
most of them appear to have at least as good prospects of
permanence as the creations of Lawrence and Gertrude
Bell.[3] I am thankful also for the periodical relief afforded
to me from the Arab world, especially eight years total
sojourn in the United States. Having had one's first
experience of America in California and the West, in the
days of Senator Knowland[4] and the China Lobby, before
moving to the East Coast, makes it easier to understand
if not to sympathise with the mood in President
Reagan's Washington.

A life-long friendship with many of the dedicated
professionals in the State Department should also perhaps
make it easier to react as philosophically as they when our
own Service becomes the object of the same kind of
public obloquy and misrepresentation as they have
endured for decades. But it does not. Even after pleading
collective guilt to occasional complacency, arrogance,
spinelessness, misjudgement, high living and other human
frailties I remain unable to fathom why journalists and
politicians who have seen us at our work (and enjoyed
our hospitality) should persist in both denigrating its
value and attributing to the Office ulterior policies of
its own; or indeed why the Treasury should choose to
devote so many of its mandarin man-hours to the
minutiae of our conditions of service. The motive of the
superficial critic is perhaps to be found in that dogged
British attachment, exemplified by Arthur Scargill, to the

stereotype and the class outlook that provides an excuse for evading the more pressing and difficult challenges of changing times. If so the only course is to redouble our efforts of recent years to demonstrate that the stereotype is wrong. But if, as I sometimes fear, criticism of diplomacy reflects a growing national preoccupation, with domestic problems and a feeling that the rest of the world – with certain exceptions – is not worth our attention, or at any rate not worth spending money on in the absence of a guaranteed return (a view expressed to me by one of our visiting ministers), then the task of a diplomat is indeed fruitless as well as thankless. There is no point in paying someone to obscure the fact that the emperor has no clothes.

At least there is honour outside one's country. The Egyptian Foreign Minister's last words to me today were in praise of the expertise, balanced judgement and consistency on Middle East affairs to be found not only among British diplomats but in British institutions as a whole, in contrast to the ever-changing scene in the United States. He hoped that these talents could be mobilised, and brought to bear across the Atlantic, in the cause of peace. This was more than just a pretty speech ad hominem, and I should like to see us doing more to justify the faith of people like him.

I am sending copies of this despatch to HM Representatives at Amman, Baghdad, Beirut, Damascus, Jedda, Khartoum, Tel Aviv, Washington and at the United Nations in New York.

I am Sir
Yours faithfully

M. S. Weir

1. *James Craig*: British Ambassador to Syria (1976–9) and Saudi Arabia (1979–84).
2. *Flinders Petrie*: English archaeologist and Egyptologist (1853–1942).
3. *Gertrude Bell*: Writer, traveller and diplomat (1868–1926). During the Second World War Bell was made a Political Officer – the only woman in the British military to bear the rank – thanks to her unequalled knowledge of the region born from years of adventurous desert travel. Bell spent her final years in Iraq, as adviser to the King (both the country and monarch being recent British creations).
4. *Senator Knowland*: Californian politician who excoriated President Truman for 'losing' China to Communism in 1949. Knowland was dubbed the 'Senator from Formosa' for championing the rival Kuomintang leadership in Taiwan.

∾

Jordan

'A singular combination of opposites . . .
consistently inconsistent'

HUGH GLENCAIRN BALFOUR-PAUL, HM AMBASSADOR
TO JORDAN, SEPTEMBER 1975

CONFIDENTIAL

BRITISH EMBASSY
AMMAN
12 September 1975

The Right Honourable
James Callaghan MP
etc etc etc

Sir,

Many good men and true, I have observed, on arrival in this eccentric principality, fall quickly under a sort of Hashemite spell (and some never break out of it). My own first impressions, recorded in 1972, might have suggested that I was sickening for a similar bewitchment. Three years' experience has proved at least something of an antidote. There have been moments when the less agreeable aspects of life under the Hashemites have taken precedence. With the passage of time the bad has tended to obtrude, the good to be taken for granted and forgotten: a familiar syndrome, no doubt. In this valedictory review of the Hashemite Kingdom, its people and its policies, I shall try to reassess them objectively.

Jordanians and their rulers, like other Arabs and theirs, display to Western observers a singular combination of opposites, are consistently inconsistent. Heart-warmingly open and genuine one moment, they can be devious and deceitful the next. Hospitable and generous to a fault with individuals, especially foreign ones, they can be singularly indifferent to social abuse and group suffering. They admire honesty but tolerate corruption; welcome outside opinion but continually disregard it. Their intellects are at once acute and sloppy, their imaginations effervescent but uncreative. They are masters of good argument but martyrs to rhetoric. Genuinely attached to their country, they know next to nothing of it, and desecrate what little they explore. They point proudly to their traditional arts and fill their houses with the vulgarest imported kitsch. The feckless hedonism of so many of the rich and the grasping incivility of so many of the poor (especially those 'dressed in a little brief authority') are balanced in both cases by virtues that Western civilization seems sadly to have discarded.

One does not need to have spent 30 years with Arabs to grow aware of these and other startling dichotomies in their make-up. (No doubt the Arabs are equally baffled by inconsistencies in ours. Certainly they swing continually, in their attitudes to Britain, from admiration to disgust, from disaffection back to affection.) I do not pretend to any special understanding of the Arab character: on good days it seems to me (like those intricate villanelles of Auden) clear as a bell, on bad ones totally opaque. But viewing as objectively as I can King Hussein's subjects as compared with the rest of the 'race', I believe them to have rather more of the agreeable qualities and rather less of the disagreeable than other Arabs of my acquaintance . . .

. . . What about their rulers – the King and the handful who contribute to his policy-making? Certainly they too have their faults – displaying an exaggerated idea of their own importance, a cavalier approach to financial priorities and proprieties, and a mistaken belief that a loyal army is a substitute for a contented citizenry. But they have virtues too – and there have been times when Hashemite resilience and purposefulness have given me a lift of the heart, just as there have been others when their waywardness has left me grinding my teeth. Perhaps the King's uncle, Sherif Nasser, provides the best example of this combination of opposites: notorious at once for buccaneering and for benefaction, his huge private irrigation project in the stony desert at Hallabat is the most imaginative of its kind in the region – and the most unscrupulous. The library in Prince Mohammad's study offers an equally revealing (if less fair) illustration of Hashemitism: 100 volumes on the Middle East, 50 on Chess, 50 on Gun Culture, 50 on Karate, one on *Male Grooming and Good Looks* and one final one entitled *My Poodle and Yours*. The Crown Prince presents a third variant, combining intellectual conceit with moral concern, now repelling popularity through his penchant for polysyllables, now attracting it with his passion for parachuting. Zeid Rifa'i, Jordan's agile Prime Minister for most of my time, was passed in the course of the farewell dinner he gave for my wife and myself a book of zodiacal horoscopes. Rifling through it for his own he found it to read: 'Gambler, gourmand, critic, crook, loyal subordinate, right-hand man . . .' and closed the book with a peal of engaging self-recognition . . .

But perhaps, on leaving the neighbourhood of Palestine, I ought to end this one with some measured valedictory nostrum for solving the apparently insoluble. You will be relieved to know that I have none to offer. My only modest suggestion is that, in addressing itself to the Palestine problem, the world would do well to encourage greater precision in the use of language. Arabs are worse than most people at linguistic flatulence, at not bothering to define their terms. Ambiguity has of course its uses in this field of diplomacy as in others. But did the Arab/Israeli situation by now enjoy a more precise vocabulary – starting perhaps with an agreed definition of 'the Palestinians' whom it is all about – there might be more prospect of handling it productively. As things are – and the Hashemites are perhaps little more scrupulous than others in this respect – Lewis Carroll (that *vade mecum* for sojourners in the Middle East) hits the nail as usual on the head:–

'When I use a word,' Humpty Dumpty said in rather a scornful tone, 'it means just what I choose it to mean – neither more nor less.'

'The question is,' said Alice, 'whether you can make words mean different things.'

'The question is,' said Humpty Dumpty, 'which is to be master – that's all.'

I am sending copies of this despatch to Her Majesty's

Representatives at Beirut, Cairo, Damascus, Tel Aviv, Baghdad, Jedda, Tehran and Jerusalem.

I have the honour to be

Sir,
Your obedient Servant,

H. G. Balfour-Paul

~

Syria

'Six or a dozen men rule Syria. They listen not, neither do they consult . . . I do not like them at all'

SIR JAMES CRAIG, HM AMBASSADOR
TO SYRIA, SEPTEMBER 1979

James Craig wrote several valedictories in his long career. His reflections on leaving Dubai are on p. 325. Given the vigour with which Craig tackles the Syrian character here, it is perhaps unsurprising that the Foreign Office declined to release his final, 1984 Saudi valedictory in response to a Freedom of Information Request. The given reason was that 'whilst in most governments senior Officials tend to serve an appointed term, many of the senior members of the Saudi Government have held the same governmental positions for many years. Trust is extremely important to these states and any potential release could have repercussions . . .' In other words, Mr Craig has insulted senior Saudis who are still in office. A quarter of a century on, Craig's valedictory from Jeddah remains not just classified, but also covered by a High Court injunction, taken

*out to stop its publication in the press after a leak (see the
introduction to Chapter 5). This valedictory from Damascus
concludes on a remarkable note, bold even for a Camel Corps
Ultra. Many politicians in the West maintain that Syria's most
objectionable contribution to world affairs has been her
sponsorship of Palestinian aggression against Israel. Sir James
effectively suggests the opposite.*

BRITISH EMBASSY

DAMASCUS

18 September 1979

The Rt Hon the Lord Carrington KCMG MC
Secretary of State for Foreign and Commonwealth Affairs
FCO

My Lord,

My predecessor, a more tolerant man than I, wrote in his
valedictory despatch that he had given part of his heart to
Syria – or some such Cymric extravagance. I am far from
sentiments of that kind. I find Syria not particularly
beautiful except in patches which are not likely to stay
beautiful much longer. Its people are kindly, but the
sophistication and stimulus of their society hardly approach
the standards of ancient Athens. The distinction and
originality of their once colourful culture are being
submerged in a cosmopolitan blur of Pepsi Cola, crumpled
suits and drab apartment blocks.

Above all, they have been ruled for sixteen years by
the Ba'th Party, which whether you look at its members
or at its institutions, is a very unattractive affair. Its
leaders have blinkered minds and an attachment to a
sentimentous ideology in which few of them sincerely or

comprehendingly believe. They speak in slogans which permit of private cynicism but never of public doubt. They know nothing of the outside world. Their experience of countries other than Syria is confined to official visits: special aircraft, Mercedes cars, government guesthouses, formal banquets. The odd Ba'thi who has really lived abroad is a different animal altogether. I know three. The rest are impervious to argument.

Moreover, Ba'this are infuriatingly secretive. They prefer to say nothing unless the need to speak is plainly inevitable; and when they do speak, their words are bland or guarded or superficial. Six or a dozen men rule Syria. Presumably among themselves they debate and discuss. But they tell no-one of their arguments or of their options. They listen not, neither do they consult. They certainly do not trust: not their people, not their allies and not, above all, foreign ambassadors. Their assumption that any story – or no story – is good enough for their audience is contemptuous and foolish.

Like all Arabs they say one thing and mean another. The influence of Arabic upon those who speak it is a long and subtle subject. Without a doubt it leads to cant, hypocrisy, bombast and self-deceit. Fine language allows Arabs to avoid their fears and their doubts and the imperatives of logic.

Finally, like all parties which rule alone, the Ba'th despite its dogma books has no true faith in democracy. It practises, though it preaches the opposite, one law for the strong and another for the weak; and it therefore permits (like many other regimes, including its predecessors) patronage, corruption and nepotism. It denies freedom of speech; its newspapers are objects of derision.

But governments, like men, are all paradoxical: just and

tyrannical, competent and feckless, thoughtful and stupid. Even the Ba'this have their virtues which merit our praise, and their problems which attract our sympathy. And I am certainly sympathetic to the Ba'this in the dilemmas which they face and the misrepresentation of which they are victims.

As you will have seen by now, I do not like them at all. But all that I have said against them could be said against a hundred other governments in this naughty world. And there is this, above all, that can be said for them: ever since they came to power, and long before, they have devoted a preponderant part of their energy to the cause of the Palestinians, to which they are called not only by self-interest but by the ties of kinship, neighbourliness and compassion. They could, long since, have settled their own relatively minor disputes with Israel, as Egypt has done. They could have saved their blood and used their treasure on their own country's needs. They could have told the Palestinians that enough was enough, that the time had come to think about Syria's GNP and inflation and balance of payments. However misguided their policies and their actions may be from time to time, it must be set to their credit that they have never been even tempted to renounce what they conceive to be their obligations. In present circumstances, they have no clear idea, and little hope, about what is to happen in the great conflict which occupies their hearts and minds; and yet they persist. Wrong-headed, inflexible and shortsighted as I take them to be, I yet find a faint but distinct spark of nobility in their obstinacy. And were I in their shoes (which Heaven forbid) I should find myself as perplexed as they.

The Lebanon

'"Heady and oppressive"'

SIR DEREK RICHES, HM AMBASSADOR
TO THE LEBANON, JUNE 1967

After four years in the country, it is the vices of the Lebanon
and the Lebanese, rather than the virtues, which more insist-
ently obtrude into the consciousness: the weakness of the
Government rather than the successful holding of the ring
among a multitude of confessions and influences, the irresponsible antics of the Chamber of Deputies rather than the
maintenance of democratic form and fact in a largely totali-
tarian area; the venality of the Press rather than the public
expression in it of the whole range of opinions and policies; the
economic ruthlessness of the rich and powerful rather than the
(hitherto) annual rate of growth of over 10 per cent; the lack of
generalised social conscience rather than the close ties between
classes of the same confession or region; the disorder of Beirut
rather than the surpassing beauty of unchanged areas of the
interior; in short, the corruption rather than the flowering.

To some extent, these feelings may be nurtured by the
atmosphere of Beirut, where, as Fedden[1] says, the haze en-
veloping the town symbolises the miasmic Levant:

> Rich and uncertain, heady and oppressive, the air blurs
> shapes and principles, precludes clarity of action and thought,
> but it drives trade, it is the heavy fuel on which the Levantine
> works. Under this haze, enterprises spawn, and coin turns
> rapidly. The obscure deal and the close contract burgeons
> into fortune.

But chiefly they arise, I think, from exasperation that a people so intelligent, diligent and charming, with ample human and adequate material resources at their disposal, should be so devoid of the will to make some personal sacrifice in the interests of national and truly co-operative action.

1. *Fedden*: The author Robin Fedden (1908–77), best remembered for *Chantemelse*, about his childhood in France. His eclectic oeuvre includes works on suicide and skiing – and on the crusader castles of Syria and the Lebanon.

~

Kuwait

'The breathtaking self-centredness of the Kuwaiti population . . . mental attitudes every bit as disagreeable as those of Qadhafi'

SIR JOHN WILTON, HM AMBASSADOR
TO KUWAIT, APRIL 1974

Kuwait cannot herself exercise a decisive influence on either the price or the volume of world oil production in the way that Saudi Arabia could if she chose to do so. But so long as Saudi Arabia does not choose either to swamp or to starve the world market Kuwait, as a country which can vary her production upwards or downwards by a million or more barrels a day without any serious practical or financial constraints, is in a position to exercise a very great influence on supplies and prices whenever she wishes. She has so far chosen to exert her pressures to increase the price and I expect her to continue to do so. She does not, I believe, thereby run the risk sometimes alleged, of being left eventually with oil in the ground that nobody wants. The cost of producing Kuwaiti crude is, because of the natural advantages of the now virtually fully-commissioned Kuwaiti fields, the lowest in the world. The necessary capital expenditure has been incurred. Little is now required but to open and close the taps. Even if the oil market should one day again become a buyers' market Kuwait will always be able to sell.

In these circumstances the weakness of the government, the bletherings of the Assembly, the acid tongue of the Finance and Oil Minister, the indecisions of the Defence Minister, the bland myopia of the civil service and the breathtaking self-centredness of the Kuwaiti population at large give rise to a disquieting sensation of insecurity among those who are in any measure dependent upon Kuwait. The position of a dependant is seldom agreeable. There is no shortage among the inhabitants of Kuwait of mental attitudes every bit as disagreeable as those of Qadhafi . . . and their views find free expression in the Assembly and the pages of the irresponsible press . . .

The overpowering silliness of the Assembly continually frustrates such few sensible schemes as the government does put to it and infallibly fastens upon some selfish, trivial or backward-looking issue over which to bicker; but so long as it provides a vent for its particular brand of folly it can, perhaps, be argued that it is a kind of safety-valve against a political upheaval that would produce something worse. For unsatisfactory and feeble though the present regime may be there is little prospect of a better one replacing it . . . New elections are due in January 1975 and in theory, on statistical probabilities alone, it ought to be possible out of a population of some 400,000 native Kuwaitis, to produce a better, more competent, Assembly and Government than that which at present runs Kuwait. But when I look at the alternative talent available my faith in statistics evaporates . . .

This is the central problem which faces the Government of Kuwait over the next decade. In almost every walk of life the plans, and the means, for a great expansion exist – except that the qualified men are not to be found. The University is to be enlarged to cope with the torrent of students now emerging from the secondary schools. There is to be a Medical School to train the doctors to staff the new hospitals. The Armed Forces are to be expanded and equipped with up-to-date tanks, aircraft, missiles and naval vessels . . . It would be difficult to see where all the necessary talent could come from even if the Kuwaitis were exceptionally gifted and exceptionally industrious. They are neither. They are about average in the matter of natural talents but their tradition inclines them strongly to commerce in preference to other professions or trades and their climate and recent prosperity have made them disinclined to work hard at anything. (The Naval Adviser remarked to me despondently that if there were a Kuwaiti with the qualifications necessary for a leading stoker he would expect to be at least an admiral.) There are exceptions but they more than prove the general rule. Any notion that Kuwait is, by virtue of its great wealth, likely to become the Switzerland (or even the Lebanon) of the Arab East can be discarded . . .

The Kuwaitis will, I think, go on for some years yet very much as they have in the recent past; but they will have more money (the first air-conditioned hearse has just arrived here).

～

Tunisia

'Even the most educated are apt to be bewildered
over the difference between left and right . . .
which means hazards on the roads'

SIR EDWARD WARNER, HM AMBASSADOR
TO TUNISIA, MARCH 1970

Warner's tirade against rules and regulations came the year after the Duncan report, which looked at ways to run British embassies abroad more cheaply. The reforms that followed included centralizing procurement back in Whitehall, and linking accommodation allowances to those paid by private-sector firms retaining British staff overseas. Obviously furious about having to quit his post early, Sir Edward's rage is directed more against Whitehall than Tunis.

I leave this varied and attractive country, with its volatile and mixed population, with regret after only two years. It has been long enough to establish contacts and get one's self known – a slow process at a 'bricks without straw' post – but not long enough to exploit the contacts made and the experience gained. Departing with a sense of wasted effort and lack of fulfilment, I hope that my successor will be left *en poste* long enough both to do my spade work all over again, and to draw benefit from it. The local population – basically Berber, cross fertilised by Phoenicians, ancient Greeks, Romans, Gauls, ancient Britons, Vandals, Byzantines, Arabs (various sorts), Crusaders, Moors and Jews expelled from Spain, Turks, Spaniards, Circassian blood via imported female slaves, Italian and French, not to mention the various armies in World War II – is not easy to get to know. Nor is the devious mentality of the friendly and attractive people resulting from this mixture easy to understand. Even the most educated are apt to be bewildered over the difference between left and right, fact and fiction, which means hazards on the roads and much patience in getting at the facts. This all takes time and effort. If postings are not to become diplomatic musical chairs – a game particularly hard on wives – I would venture to suggest that the local facts of life need to be more seriously taken into account.

I would also plead for a halt in the ghastly process of reducing everything to quasi military rules and regulations, applied regardless of local variations. The armed services have to have such rules and regulations but, in my humble estimation, the Diplomatic Service is something quite different. Its very essence is variety and variables; adaptability and improvisation. Rules cannot be applied without exception. Everything cannot be reduced to the precedent of somewhere else. Nor, in a place where the Head of Mission, for historical reasons, lives in a Moorish palace, surrounded by a small estate containing the cottages of the staff, granted free of all cost by a former Bey, can it be said that his domestic arrangements must be governed by the local good employer practices of the Manager of Shell, and Missions occupying small suburban villas with non-resident staff. Far too much time has to be spent fighting against rigid instructions based on uniform rules and regulations, and trying to get the most obvious tools for the trade – such as adequate equipment for buffet dinners, the main medium of entertainment in a country where Ministers and officials dislike committing themselves to set dinner parties, but may well attend on more informal and less binding occasions. I hope that some flexibility can be re-introduced so that Heads of Mission can be given wide discretion in matters of local administration (such as I believe the Germans enjoy); and that equipment can be supplied to meet what an Ambassador regards as locally necessary, rather than on the basis of standardised world-wide issue. There need be no exaggerated fear of setting dangerous precedents. Conditions, mercifully, still vary from country to country, and the deadly world-wide uniformity, apparently beloved of Whitehall and its computers, has still to be achieved.

~

'The Tunisian temperament, like Tunisian toilet-paper, tears in such unexpected directions'

HUGH GLENCAIRN BALFOUR-PAUL, HM AMBASSADOR TO TUNISIA, SEPTEMBER 1977

A true Arabist, Balfour-Paul served as Head of Mission to three Islamic countries, Iraq, Jordan (see p. 248) and Tunisia. In Iraq he met Saddam Hussein, then head of Ba'athist security (whose powers of argument, the ambassador recalls, were 'skilful enough to wrap me around his little finger'), before being expelled when the regime of Colonel Ahmed Hassan al-Bakr broke off relations with Britain. Balfour-Paul considered his last post as ambassador in Tunis 'the least inspiring job in the service but the most inspiring Residence to do it from'.

(CONFIDENTIAL)   *Tunis,*
                                          19 September, 1977

Sir,

My Last Impressions of Tunisia represent so small an advance on my First that it would seem emptily repetitious to commit them to paper. After almost two years I still find myself suspended between the same two opposing views of this country as I did in my first despatch (and which I there entitled the Dyspeptic and the Lotophagous[1]). It would, I suppose, be cheating simply to refer the imaginary reader back and sign off. So rather than re-submit the same old wares in a different wrapper I shall, with your permission, only pinpoint a few salient features of Tunisia and then, provoked by thirty-odd years in the Arab worlds venture one or two observations of a wider reference. This is after all the last despatch I shall ever burden you with.

During the visit here in 1976 of Her Royal Highness The Princess Margaret we stood for some minutes in the room at Monastir where President Bourguiba[2] was born (a national shrine filled with the *sacra* of the Republic's founder). The conversation, led by Habib Bourguiba Junior, turned for some reason to the Watergate scandal and the bugging of the Democrat headquarters. 'And did you know, Ma'am,' he concluded in his (almost) faultless English, with the air of a conjuror producing (as indeed he did) a rabbit of an unexpected kind, 'Did you know that the plumbers were the buggers?' Princess Margaret's eyebrows rose almost imperceptibly; but the phrase has stayed with me as a kind of encapsulation of what is amiss in Tunisia itself.

I am not referring in the literal sense to the defects of Tunisia's sanitary engineering – striking though they are, and true though it is that one of the capital's main hotels has to keep all its windows hermetically sealed. Nor am I thinking of the shoddy nature of so much workmanship and the casual nature of so much behaviour which in Tunisia, as in other Third World societies, drive visitors from our own to drink or apoplexy. It is in the political sense that I would apply Bourguiba Junior's memorable phrase to his own country. For the root fault of this republican regime is that it too interferes – needlessly as well as improperly – in the legitimate activities of its democratic rivals. Bourguiba's Constitutional Socialist Party is led by men of intelligence and skill, it has much to its credit – trades union rights, imaginative planning, an advanced educational system, an air of general tolerance, all of them without parallel in the Arab world – and it is well established. But it does not have the courage of its convictions. Its political critics linger unnecessarily behind bars, its Press is drearily controlled, its Human Rights champions are muzzled. The singular conceit which so disfigures the Tunisian persona is matched by a singular sense of insecurity. Maybe this is why the Tunisian temperament, like Tunisian toilet-paper, tears in such unexpected directions . . .

. . . [B]ecause this country has enjoyed (and suffered) a particularly close relationship with part of Europe, I believe it is better placed than bigger and remoter bits of Afro-Asia to teach us something . . . During my farewell call on one of the Tunisian Ministers he said something that I think worth passing on – with no less diffidence than he passed it to me.

The Minister concerned is a pronounced lover of England and the English, and he has seen the world both as a diplomat and as a politician. What he said was this: 'Your country is no longer a power of the first order. But she has unrivalled experience of world affairs and an influential role to play. Why cannot she adjust her dealings with the Third World to suit her new situation – not, as your Think Tank[3] has apparently recommended, by a feeble contraction of her overseas posture, nor by the vulgar reduction of her diplomatic criteria to cost-effectiveness and of her diplomats' qualifications to degrees in economics, but by giving your profile a new and less ungracious expression?

The Third World has a great respect for your cleverness, but a sad disbelief in your sincerity. Even when your thought processes lead you to make concessions to Third World opinion, you make them with a cold and grudging air. Perhaps because of some imperial hangover your public attitudes to the Third World still sound *de haut en bas*, liverish if not arrogant. The Third World will not say so to your rulers because it would be impolite; and your diplomats resident abroad are unlikely to reflect it if London's ears are open only to the crudities of economics. But that is what the Third World thinks – I know this (he went on) because I belong to it and live with it. The Third World has come to stay and is growing. We are emotional people: coldness and calculations of cost-effectiveness give us the shivers. Why do you British not realise this and (in your own interests as well as ours) condescend to it – without an air of condescension. It is not so much a matter of what you do (or don't do) as of what you say (or don't say) and of the way you say it (or don't say it). Look at the way de Gaulle changed the whole course of Franco-Arab relations with a single phrase!4 Whereas in your country . . .' Could he, I wonder, have a point?

I must bring this scrappy and sententious submission to an end. I leave Tunisia with much less regret and much less affection than I leave the Service. In Tunisia little has changed in the 22 months I have known it. In the Service on the other hand much has changed during the 22 years it has found employment for me – some of it but not all of it for the better. Many of us, I suspect, are haunted (quite apart from Berrill and all that) by a ghostly sense that the Service is losing its vigour of bone and other ancestral virtues. An empty ghost perhaps. But may I conclude by quoting the engaging malapropism of a lady of my acquaintance, and suggest that it is 'high time this ghost was circumcised'.

I am sending copies of this despatch to Her Majesty's Ambassadors at Algiers, Tripoli, Rabat and Cairo and (because of its references . . . to the CPRS Review) to Sir Andrew Stark.

I have, etc.,

H. G. Balfour-Paul

1. *Lotophagous*: Lotus-eating; indolent daydreamers. Used here in contrast to the unsettled demeanour that comes with indigestion, or dyspepsia.

2. *President Bourguiba*: Habib Bourguiba, the first President of independent Tunisia, 1957–87. His son, born from a French wife, shared the same name (Habib Junior).

3. *Think Tank*: In 1977 Sir Kenneth Berrill, head of the Central Policy Review Staff (the 'Think Tank') proposed cuts to the Foreign Office budget and made a recommendation – never carried out – that the diplomatic corps be merged with representatives of other foreign-facing departments such as the Ministry of Defence. Reporting and despatch-writing in the FCO, the report concluded, was 'done to an unjustifiably high standard'. The Diplomatic Service, it said, 'tends to err on the side of perfectionism in work whose importance is not always commensurate with the human and material resources devoted to it'.

4. *de Gaulle . . . single phrase!*: Probably de Gaulle's famous condemnation of Israel in 1967, after the Six Day War: 'Le peuple juif, sûr de lui même et dominateur' ('The Jewish people, self-confident and domineering').

∾

Libya

*'Observers in aircraft and ships leaving
Tripoli have noted almost hysterical
manifestations of relief'*

PETER TRIPP, HM AMBASSADOR TO LIBYA,
MARCH 1974

Three years in post-revolutionary Libya have on the whole
been a depressing experience. Qadhafi's one-man rule, the
chaos he has created, his unbalanced character and his
ingrained prejudices have frequently produced situations
inimical to British interests and obstructive to our work . . .

Had his policies at home made Libya a happier place for
the Libyans themselves, he might be excused some of his
excesses. But the plain fact is that Qadhafi is indifferent to
and contemptuous of Libyans as a whole. He uses them
for his own ends and to further his own ambitions.
Extraordinarily apathetic and backward, they signally fail
to match up to Qadhafi's requirement of a dynamic,
Muslim elite . . .

The power which vastly increased oil revenues confers
has – quite apart from Libyan xenophobic arrogance and
egocentricity – made the regime indifferent to the
admonitions and criticisms of the rest of the world. There are
constant supplicants for Libyan hand-outs and, in a more
sophisticated context, contenders for fat Libyan contracts . . .
Yet Libyan meanness drives away many competent foreign
technicians and she is paying dearly for botched work . . .

Major difficulties for anyone working in Libya include
the abysmally low standard of administration, the
incompetence of civil servants, the absence of qualified

Libyans of all sorts, the pathological meanness of Libyans and the lack of co-ordination between different departments and strata of government. Add to this officials' fears of making a mistake, of being over-ruled or cast into gaol, and it is easy to understand why the Libyan Government machine labours so badly. National pride will not permit Libyans to admit that they do not know, or cannot do something. All major decisions are taken by Qadhafi or by the RCC.[1] Ministers are rarely consulted on policy, only on execution. The Ministry of Foreign Affairs, the only Ministry with which foreign missions are allowed to deal direct, has been without a Minister for all but seven months of my three years here. The job is now passed round from hand to hand – Qadhafi continuing to make his own foreign policy without advice and often without informing his colleagues . . .

I hope there will be a better future for Libya than a perpetuation of Qadhafi's rule. He is too egocentric and erratic ever to make a benevolent dictator. Granted Qadhafi broke with the colonial past and made Libya truly independent – (he now seems unreasonably keen to lose that independence by merger with other more developed Arab States), but he has virtually isolated his country by his abrasive and destructive policies and made only enemies among the Arabs. Even given the Arabs' propensity for trying to kill each other one day and, the next, kissing and making it up, even given that their staple diet is all too often their own words, Qadhafi's hostility and contempt for other Arab leaders will be hard to swallow . . .

It is a very great shame that Libya with all its attractions, its magnificent coast-line, exciting hinterland, superb archaeological remains and relatively good climate, should have been turned into such an uninviting and depressing place. I contemplated entitling this despatch: 'Where Every Prospect Pleases . . .'[2] but was persuaded that this would be an offence against the accepted convention that an Ambassador should not 'knock' the people who have, however ungraciously, received and tolerated him! But what impression should one retain of a country, so very different from any other Arab State, where personal contacts are excluded because people are too frightened by the secret police to respond to one's friendly overtures and where officials carry vindictiveness to unbelievable lengths, both in their dealings with foreigners and with each other? Contacts with officials are in any case minimal because the regime forbids officials from mixing socially with foreign diplomats. My Embassy is not alone in this, even some Arab Missions are shunned. There are of course rare and unscheduled friendly contacts, particularly in the countryside, which are the more memorable because they are so rare. At the popular level there is some goodwill for Britain. Sometimes, when Qadhafi has attacked us, Libyans have privately apologised to myself and members of my staff. But they are afraid – afraid to speak up and afraid to act. They therefore count for very little in our current relationship, although they are worth cultivating for their possible long-term value . . .

There is a well-known syndrome affecting expatriates leaving Libya either on holiday or finally. This shows itself in an exaggerated and irrational feeling of euphoria and an urgent need for strong drink. Observers in aircraft and ships leaving Tripoli have noted almost hysterical manifestations of relief. Curiously enough, many Libyans are similarly affected. This is a legitimate (and revealing) comment on the state of affairs in Libya today. Perhaps Qadhafi started out with good intentions but 'Virtue itself turns vice, being misapplied'.

I am sending copies of this despatch to Her Majesty's Representatives at Algiers, Beirut, Cairo, Paris, Rome, Tunis, Valletta and Washington; and to Her Majesty's Permanent Representatives to the European Communities and to the North Atlantic Council at Brussels, and to the UN at New York.

I have, etc.,

PETER TRIPP.

1. *RCC*: The Revolutionary Command Council.
2. *'Where Every Prospect Pleases . . .'*: The line concludes 'and only man is vile'. Reginald Heber's missionary hymn, written in 1819, roused the ire of no less a figure than Gandhi, who said it 'always left a sting' with him. Heber was Bishop of Calcutta, and he was writing about Ceylon (Sri Lanka).

6. Now, If I Were Foreign Secretary . . .

Matthew Parris found during his short stint as a trainee diplomat that colleagues divided into two quite distinct types. They are well represented among ambassadors. One type of diplomat is really a government minister manqué. His duty may be to carry out the Foreign Secretary's orders, but in his imagination he would like to be giving them; and he frets about policy, always asking how it might be better framed and conducted. The other type – often no less intelligent or probing in his intellect – is relatively untroubled by the question of whether he agrees or disagrees with the policy line it is his job to serve. His job is to serve it. From time to time, and if asked, he may offer advice on how it might be improved, but he is professionally careless whether his advice is taken or ignored.

The second type of diplomat is likely to sleep easier and live longer. Examples of the former abound below.

～

'Our world is dying'

PETER JAY, HM AMBASSADOR TO THE UNITED STATES
OF AMERICA, JUNE 1979

Peter Jay came to diplomacy after a career at the Treasury and ten years as Economics Editor of The Times. Described by his tutors at Oxford as the cleverest young man in England, Jay was an unabashed elitist. A startled sub-editor who once complained to Jay that one of his articles was hard to understand was told: 'I only wrote this piece for three people – the editor of The Times, the Governor of the Bank of England, and the Chancellor of the Exchequer.'

However, as a 'non-careerist' in the diplomatic jargon, Jay's appointment to Washington at just forty may have owed something to the fact that James Callaghan, the Prime Minister, was his father-in-law, and the Foreign Secretary, David Owen, a friend. Owen had discovered that senior Foreign Officials were, as he saw it, freezing him out by exchanging information in telegrams marked 'personal and confidential' and he was determined to break up this circle. Jay says Owen appointed him as 'my man, whom I can trust not to be part of a network which excludes me'. A fierce nepotism row ensued over the appointment. Even Jay was surprised by the scale of his promotion; when Owen summoned him to the Terrace of the House of Commons, Jay thought he was being offered the post of Economic Minister at the embassy, a post two full rungs below ambassador. When it became clear that Owen was actually offering him the top job, 'I actually fell off my chair,' Jay recalls.

In 1979, with a change of government in Whitehall, Jay was replaced. Packing his bags after just two years in the Diplomatic Service, Jay was not steeped in its traditions. But he embraced the customary farewell despatch with vigour, not to say volume. Jay's overall message, much of it cast, as he put it, in 'highly abstract, even philosophical, terms', is an enduring one – that Europe and America must not allow their petty disagreements to undermine the stability and security of the West. In 1979, the biggest danger to the established order on the European side was, as the ambassador saw it, nationalism. This last argument is not helped by the obvious reflection that Europe was more often seen as an anti-nationalist than a *nationalist force. In an interview with us Jay said he regards nationalism as dangerous because 'it excites and inflames emotions which are not about important objective things like prosperity and people's welfare, but about a kind of Olympic games version of political life where each nation is trying to come out top dog over the rest'. One can sense why he was not Margaret Thatcher's choice for Washington.*

But this valedictory essay, though it has its longueurs, can make heavy verbal weather of straightforward thoughts, and is prone to lose the thread of its argument, remains important. European disappointment with President Carter was, in Jay's view, both a cause and an effect of the cracks which had opened up in the transatlantic relationship. In this despatch the ambassador paints a sympathetic picture of the beleaguered President. In June 1979 Carter had plenty on his plate – an energy crisis, spiralling inflation – but things were to get worse in November, with the seizure of fifty-three Americans at the US Embassy in Tehran. American prestige was diminished and American voters enraged by the inability of the White House to free the captives. The Iran hostage crisis lasted for the remainder of Carter's first term of office, putting paid to any hopes of a second.

In terms of the direction of British foreign policy, the passage of time has shown Jay to have pointed the way on the issue, at least, on which he and Thatcher would have agreed. The ambassador's desire for the Atlantic alliance to be nurtured and not taken for granted became the Thatcher government's policy: her outlook was altogether more Atlanticist than European. On the more prosaic matter of electoral forecasting Jay had less success. He got it wrong on three out of three counts: Edward Kennedy did challenge Carter for the Democratic nomination in 1980 – and lost. Carter went on to lose the election to Reagan, by 8 million votes.

His two years as HM Ambassador in Washington were pro-
fessionally rewarding but personally trying; Jay's wife embarked
on an affair with the Watergate journalist Carl Bernstein, and
Jay fathered a child with the family's nanny. After Washington,
Jay plunged back into the media, as the founding Chairman and
Chief Executive of TV-am, Chief of Staff to the later disgraced
Robert Maxwell, and on screen as the BBC's Economics Editor.

Foreign and Commonwealth Office Diplomatic Report   No: 149/79
General Distribution

THE WEST: THE PERIL WITHIN

Her Majesty's Ambassador at Washington to the Secretary
of State for Foreign and Commonwealth Affairs

Washington,
20 June, 1979.

My Lord,

Our world is dying; and its death is being hastened by errors
and myopia in our own ranks. Forty years ago Winston
Churchill saw the need to bring in the New World to redress
the balance of the Old. Now we risk driving out the New to
indulge the *amour propre* of the Old; and thereby we are
putting at hazard the foundations of the peace and prosperity
which have been the fruits of the Churchill doctrine.

When the Prime Minister goes to Tokyo at the end of this
month to meet President Carter and the other leaders of
the Western world she will face an historic choice between
swimming with the new tide of economic nationalism
and refighting the unending battle for the broader
principles that have underpinned transatlantic cohesion
since the war . . .

The spirit of 'the West'

By 'our world' I mean the political, military and economic order which has sustained the stability, freedom and prosperity of the 'Western' nations through thirty almost unprecedented years of peace and progress. That order was first conceived, extraordinarily enough in the darkest days of the war, by Winston Churchill and Franklin Roosevelt and foreshadowed in the Atlantic Charter of 1941 . . .

The philosophic worm in the bud

. . . Understanding is side-tracked by superficial and unilluminating arguments between 'capitalism' and 'socialism' and between 'the Atlantic' and 'Europe'. We can have democratic capitalism or democratic socialism to taste. We can lean in day-to-day affairs to the US or lean to the Common Market to taste. What we cannot safely do, but are doing, is to trifle with or to neglect the basic foundations of the security, stability and prosperity of the free world or its necessary relations with Russia, China and the Third World. Those foundations . . . are undermined by nationalism in politics, isolationism (or 'decoupling') in defence and mercantilism in economics in whatever part of the free world they occur.

That they are occurring, that the framework of the West – and the security, freedoms and prosperity which depend on it – is being dangerously eroded and that the growing 'prevailance' of the Franco-German concept of 'Europe', both nationalist and autarkic, is powerfully contributing to this peril are the themes of this despatch. To put it more baldly, the way things are going we are set fair to lose during the 1980s the substance of NATO, the utility of the UN, the essentials of the GATT, the spirit of the OECD and the purpose of the IMF. The challenge we face is not to find the imagination, courage and statesmanship which enabled Churchill, Roosevelt and the rest to conceive and to create the post-war order, but more modestly to produce the leadership, common sense and restraint, to preserve it from internal destruction . . .

'Europe': Liberal or Nationalist?

. . . It is no part at all of the argument that the search for greater political and economic unity in Western Europe is, as such, wrong . . . or that any tendencies or attitudes in Europe are exclusively to blame . . . There is, however, a 'good' Europe and there is a 'bad' Europe, just as there are 'good' and 'bad' Americas . . . The 'good' Europe is easily recognised. It is the Europe of Monnet, a monument to the internationalist ideal and, so it was intended, an antidote to the specific evil of the old nationalisms of Germany, France, Britain, Italy, etc. It is the Europe of free internal industrial trade, open frontiers and mobility of people and capital. It is the Europe which promptly embraces all democratic European nations who wish to join . . .

But there is a 'bad' Europe, too. It is the Europe that sees its own unity as a vehicle for a new nationalism on a sub-continental scale, as an escape from the post-war impotence of the old petty, Balkanised nationalisms of France, Germany etc. into the headier league of superpower or regional nationalism. It is the Europe of the common agricultural policy . . . It is the Europe that is tempted to proclaim its identity by grandiose gestures and ridiculous standardisation rather than by steady practical achievements: the Europe of monetary union and the EMS,[1] of heavy lorries and of uniform beer mugs . . . It is the Europe of vulgar anti-Americanism and elite anti-Carterism, that has neither the inclination nor the aptitude to understand contemporary America and that smugly delights in every American mistake or misfortune, real or imagined. Above all and embracing all, it is the Europe that cares more about Europe than the West, about the dash it cuts than the crash it causes and about displaying its own identity and prestige than about sustaining the broader Western framework of security and prosperity on which it depends.

A similar examination of the 'good' and 'bad' faces of America could be made; and some of its unacceptable features would be comparably gross. Protectionism and autarky are growing. Isolationism still stirs. Anti-Carterism here is streets ahead of its European counterpart. Dark forces – anti-semitism, cold-war hysteria and panicky self-doubt – are visible not all that far below some surfaces to the regular traveller away from Washington . . .

Carter and contemporary America
One of our European Ambassadors, in a letter of 7th May, 1979, to the department on US Foreign Policy, refers to 'the general European disenchantment with President Carter'; and, as a description of the private attitudes of many influential people in and out of government on the Continent, this is clearly accurate and has its full counterpart in the US . . . [let us] beware of the fallacy that we make Europe strong by depreciating the US or its President; for, as I have said before, Mr. Carter is the only President of the US we have got . . .

I have described elsewhere . . . Mr. Carter's correct insight into the bankruptcy of pressure group politics, once more than half the nation is so organised, and his commendable determination to take the high road of national leadership, mobilising the general will of the public as ordinary citizens behind decisions which will benefit the whole society against the sectionalised will of organised interests. He has trodden that road unflinchingly. Indeed, if anyone is still tempted to find Mr. Carter unpredictable, they should recognise that the defect lies in their own comprehension. Line up any set options with the most immediately unpopular but, on merits, correct on the left and the most immediately popular but, on merits, wrong on the right; and you can rely upon it that Mr. Carter will choose from the left. It is not the kind of facile predictability that comes from being easily labelled 'hawk' or 'dove', 'liberal' or 'conservative', 'idealist' or 'realist'. It is the predictability of a subtle, penetrating and ice-cold mind studying the detailed merits of issues and deciding them accordingly. To describe him as a man whose heart rules his head is about as apt as calling Aristotle a hysteric or Euclid a pornographer.

Politically Mr. Carter is failing. He has chosen, bravely, a highly unconventional style of Government; and he has failed so far to win sufficiently widespread understanding of the virtue and necessity of this radical departure. The explanation is not the substance of the policies, still less public doubt of his integrity, decency or mental ability. It is rather that, if a leader takes on the entire apparatus of organised political opinion – and so the press and broadcasters who are geared to amplify those special pleadings – then that leader will be widely and vigorously bad-mouthed. His only weapon is his own direct access to public attention; and to use that he must articulate effectively, not just the detailed justification of his individual decisions, but the unifying conception of what he is doing and why. Mr. Carter has never yet managed to do that, his great skills at the quite different art of electioneering notwithstanding. He is, perhaps, too fastidious to trust the generalisations and memorable phrases that a Churchill or a Roosevelt used so skilfully, too proud to fight, as was said of Woodrow Wilson, with rhetoric and ideologies that he intellectually distrusts.

So he stands low in the polls and could indeed be denied re-election or re-nomination in 1980. If, as I still think unlikely, Senator Kennedy sought the Democratic nomination against Mr. Carter, the Senator would almost certainly get it. Against any other Democratic contender the advantage of the incumbency, even one so fastidious (or, according to your view of the baser political arts, inept) as Mr. Carter, still seems at this stage likely to prevail, though a year is an aeon in Presidential politics. If nominated, it now seems likely that Mr. Carter would face Governor Reagan, whose entrenchment with the Republican faithful is being prematurely discounted, or Governor Connally, though Senator Howard Baker and others are still in the race. Against Mr. Reagan the odds still favour Mr. Carter as incumbent and as a man whose merits may be expected to gain wider recognition when it comes to a choice between two real candidates rather than between one President and the Archangel Gabriel. Moreover, Mr. Reagan's reputation is not such as will enable him easily to capture the floating vote in the centre from as moderate a Democrat as Mr. Carter . . .

In short the odds now on Mr. Carter being re-elected are probably little better than evens, though shorter than on any one other potential candidate (given Mr. Kennedy's reluctance to run). This means that the dangers of unchecked anti-Carterism in European counsels can by no means be assumed to expire by January 1981. It may well be more useful to understand him and to cultivate him, indeed on the merits of the issues to support him, than to revile him, dismiss him or misrepresent him . . .

Tokyo summit
When the Prime Minister meets President Carter bilaterally at Tokyo, she will have many specific issues to discuss and

she will be looking to confirm, as will he, a good personal relationship. He may by then be tired from his travels; and he has plenty of domestic political worries on his mind, although he is not a man to show either or to appear bothered. He has a keen intelligence and enjoys solid discussion of complex problems with other good minds. He is more a man for the particular than the general (hence his political problems). He likes to make friends and usually makes a good impression in private. He is an exceptionally good listener.

The Prime Minister has already met him and will know best how to approach the meeting. Without being drawn too far into philosophy, I think the President would most value Mrs. Thatcher's appreciation of the state of and prospects for US–West European relations and of the role her Government hopes to play in them. I hope this despatch will be helpful as background.

I am sending copies of this despatch to Her Majesty's Ambassadors at European Community Posts, Moscow, Tokyo, Peking, Tel Aviv, Cairo and Jedda; British High Commissioners at Ottawa and New Delhi and the UK. Permanent Representatives to the UN on the North Atlantic Council, to the OECD and to the European Communities; and to Her Majesty's Consuls-General in the US.

I am, Sir,
Yours faithfully,
PETER JAY.

1. *EMS*: Exchange-rate pegging. The European Monetary System was a fore-runner of Economic and Monetary Union, which in turn led to the Euro.

∽

'A betrayal of that history which others in the world . . . will neither understand nor forgive'

SIR BRIAN BARDER, HM HIGH COMMISSIONER
TO NIGERIA, JANUARY 1991

Not all valedictory despatches were given a wide circulation. Some were hushed up.

In 1991, Brian Barder was preparing to leave Africa to take up his final post in the Diplomatic Service, as High Commissioner in Australia. Barder had come to know the continent well, spending the last three years as British high commissioner to its most populous country, Nigeria. That followed four years as ambassador to Ethiopia, a period which included the 1984 famine in which one million people died. The catastrophe (and reports and campaigning by the likes of Michael Buerk and Bob Geldof) triggered an unprecedented flood of private donations from Britain to Africa; but as the decade drew to an end Africa and its problems were losing the public's attention. Newer priorities, such as rapidly unfolding events in Eastern Europe, were keeping ministers awake. It was against this backdrop that Barder was asked to put down some final reflections on leaving the continent.

The result was a despatch that pointed out the 'sorry story' of British aid. In 1991 HM Government was giving less per capita in aid to the Third World than any other member of the EEC bar Austria. In seeking to downgrade Africa in its priorities and further disengage from the continent, we were (Barder wrote) shirking obligations and betraying our history. One can see why his well-argued case cut little ice with much of its likely audience: he addresses every argument for diminished aid to Africa except the one which will have weighed most with an incoming government: would an increase in aid along the lines the ambassador urges, in fact have achieved the human and policy goals he lists?

Sir Brian, a prolific blogger in retirement, recalls on his website (www.barder.com/ephems) that his African valedictory was given

> a far more strictly limited domestic and global distribution than was then customary for this kind of document. The sentiments it expressed seemed controversial, even provocative, in the climate of the time; there was some suggestion (as I learned later on the grapevine) that when I wrote it I must have forgotten that there was no longer a Labour government in office at home.

Baroness Lynda Chalker, the Conservative Minister for Overseas Development at the time, was said by some to have ordered that the despatch be suppressed. She became, however, a considerable champion of aid to Africa.

BRITISH HIGH COMMISSION
LAGOS
7 January 1991

The Rt Hon Douglas Hurd CBE MP
London

Sir,

DOES AFRICA MATTER?

Next month I leave Lagos and complete 17 years' involvement in African affairs, 10 of them dealing with west Africa or southern Africa in London, and 7 as head of mission in the two most populous countries of black Africa, Ethiopia and Nigeria. Tidily, I end where I began, with Nigeria, whose constitutional and political problems I first tried to grapple with as a new entrant in the Colonial Office in Great Smith Street a third of a century ago. I leave Nigeria with many of the same problems unresolved – not, I think, for any lack of effort by ourselves as the colonial power or by the Nigerians themselves, but chiefly because of the inherent difficulties we bequeathed when we gummed together such a big, unwieldy entity in such a casual manner 90 years ago.

As I leave the continent, Africa ranks at its lowest in any British Government's scale of global priorities for 100 years or more. There are intense pressures, from Ministers downwards, for sharp cuts in the resources we devote to Africa in money and manpower; and for some reduction in our commitments in Africa . . . As I shake the African dust from willing feet, it is natural to wonder why this down-grading of Africa is taking place; whether it is politically and economically justified; and what might be the implications for British interests.

Why are we demoting Africa in our priorities?
There seem to be 5 main factors:

(a) *Decolonisation fatigue.* Shedding our colonial responsibilities in Africa has been a long, wearing process, bringing us more obloquy than ovation and often yielding more disappointments than evident successes. For 3 decades, completing this process – especially in Kenya and then Rhodesia – and ridding ourselves of the international incubus of our involvement in apartheid South Africa have been our overriding aims in the continent. Now that they are achieved (or, in the case of South Africa, within sight of being achieved), it is natural to feel that we are entitled to turn our attention elsewhere. To recognise, define and substitute new needs and objectives requires an effort of imagination and will that does not come easily to the exhausted.

(b) *Humanitarian fatigue.* For decades we have given aid to Africa – sometimes generously, sometimes not. We have responded to famines with humanitarian relief aid, although often without the development aid needed to avert renewed famine in the future; and to poverty (in countries where we have recognised special responsibilities) with development aid. Yet we see a situation in Africa where poverty and need are as great as ever: in some places, greater than ever. It is understandable enough that some should begin to see Africa as a bottomless pit, and resources directed to Africa as wasted – understandable, but profoundly misguided. It is a short step from this to the conviction that Africa's failure to make better use of the aid it has received is Africa's fault: a notion with a big enough germ of truth to be all too plausible, especially in the eyes of those who are charged with cutting public expenditure in all directions . . .

(c) *The end of the cold war.* As long as the Soviet Union and its erstwhile allies were competing for third world hearts and minds, the west perceived the penalties of turning its back on the more western-oriented of the developing countries as unacceptably high. That constraint has gone.

(d) *The lack of an obvious economic role for Africa.* Until relatively recently, Africa has been regarded as a useful – even necessary – source of cheap raw materials, and a worthwhile market for the developed world's finished products. But as cheaper artificial substitutes for Africa's raw materials have become available, as well as for other reasons, the terms of trade have turned against Africa, with disastrous consequences for the continent's earning power; and thus for its value as a market for the west's exports. The process has been further aggravated by corrupt and incompetent management of production processes, leading to falls in the quality and reliability of African traded goods . . .

(e) *Perceived mismanagement by Africans of their own affairs*. Again, undeniably true, although some at least of Africa's most pressing problems are not in fact attributable to the short-comings of African leaders. However, the issue is not who is to blame for the African mess, but whether we can safely and cheaply afford to ignore it.

It is evident that all 5 factors have substance. But the striking thing which they have in common is that they explain growing indifference to Africa: they do not *justify* it, nor do they demonstrate that indifference is necessarily in our own interests.

Are we politically or economically justified in reducing our commitment to Africa?
Africa certainly has little commercial significance. In 1988 it accounted for a mere 2.61% of world trade . . . However, the African countries which produce and export oil (and gas, now or soon), while relatively few in number, include Nigeria, which alone contains almost a quarter of the population of black Africa; and energy supplies from an area which is not subject to the stresses and conflicts of the Middle East are not to be sneezed at . . .

Politically, the end of the great confrontation between international Leninism and western liberal values makes Africa more, not less, relevant to the kind of world we and our children are going to live in. The remaining global fault-line is that which separates the rich white (and, increasingly, brown or honorary white) section of humanity from the poor and mainly black. It is this division more than any other which now threatens future conflict, insecurity, violence and destruction. How this explosive incongruity comes to be resolved – bloodily or peacefully – will depend significantly on events in Africa. The escalating clash between western values and radical Islam, which is in part a function of the rich/poor, white/black divide, will also play itself out in Africa among other areas: the seeds of that conflict have already been planted, the first shoots manifestly appearing. It is difficult to see how a western country which aspires to a global role can contemplate even partial withdrawal of interest from one of the two or three most pressing issues of our generation; disclaim its responsibility for carrying its share of the burden; or seek to reduce its ability to play a part in bringing about a resolution of the next act in the drama.

Finally, we have to consider the potential for a wide-spread economic and social collapse in Africa . . . There is at last in Africa an almost universal realisation of the calamitous mistakes and mismanagement of the decades since independence and a willingness to put things right. But it becomes more and more evident that Africa's problems simply cannot be solved by Africa's own unaided efforts . . . A very large-scale transfer of real resources to the poor countries of Africa is an absolute necessity if Africa is to stand any chance of overcoming the enormous problems of declining demand for its raw materials and agricultural products; foreign indebtedness; environmental degradation; and population growth at rates which outstrip the increase in both national income and labour productivity. All these problems can be overcome, but not without western help on an unprecedented scale.

If that help is not forthcoming, the prospect of a general collapse, although still only a worst case scenario, is bound to become much more real. We cannot always base our plans on the gloomiest assumptions, but we need to be clear about the possible consequences of the policies we adopt. Increasing impoverishment and unemployment in the towns, spreading break-down of basic services (including health, communications, food distribution networks), failure of the security forces to contain violence and theft, growing inter-tribal and inter-regional conflicts – all this can already be seen in embryo in many parts of Africa; and if it becomes general, it will cause a swift descent into massive starvation, disease, violence and collapse. These will in turn prompt significant movements of populations in search of food, safety and a future for their children. A disaster on such a scale could not be quarantined inside Africa. The rest of the world could not turn its back while more than half a billion people were exposed to an experience of this character. But once the collapse begins, the cost of arresting it will rapidly become immense. Prevention is cheaper as well as better than cure . . .

. . . The aid performance of the 17 major donors, including the Twelve,[1] in 1987 tells, from our point of view, a sorry story. Britain's aid as a percentage of GDP was the lowest of any of the 17 apart from Austria (an anyway embarrassing analogue) and the United States (whose total aid programme was more than 4 times as big as ours).

Although a healthy share of the aid which we do give is allocated to Africa, the size of our aid in total is not something to be proud of. The promise of some increase is welcome, but nothing so far envisaged comes near to matching the scale of the need or the extent of our responsibilities as Europeans . . .

Conclusions

Nothing that is likely to occur in the foreseeable future in central or south America, in Asia or the Pacific, is likely to impinge half as directly on British and western interests as the danger of degeneration or outright collapse in Africa. Only events in Europe itself, and arguably in the Middle East, should be rated as of obviously higher priority for Britain; and whereas in the rest of Europe and in the Middle East Britain is not the principal player, in most of Africa we are; no other country has the close links, historical ties and depth of understanding with Africa that Britain has built up in the past 100 years and continues to enjoy (if that is the right word). Our influence in Africa and capacity for understanding its dynamics are important elements in our international standing. This is a national asset which, once thrown away in a fit of instant cheese-paring, could never be retrieved.

Against this background, for Britain to start a process of disengagement from Africa, principally for reasons of financial stringency, would be widely and justifiably seen as implying at best a sad failure to understand and accept our own history; and at worst as a betrayal of that history which others in the world, and many among our own compatriots, will neither understand nor forgive.

I am sending copies of this despatch to the Minister for Overseas Development and to HM Representatives or High

Commissioners at Nairobi, Addis Ababa, Pretoria, Accra,
UKMIS New York and UKREP Brussels.

I am
Sir
Yours faithfully

Brian Barder

1. *the Twelve*: Until 1993 the European Economic Community consisted of
twelve members.

~

'The Bosnian poison has circulated in the veins of the UN'

LORD HANNAY, HM PERMANENT REPRESENTATIVE
TO THE UNITED NATIONS, JULY 1995

Diplomacy used to be a largely bilateral affair. Through our ambassadors and other representatives abroad, Britain would talk directly with foreign governments, and where deals were struck, two parties would usually be at the table. But over the past thirty years or so, things have changed; the institutions of the European Union have grown in stature, along with international organizations such as the UN, and nowadays much more of what the Foreign Office does takes place within their confines. Today, multilateral diplomacy is often where the action is.

David Hannay's career saw him in the thick of that action. In 1970 he helped negotiate Britain's entry into the European Community, and for most of the twenty-five years that followed Hannay continued to work on European affairs in a succession of posts, culminating in his appointment as the

UK's Permanent Representative to the EC, an ambassador-grade post. In 1990 he moved to New York to take up the same role at the United Nations. His valedictory written upon his retirement five years later is a masterly survey of the difficulties into which the UN had by then fallen. It reads as sharply today as it did in 1995 – and gives some background to today's complaints.

UNITED KINGDOM MISSION
TO THE UNITED NATIONS
NEW YORK
26 July 1995

The Rt Hon Malcolm Rifkind QC MP
Secretary of State for Foreign and Commonwealth Affairs
Foreign and Commonwealth Office
London

Sir,

UNITED NATIONS: VALEDICTORY

I arrived in this post almost exactly five years ago. They have been tumultuous and innovative years, with the UN in the thick of the action, in a way it had hardly ever been before and never over such a sustained period. Now, with slightly over one-third of all Security Council resolutions adopted in the United Nations' first fifty years negotiated and voted in that time and some 20,000 outgoing telegrams from this post later, it is the moment to take stock and to make some kind of overall assessment.

Three developments, which occurred far from New York and in which the UN played little direct role, fundamentally transformed the background to all its work. The end of the Cold War and the collapse of the Soviet Union brought a whole series of disparate consequences . . . In South Africa the fall of the apartheid system and the emergence of a multi-party democracy was almost as revolutionary in its impact . . . And in the Middle East the transformation of the peace process from a slogan lacking any real credibility into a reality producing steady, if painful, progress removed a threat to peace which had burst into dangerous and divisive warfare on a number of occasions.

The effect of all this on the UN was largely, if not exclusively, beneficial. When Saddam Hussein fatally miscalculated the international reaction and sought to wipe Kuwait off the map in 1990, the UN was the means chosen to reverse his aggression; and it worked . . . Elsewhere, in Namibia, in Cambodia, in El Salvador, in Mozambique and now, hopefully, at last in Angola too, the UN helped to broker and then to implement peace settlements which put an end to a string of civil wars . . . But success brought with it excessive expectations and overstretch. Heady new wine was being poured into some pretty old and cracked bottles. The UN's peacekeeping machinery creaked and groaned as the number of active operations jumped to seventeen, the peacekeepers deployed went from about 10,000 to nearly 100,000 and budgets doubled and doubled again. The time taken to deploy troops lengthened, command and control problems surfaced with a vengeance and that dread disease 'mission creep' became the talk of the town. In Somalia what began as a laudable and successful humanitarian mission to put an end to mass starvation, exacerbated by the ruthless manoeuvring of warlords, slid gradually across what has come to be known as the 'Mogadishu line', when the peacekeepers themselves became a party in the civil strife and the level of internecine warfare was actually greater when the UN was there than after it left. In Rwanda three lightly armed battalions, sent to monitor a peace settlement, suddenly found themselves in the middle of genocidal massacres which they had no means of checking; and, when no single troop contributor showed the slightest inclination to despatch troops until the military die was cast, the UN was left with part of the blame for what had happened and much of the responsibility for clearing up the mess.

But of course the UN's worst headaches have come in the former Yugoslavia, in Bosnia in particular. Here too, as in Iraq, the UN was the international community's chosen means of dealing with a major instance of new world disorder. But on this occasion it was denied the firmness of policy direction and the sufficiency of resources which characterised the handling of Iraq. The underlying problems in the former Yugoslavia were in any case far more complex and far more intractable. This was no simple war of aggression which could be ended by the expulsion of the aggressor from the territory of its victim. Rather it was a complex hybrid, a civil war with a strong dash of aggression, in which any settlement had to find an appropriate place for all the parties. The objectives pursued, of containment, of the avoidance of direct external involvement in the fighting, of humanitarian relief and of fostering a peace process were sound enough. But the insufficiency of the resources supplied for the tasks in hand, the endless, kaleidoscopic shifting in the attitudes of the main players trying to manage the crisis, the United States in particular, and above all the stubbornness, brutality and deviousness of the parties, none of whom has so far wholeheartedly sought a peaceful settlement, has resulted in an operation which looks more like a failure than it ought to. The Bosnian poison has circulated in the veins of the UN as it has in those of NATO and the EU; it may not be lethal, but it has certainly been debilitating.

Now, in the middle of 1995, the triumph of the Gulf War and the success of several other UN missions stand in the deep shadow cast by Bosnia and Somalia. The pendulum which swung too far towards euphoria after the Gulf War has swung too far towards despair. From being an organisation which was wrongly thought capable of solving everything, the UN now tends, equally wrongly, to be regarded as incapable of solving anything . . .

. . . We will need however to be a bit cautious and conservative about what we ask the UN to take on in future. It needs a higher success rate than it has recently achieved if it is not to be discredited. It cannot afford more Bosnias and Somalias. So enforcement should be off limits, to be undertaken either by 'coalitions of the willing', if possible with UN authorisation, or not at all.

~

'Time to look at the legalisation of drugs'

RICHARD THOMAS, HM HIGH COMMISSIONER
TO BARBADOS AND THE EASTERN
CARIBBEAN, FEBRUARY 1998

Further extracts from Thomas's despatch are on p. 322. Note that this Richard Thomas is not to be confused with his earlier namesake whose valedictory from Puerto Rico appears on p. 115.

Close proximity for the last three years to the international drugs control scene has not reinforced my faith in the prescriptions at present favoured to deal with the narco menace.

Britain spends millions, maybe hundreds of millions, of pounds every year, at home and overseas, to try to stem the flow, fight the traffickers and cure the addiction. So do all other developed countries. The United States spends billions. And yet the supply of drugs, soft and hard, shows no signs of diminishing. On the contrary, it is growing. Drugs are now the most traded commodity after oil, and almost all the trade is illegal. So not only do we have thousands, maybe millions, of people ruining their health world-wide, at the expense of scarce healthcare which could be put to other, more beneficial purposes; we also have world-wide organised crime whose sole purpose is to produce, transport and distribute these evil substances in order that the trade can grow still greater, and its perpetrators even richer. One of their objectives – perhaps the most horrible of all – is to ensure the dependence and addiction of those involved along the trading routes and at the destination. It is the criminal nature of the trade, with its ruthlessness and secondary effects such as money laundering, that first drew our attention in the Eastern Caribbean to the effect which it was having on regional security. Drugs criminals will stop at nothing, including the subversion of small, fragile democracies. If they can suborn places like Antigua and St Vincent now, who knows where they will stop in the end?

It is time that counter-narcotics strategists started seriously to examine the merits of legalisation of all drugs, not just cannabis. There must be another way of controlling drugs abuse, and that way could well in the end turn out to be a mix of medical prescriptions for registered addicts, treatment and fiscal regulation, as for alcohol and tobacco. At present anyone who advances legalisation as an alternative policy is dismissed as simplistic. Three years of work in support of classic law-enforcement methods, with their patent lack of effectiveness, have begun to propel me into the simplistic school of thought. Legalise drugs and you pull the rug from under the feet of half the world's organised criminals. You also, in the Caribbean, remove the main threat to the region's security.

7. Privileges and Privations

Someone once said that, distilled, the essence of diplomacy is 'protocol, vitriol and alcohol' – but nobody mentioned the sweat. Privilege and privation make a strange cocktail, a cup it has been many diplomats' experience to sip through a long career, though times have changed from the days in the 1940s when (as one despatch put it) 'Administration was primitive and gentlemanly. You could take overseas a "reasonable" amount of luggage and servants. The borderline of reasonableness lay between pianos and grand pianos.'

Along with the perks, the hardships could go beyond the physical. Being an ambassador was more than a day job: spouse, and sometimes children too, were bound into a routine of entertaining and being entertained. You, your house, and often your family, were always, at least a little bit, on parade. Offering hospitality went with the job. Domestically, there were cities and societies that presented particular challenges, and those diplomats whose career has taken them away from the Service's easily defensible functions in the EU, NATO, the UN, the GATT, the WTO and other acronyms, and away from Britain's First World working relationships within Europe and with the United States and Russia, have sometimes felt thrust into what, with bitter sarcasm, we used to call the 'Outer Darkness': no doubt a word-play on the division made by the despised 1960s Duncan Review, between an Area of Concentration and an Outer Area (see Chapter 2).

Doing a sophisticated job, with the trappings of a sophisticated lifestyle, in an unsophisticated place, hasn't got any easier as resources have been cut. Successive performance reviews of the FCO as an institution have tried to create grids of goals, roles, objectives and means, to find ways of measuring and ordering priorities, to tighten the definition of entitlements, and – ever and anon – to save money.

Until very recently diplomats had to retire at sixty – at the height (many thought) of their powers. Women – admitted to the Diplomatic Service since 1946 but under special rules, limited to 10 per cent of the intake – were paid 20 per cent less than men doing the same job and they had to resign when they married. Equal pay was conceded in 1955 (fully implemented only in 1961) and the marriage bar was rescinded only in 1972.

'There is an outside vision of diplomacy and of ambassadors,' Sir Christopher Meyer told us, 'that is impossible to eradicate from the public imagination and particularly from the imagination of journalists, whose Pavlovian default position when they write about ambassadors is to write about envoys quaffing champagne and sucking on cherries dipped in asses' milk and that they are all living the most glorious life. Now, let's not beat about the bush – when I was entertaining Americans, they did not expect fish fingers; if I was going to influence members of the American cabinet or White House I didn't serve them fish fingers. I enjoyed a high standard of living when I was ambassador to the United States but the balance to that was having two tours in our Embassy in Moscow in the depths of the Cold War when Russia was the Soviet Union and Moscow in those days was quite clearly a hardship post. It was a hardship post for all kinds of reasons.

'A hardship post is a place where the material and psychological conditions of service are particularly arduous. The pressure put upon you by these circumstances actually makes it difficult for you to do your job. You get paid a bit more money for serving in a hardship post and I think it gains you some extra pensionable years.' In Moscow, said Meyer, hardship meant: 'difficulty in getting fresh fruit and vegetables and decent food to eat on a daily basis; it meant a highly restricted movement because the Soviet authorities didn't like diplomats travelling around the country, or even far beyond the city of Moscow, so you were in a claustrophobic bubble from the moment you arrived. And then there was the psychological pressure, which was unrelenting, of the old KGB constantly up to tricks to ensnare you in some embarrassing blackmailable situation, as they tried several times on me. I actually found that type of hardship stimulating and terrifically exciting, but for some people it was terribly oppressive and they didn't withstand it very well.'

Lord (Chris) Patten seconded that view: 'I've seen over the years the Foreign Office subjected to one round of cuts after another and I've seen it put in the dock again and again to demonstrate that it's useful; and I think it's completely absurd. I've always believed that part of the problem is that you get some of the Stakhanovites in the public-spending division of the Treasury going home from Waterloo on a wet cold Tuesday night in February, with papers in their box including the latest public spending bid from the Foreign Office. They sit down in their little corner of the compartment, damp and cold, at half past eight or quarter to nine in the evening and have this vision of diplomats – of their equivalents in the Foreign Office – slipping into swimming pools in tropical climes with butlers in white bumfreezers waiting on the edge with crystal cut glass with gin and tonic clinking away. And it's a complete nonsense. Of course ambassadors very often live in nice houses and have staff, but they are also just as likely to be living in pretty difficult places with junior staff who are having a tough time. And they do a very, very good job.'

Denis MacShane told us that 'I stayed recently since I stopped being a minister with an ambassador in one of the most important posts in Europe. I was given one of the guest bedrooms and I froze that night because he didn't have enough money to fully heat his embassy . . . I don't think the Foreign Office, as part of the Whitehall machine, is anything other than quite mean and quite hard.

'There's an endless argument: should we maintain the splendid embassy in Paris? Well, should we maintain Buckingham Palace or Lancaster House? I think on the whole yes. Ambassadors are only there for a short time, and if we sold the embassy in Paris for a little fortune now and shunted the fellow out to the suburbs and put him into an anonymous office block somewhere I just don't think anyone would come to see him.'

Warming to his theme (though in fact the Office pays boarding-school fees for many British diplomats posted abroad) Mr MacShane continued: 'The question of how you educate your children is a huge problem. The French have a network of international Lycées in every major capital city, we don't . . . You can't seriously expect a man to go to Afghanistan or Iraq, places where ambassadors have been kidnapped or diplomats have been killed – and have his children tootling around on the pavement playing hopscotch.' MacShane has a point, certainly – though one is tempted to ask if, in this case, it is not the minister who has gone a little native.

~

'A really good man for Bogotá'

SIR ANDREW NOBLE, HM AMBASSADOR
TO MEXICO, OCTOBER 1960

The first post abroad in which I served was Rio de Janeiro, almost thirty years ago. In those days the Diplomatic Service regarded Latin America as a jungle, better perhaps than Central Africa, but no more important in the scale of world values. We paid lip service to the importance of the A.B.C. countries, Argentina, Brazil and Chile, largely because of the important British investments, and therefore dividends, to be protected; to be sent to any other Latin-American post was banishment. The Service view was aptly parodied by a small picture hanging in the room of Mr. Collier (now Sir L. Collier), the Head of the Northern Department. This reproduced one of his father's problem pictures, which showed an older man sitting behind a desk in serious pose; opposite him was a young man clearly struggling with tortured apprehension. The caption below described the older man as the Diplomatic Private Secretary, then master of our postings, and put into his mouth the ominous sentence: 'We want a really good man for Bogotá.'

∽

'My first experience as Her Majesty's Ambassador was to shave out of a kettle'

ROGER PINSENT, HM AMBASSADOR TO
NICARAGUA, JULY 1967

More from Pinsent can be found on p. 106.

Perhaps it may be useful at this point to give some comments on the personal aspects of life at Her Majesty's Embassy in Managua, Nicaragua. Managua is undoubtedly a difficult post, both from the point of view of climate and amenities, and because the staff position is always critical, leaving virtually no margin for leave or sickness. Fortunately, we now have an air-conditioned office ... The main problem from our point of view has, of course, been the necessity of living in a totally inadequate Embassy Residence without proper room for entertaining or living, or even basic facilities such as hot water – my first experience as Her Majesty's Ambassador was to shave out of a kettle ...

In spite of the difficulties, unpleasantness and even violence to which we have been subjected at times during our tour in Managua, I must admit that we leave the country with some regret. Not, I may say, for Managua itself, but paradoxically for the sunny Nicaraguan climate as experienced in the mountains above the two great lakes and among the hundreds of little volcanic islands on Lake Nicaragua with their palms, mangoes and other tropical fruit, to which spice is added by the presence of sharks.

~

*'I hope that my successor will unearth
no such skeletons of mine'*

SIR DENIS WRIGHT, HM AMBASSADOR
TO IRAN, APRIL 1971

I now leave Tehran with much sadness but feeling that after eight years it is time to go. In the 160-odd years since regular diplomatic relations have existed between the United Kingdom and Persia only Charles Alison (1860–72) served longer than I have done as Her Majesty's Representative. Alison left behind him an illegitimate daughter, patriotically named Victoria; a packet of trouble arising from his purchase of land in what is now part of our Gulhak compound; and his own grave in the old Armenian church near the site of our original 'Mission House'. While I hope that my successor will unearth no such skeletons of mine, at least he will find a new and well appointed Protestant Cemetery . . .

~

'Each slice of smoked salmon being folded round a gold half-sovereign'

THOMAS SHAW, HM AMBASSADOR TO MOROCCO, NOVEMBER 1971

A glimpse here of the high life; and its dangers. The spring party which Shaw describes was certainly lavish. The 'later birthday-party at Skhirat' however, to which he refers at the end of this extract, was in fact the scene of an attempted coup. Hundreds of soldiers stormed the royal palace, where the diplomatic corps had assembled to mark the King's forty-second birthday. The Libyan-inspired plot failed, but only after five hours of desperate fighting, in which the Belgian ambassador was killed by a bullet. Shaw told a newspaper reporter afterwards: 'Bullets were whizzing all around us. Back at the swimming pool, I found the Yugoslav ambassador, who had long partisan experience in World War II, lying on the floor with a chair over his head, so I lay down beside him and did likewise. Then I saw a hand grenade come flying over the wall.' The soldiers had apparently been drugged, and tricked into storming the palace, believing the diplomats were holding the King hostage. Upon his appearance, they cheered and threw down their arms. King Hassan told foreign press the ringleaders were unlikely to divulge much information in prison: 'I am afraid it may no longer be possible to interview them as they will probably be executed by firing squad.'

The dinner-party which the King gave for the Diplomatic Corps in the spring was characteristic of his taste for lavish display regardless of growing popular criticism. The occasion – I forget whether it was his second son's first birthday or his elder son's circumcision – was not impressive, nor were the guests, principally ourselves and our wives, in need of being impressed. A Russian choir was flown from Paris to entertain us; we were lavishly fed, each slice of smoked salmon being folded round a gold half-sovereign; and to conclude we were taken on to the Palace roof for an hour's breath-taking display of fireworks activated personally by the King from a console of press-buttons and accompanied by a 'Son et Lumière' commentary in Arabic. I am told that Messrs Brocks going rate for an hour is about £10,000. As the spring night was cold, the luckier guests were provided with scarlet cloaks taken from the backs of the Royal Guard on duty as lantern-bearers in the gardens below. The rest of us shivered while flocks of pigeons and storks wheeled distracted above in the pyrotechnic glare – altogether a party which was a worthy predecessor of the later birthday-party at Skhirat.

∼

'*The Embassy staff have kept up their water-skiing despite the proximity of explosions*'

ANTHONY WILLIAMS, HM AMBASSADOR
TO CAMBODIA, JANUARY 1973

... [A] tribute to the succeeding generations of this Embassy's staff, during my time, comes specially appropriately. I am glad to record that no member of it – or of the community – has suffered death or even injury during the fairly regular rocket, *plastique* and commando attacks which have punctuated the whole of my sojourn in Phnom Penh. But it has always, of course, been at the back of our minds that it could happen – and to ourselves. The enterprising cheerfulness with which this Embassy at all levels has 'carried on as usual' – and indeed got a lot of fun out of this life under siege – has caused admiring remarks, not only from more pusillanimous colleagues, but from the Khmers themselves . . . The fact that we have never, like most missions here at one time or another, started shipping out our families or stopped children coming out for holidays . . . even the fact that the Embassy staff have kept up their water-skiing despite the proximity of explosions – all these have, I think, genuinely helped the Khmers to hold on and believe in themselves.

~

'"You aren't paid for doing things: you are paid for being here"'

SIR PATRICK HANCOCK, HM AMBASSADOR
TO ITALY, JUNE 1974

A lot is written nowadays about the job of an Ambassador. To my mind, the most unsatisfactory thing about the job is that it is often not clear what an Ambassador ought to be doing or what he is trying to achieve. Is he being sufficiently active? Or, on the other hand, is he bothering people unnecessarily? Does he report too much or too little? Does he know the right people? Does he travel too much or not enough? And so on. Most Embassies have slack moments, when an

Ambassador wonders if he is earning his keep. At such times, I take comfort from the scene in a long-forgotten play by Maurice Baring, in which the staff of an Embassy complain to the Ambassador that they do not have enough to do. The Ambassador dismisses them with the remark: 'You aren't paid for doing things: you are paid for being here.'

~

'Our specific calling's snare is drink'

RALPH SELBY, HM AMBASSADOR
TO NORWAY, MARCH 1975

Ralph Selby's career valedictory from Oslo was the starting point for Parting Shots. *Back in 1975 it passed through my hands as a junior desk officer (see the main Introduction to this book). My signature can be seen on the cover sheet, along with the handwritten comment 'I think this is a very good despatch.' The image of the ambassador creeping along corridors late at night to collect shoes for polishing certainly sticks in the memory – as do his views on alcohol.*

This was the first valedictory that we unearthed from the vast stacks at the National Archives. Several hundred despatches down the road, its refreshing mix of eccentricity and candour still stands out. (Sadly, Sir John Russell's final valedictory, to which Selby frequently refers, is not to be found at Kew, although his Brazilian sign-off is a treat – see p. 51.)

Selby actually wrote two valedictories in 1975, and the record shows 475 copies were printed of his 'serious' effort on the political situation in Norway (see p. 213). But the broader Whitehall audience was denied the chance to read these,

Selby's less po-faced 'animadversions' on his thirty-eight-year career. They failed to move my then boss, Christopher Hulse, who wrote: 'On the whole I find these slightly quaint . . . I doubt if it deserves printing.' Another officer scribbled: 'He says a lot of sensible things, though I agree that the style is a little bit "knife and fork".'

The Department did make a few copies, for the Personnel Department, Chief Clerk and Permanent Under Secretary ('very much voluntary reading').

RESTRICTED

BRITISH EMBASSY
OSLO
12 March 1975

The Right Honourable
James Callaghan MP
etc etc etc

Sir

Two senior members of the Service have expressed the view that the animadversions about the Service, frequently included in retiring Ambassadors' valedictory despatches, should more properly be incorporated in a separate despatch. As one of the Ambassadors concerned was my boss in my last post, I feel I should follow his advice. I am of course very conscious of my place – specifically, No 109 in the latest Diplomatic Service List, which is no very big advance on No 209 in the 1938 List. Nevertheless I have for some months been able to claim that I have served longer in Her Majesty's Diplomatic Service than anyone else now in it; and my experience extends over two generations, and indeed in some respects over three, for my wife's grandfather was, like my father, an Ambassador. My own first post abroad was Cairo in 1921. I was then five . . .

... [D]iplomats of the old school ... did not have to deal with such a flood of paper. Sir Terence Shone, who was High Commissioner in India when I was posted there in 1947, said that at his first post abroad his Ambassador had refused to allow a typewriter to be used in his Embassy (Lisbon). Any copies of despatches made had to be written in long hand. The flood of paper which has thus grown within a single generation is fantastic. Far too much is copied or repeated to too many posts. Papers containing 40 paragraphs, of which one might be of interest to all, are copied everywhere, without deletion of the 39 paragraphs which might be of interest to a limited number of posts only. Telegrams seem often to be sent because there is still a widespread impression that they are the only form of communication which cuts any ice in the Foreign Office. The summaries of printed despatches are often not summaries at all, but mere catalogues of contents. At the end of it all I do not feel we are always particularly well informed about matters which are of major concern to the countries in which we are serving.

In this latter context increased contact between ministers and ambassadors abroad is, as Sir John Russell inferred, very desirable ... I am quite sure a conscious effort should be made in London to make Ambassadors visiting the United Kingdom feel that Ministers and Under Secretaries would actually like to see them when they are at home, even if in reality it would, as most of us suspect, bore them to sobs. I am also quite sure, having been exiled for 20 years, that it is a great mistake to leave people abroad too long. It is impossible to be an effective Ambassador without a relatively recent acquaintance not merely with the senior hierarchy of the Office but also with the procedures by which decisions are reached at home.

What is an effective Ambassador? Sir Patrick Hancock expressed the self questioning on this score which must I imagine occur to most Ambassadors. There seems to be a widespread impression that a principal characteristic of pre-war diplomacy was 'cookie pushing'[1]. My father used indeed to tell me that the quality of an Ambassador was determined by the skill of his cook. A friend of his who was ambassador in Paris in the twenties complained that he was nothing but a glorified head waiter. But I often wonder myself whether one is not, and ought not still to be very much the same thing, albeit rather less glorified . . .

If entertaining is to be effective in a country where the standards of entertaining are high, the possibility of achieving high standards must obviously be maintained. Beautiful embassies must not wantonly be discarded because they seem to belong to a bygone age. Visiting Tribune Group MPs who argue for such a course, seem unable to understand that it is perfectly possible even in a socialist paradise for people to be 'simple in their lives and splendid in their public ways'[2]. A modern Ambassador's life is not always quite as luxurious as it still sometimes looks to outsiders, or even to some members of the Service itself. When for instance my more exigent house guests put their boots out to be cleaned, they are cleaned all right, and I hope to Brigade of Guard standards. But I have in fact to clean them myself. I do not nowadays find it easy to recruit staff who are willing to lick other people's boots. Admittedly the government pay for an adequate domestic staff though usually alas on a scale adequate to recruit them a year or so previously. But when, as is inevitable, staff are in due course lured away to better paid jobs elsewhere, they are not always easy to replace at short notice. One often has to take and train up from scratch what one can find, be they but stray, cycling Sikh students as found for me here on one occasion by my Naval Attaché while sauntering in Frogner Park. They also have to be man-managed. To retain the services of my first butler, I found myself organising and eventually playing in an Embassy soccer team, a game which I had never played since I was twelve.

All that is fun. With all the difficulties and anxieties, we have loved living in this perfectly beautiful house. There are however some much more serious disadvantages about service abroad. The constant shifts of abode become more painful each time. Floods, riots or even souvenir hunting by guests are bound to take their toll on personal possessions. Hard climates inflict their own wounds on the unlucky. Above all the children suffer. As indicated in the first paragraph of this despatch I have had experience over three generations in this field. On the basis of it, I would guess that in about 50 per cent of cases, service abroad constitutes for the children concerned a very seriously unsettling influence in their lives, which the broader horizons offered do not fully offset. I hasten to add that I personally was not affected in this particular way. From the age of 7 to nearly 18 I had the enormous advantage, in my own view, of having my parents serving at home.

Sir John Russell referred to the prospect for most diplomats of impoverished retirement. I hope myself, despite inflation, to escape relatively lightly; but it is certainly true that while the Service offers people a higher standard of living abroad, it also engenders expensive habits which are not all that easy to break. It is moreover I suppose one of the few careers in which it is, in a sense, indecent to save anything. Those who sold their houses when posted abroad must, unlike their colleagues who stayed at home, look forward to a much more modest establishment when they return, unless they are fortunate enough to inherit something better. A returning diplomat obviously has few friends in the United Kingdom and is faced with the problem of making from his more modest surroundings a new set of friends in an England which seems, depressingly, to be growing more rather than less conscious of social status. Many of the friends he will have made abroad will, inevitably, come from the richer elements of society. These all promise to come and accept his hospitality in his retirement abode, where naturally there will be no allowances to help him cope.

It is true, as Sir John Russell suggests, that honours used in the old days, to offer some compensation for all this; and it is, in my view, absurd to argue, as some do, that honours are fundamentally an irrelevance and that it is a sufficient honour in itself to represent Her Majesty abroad. Of course it is while it lasts. But journalists in England do not seem to hold the job of an Ambassador in any very high esteem. The appointment of my successor to this post was the third to be mentioned among the day's appointments listed in *The Times*, and the tenth among those listed in the *Financial Times*. It is still essentially honours which give to the public an indication of the esteem in which jobs are and ought to be held. I am not however at all sure that this argues for more honours for the Diplomatic Service. I personally do not think that it is inappropriate that Ambassadors in Grade 3 posts should be equated with Major Generals. I think it would be very wrong to try to attract into the Diplomatic Service, now I believe some 6,000 strong, the calibre of candidate it was legitimate to try to attract into a service of 210. We still need the high flyers for the big jobs. I am not sure that one needs the same calibre of brain for the lesser jobs. If I had a son, which I have not, and were asked by him for my advice, which I would not be, as to whether to join the Diplomatic Service or not, I would I think be tempted to say 'yes' if he was an Oxbridge First, or an Oxbridge Third. If he had a good brain but not of the top calibre, I am not at all sure that he would not serve his own and his country's interests better by using his talents elsewhere. I have enormously enjoyed my years in the Diplomatic Service, but I am very conscious of the fact that I have been an observer rather than an actor on the world's stage.

While in fact brains are still obviously important in the Service, they are not the only thing that matters. Whenever I have had occasion at this post to express an opinion about the qualifications which I would like to see in prospective members of my staff, I have always laid a certain stress on that degree of physical fitness which will enable people to ski. This is because skiing is what all Norwegians do in Winter, and enjoy doing. My advice in this regard never seems to have been taken very seriously, except perhaps in one instance; and I am bound to say that it is my firm belief that more attention could with advantage be paid to the merits of physical fitness and stamina for diplomatic life generally. Apart from the hymn's 'gilded baits of worldly love'[3] our specific calling's snare is drink; and it is profoundly depressing to see the number of members of the Service who are engaged in the process of destroying themselves by it, without any serious attempt to apply the remedies of which there are at least two. One is total abstention each year from hard liquor for a prolonged period whether over Lent or the annual holiday or both. A second is exercise. And quite apart from its potential, health giving aspects, an ability to indulge in any sport available is an enormous help in Diplomatic life. Half the fun I have had in the Service and half the useful contacts I have made, have been made through sport; and I have enjoyed and profited, from the sports which have brought me into contact with humble people, just as much as I have enjoyed the sports which have brought me, literally, into contact with Kings.

Before concluding I would like to say that I am profoundly sad to be leaving the comradeship which exists in the Diplomatic Service from the highest grade to the lowest. It is frankly amazing that it does still exist and that morale has throughout remained so high. For 10 years the impression that I, and many of my contemporaries, derived from a visit to Personnel Department was that the greatest service that we could render to our colleagues and the state would be to drop dead . . . It is, however, in my view, very important that members of the Diplomatic Service should be made to feel, especially in the letters appointing them to new posts, that they are actually wanted . . .

. . . It used to be a convention in the pre-war Diplomatic Services overseas, that people who had had the honour of representing Her Majesty abroad should not visit capitals where they had done so, for a period of at least three years. Does such a convention or something like it still exist? If it does, it should be more widely known. If it has fallen into desuetude it should I think be revived in some form or other although, I hope it will not preclude my paying strictly private visits to the mountains and fjords of this beautiful country in which,

Sir,
It has been my honour
to be
Your obedient Servant

R. Selby

1. *'cookie pushing'*: A term which has gained traction in the United States as a pejorative description of diplomats' work; talk-radio hosts often refer to 'those pinstriped cookie pushers in the State Department'. In *Brewer's Dictionary of Phrase and Fable* it denotes a junior diplomat playing the waiter at embassy functions, forcing canapés on to unwilling guests.

2. *'simple in their lives . . . public ways'*: From 'These Things Shall Be'. John Ireland's idealistic 1937 hymn was much sung by Labour politicians and public schoolboys.

3. *'gilded baits of worldly love'*: Charles Wesley's hymn from 1749. Bachelor diplomats overseas must let their head rule their heart, because an unwise romantic attachment could jeopardize their career – especially if it turns out be a honeytrap.

~

'. . . who now closes both his career and this impossibly long sentence'

PETER OLIVER, HM AMBASSADOR
TO URUGUAY, MAY 1977

An example of how the proximity to events of an ambassador in the field can lead him to draw very different conclusions – in this case, over the harsh treatment of rebels – to those of his superiors watching from a distance back in Whitehall. In this case Oliver had very good personal reasons for what he called his 'preference of the enforcement of law'. As well as the abortive attempt to kidnap him in Cuba, Oliver alludes to another far more serious and recent precedent: his predecessor as HM Ambassador to Uruguay was kidnapped by the left-wing Tupamaros guerrillas in 1971. Geoffrey Jackson spent eight months in captivity and was only released after negotiations involving the Prime Minister, Edward Heath, and a ransom payment of £42,000.

The Uruguayan government responded to the Tupamaros with brutal martial law. In his despatch Oliver backs this tough stance, but the file shows his bosses in the South American Department in London disagreed: 'Mr. Oliver's implied justification (through the medium of a "cynical observer") of the Uruguayan human rights policies will not enjoy a receptive audience. Nor does it deserve one. Torture, brutality and murder apparently do not feature in Mr. Oliver's vocabulary. But he has always been incorrigible on this question.' This seems harsh, given the history. And Oliver's style, elegant if sometimes slightly laboured in its elegance, has a playfulness that sourer observers in Whitehall appear to have overlooked.

The same official concedes that Oliver's despatch (from which only selected paragraphs appear here) is 'very readable', but that is the only praise – and, from the lips of a mandarin, double-edged. Elsewhere in the document, the ambassador's prose is peppered with references to Zeus and Aesop – as well as the nods to Sherwood Forest in the extracts below – 'and the somewhat confusing switches in allegorical characters, writes the rather sniffy official, 'give it a carnival character . . . The result is perhaps best summed up in Mr. Oliver's own words "sweet white wine, with just a touch of Angostura", a concoction which, if taken in too great a quantity, is likely to cloy the palate and turn the stomach.' The clerks also rounded on Oliver in their marginal notes for his 'unfortunate' reference to the embassy being downgraded; and for spelling mistakes.

The Right Honourable
Dr David Owen MP
etc etc etc
Foreign and Commonwealth Office

Sir

I am writing this despatch on the eve of my departure on retirement after close on five years' service as Her Majesty's Ambassador in Uruguay. If I start with a reference to earlier experiences in Cuba, it is not without relevance, both personal and political. For some months in 1958, when Castro was working his way westward from Oriente, I was acting as Chargé d'Affaires in Havana . . . and it was in that capacity that I deciphered a 'strictly personal' telegram from your Department, informing me that it was believed that there was a Castro plot to kidnap me, and suggesting that I took suitable precautions. This seemed eminently sensible advice, which I proceeded to follow, and I was relieved to find that the precautions proved successful. I was also interested to learn, some weeks after the fall of Batista, that they had been justified; a young Cuban student confided to my daughter that he was very glad to have met me at last, as he had been a member of a commando with orders to kidnap me – orders which, he added charmingly, had fortunately proved impossible to carry out. I must as a consequence confess to a certain preference for the enforcement of law and order in dealing with guerrilla tactics, especially when the latter (whatever their motivation) are directed against comparatively harmless persons such as my predecessor or myself, although I would be the first to agree that 'enforcement' is too comprehensive a word and requires some qualification. I can only apologise if that preference tends to colour this account of my stewardship here.

Much has been written and published about the Tupamaros and I need not describe in detail their origins and early activities. They saw their heyday in 1970–71 and by the time I arrived in June 1972 they were, thanks to President Pacheco's decision the previous year to bring in the Armed Forces to help the Police, already on the defensive although still remarkably active. They had also lost a good deal of their original anti-corruption 'Robin Hood' glamour and were becoming increasingly influenced by communist ideas, even though the official Communist Party disclaimed any connection with them . . .

So much for the stage setting and the actors. How about the audience of the outside world, and their reactions? And how have these reactions affected the players themselves? A disinterested but cynical observer would probably derive a certain amount of quiet amusement from studying the scene. Ten years ago, when the Tupamaros were playing in Sherwood Forest and generally discomfiting the bad barons and the greedy Sheriff of Nottingham, they attracted some tolerant sympathy abroad. But then they started playing rough. They shot people. They murdered a United States official adviser. They kidnapped foreign diplomats, including a British Ambassador. By so doing, they forfeited such sympathy as they had enjoyed, and even when the Armed Forces were brought in and repaid toughness in kind, there was at first remarkably little talk of human rights. That, the same cynical observer might also note, only came later, when 'domestic' Tupamaros and more internationally-oriented communists came to be lumped together as 'sediciosos' . . .

Finally, there is one Ambassador who (despite some slight lingering resentment that, for reasons still undisclosed to him, it was decided to downgrade the post before his arrival) has thoroughly liked being an Ambassador; who, with his wife, has found the last five years the most enjoyable of his service, and indeed the most rewarding in the non-financial sense; who has throughout had the loyal help, not only of an excellent staff but also of a British community more co-operative than any he has met elsewhere; who, reverting to the first paragraph of this overlong valedictory despatch, has gratefully contrived to avoid the unfortunate experience of his predecessor; who will always remember with appreciation the friendliness and the cheerfulness he has met throughout the length and breadth of Uruguay; and who now closes both his career and this impossibly long sentence by having the honour to remain,

Sir

Your most obedient Servant

P. R. Oliver

∾

'I am not the man I was'

RONALD HOPE-JONES, HM AMBASSADOR
TO BOLIVIA, JULY 1977

Today is my fifty-seventh birthday. I reach 'notional 60' in another three months and am retiring from the Service. I am exercising this option for two main reasons. One is that after five years in the Army during the war (I went a bridge too far) and another 31 in the Service, eight of them at an altitude of over 9000 feet, I am very conscious of the fact that I am not the man I was, either physically or mentally. O quanta qualia sunt illa sabbata![1] The other is that after La Paz there is really no other post that I would want to go to. We have been very happy here.

1. *O quanta . . . sabbata!*: 'How great and wonderful the sabbaths will be in heaven!' A twelfth-century hymn, written by the monk Abelard, one of history's star-crossed lovers. The afterlife was all he had to look forward to; Héloïse's uncle had him castrated.

~

'Most foreigners in Vietnam, diplomats or not, are on the verge of insanity'

ROBERT TESH, HM AMBASSADOR
TO VIETNAM, MARCH 1978

I should like to put on record the very intimate collaboration between the European Community Missions here. Of six of us, with the Danes planning to join, four live, and three have their offices, in rat-infested hotel bedrooms. We have done a lot to assert our Community solidarity, have made our first attempts at joint reporting, and are close personal friends . . .

I should like to pay more than the normal tribute to my staff, even though they are all comparative newcomers by comparison with us. It can only be done by dramatic illustration. Time: 6.00 p.m. (to eliminate our raucous interpreter on the communal telephone). Scene: the strong-room and registry (each 10′ × 10′) and the corridor outside (5′ × 16′). Characters: my secretary, pounding out a telegram on our primitive cypher machine; my communicator/archivist on his back on the floor in the middle of the bits of the latest machine to go wrong; at the registry desk my large Administration Officer/Accountant/Vice Consul doing archives; in the corridor, his tiny archivist/secretary wife, alternately advising and bullying him while taking over her shoulder dictation from my First Secretary/Consul; my Honorary-Consul wife writing up her latest consular visit to the South in the middle of the tea cups; and myself treading through them all in search of a file. Even in theory we are all polydextrous. In practice, my First Secretary has had to spend almost all her time on the humanitarian task of evacuation from the South. Remember, when you judge us, that through an informal local arrangement we have 're-united with their families' in Hong Kong nearly 5,000 people – probably more than have left by illegal boat trip . . .

I must close by trying to illustrate the Vietnamese character. Anecdotes serve best. One early one was my driving test. Gossiping afterwards I discovered that their main traffic problem was bicycle crossbar riders. If the passenger baled out to the left *he* fell under the oncoming lorry: if to the right the bicycle did. Clearly there must be a law. But the debate went on unresolved on whether to 'veer to the right or to veer to the left'.

I also commented that the cyclists did not seem to obey the same rules as the motorists. 'Of course not: they have a different set of rules.' They might have told me.

Much more recently, my wife asked our interpreter (ancient, pig-headed Vietnamese) to have my chimney cleaned. With rare electric power, our home was being kippered by our log fires. He insisted, as always, that there were no chimney-sweeps in Hanoi. She told him sweetly to ask the advice of the Indian Ambassador's interpreter, who knew how to get it done. He was not to be defeated: she found one servant on the roof and two below, trying to clean the chimney – with the fire still alight. In the face of fact, few Vietnamese will lose face, admit they are wrong, or use common sense.

Talking in the main port, Haiphong, to a Vietnamese shipping official, I suggested they mobilize the army to sort, list and clear the mountains of waiting and decaying goods. He said, sadly, 'We keep doing that. It never lasts long. As long as one authority controls discharge, and another collection, and they refuse to speak to one another, things will stay as they are.'

They leave everything to the last moment, then blandly rely on outsiders to extricate them from their own mess. They are infinitely charming and will give ten different reasons for not doing something which they have for months said they wanted to do and over which one has gone to endless trouble. After months of silence they will demand immediate and almost impossible action. Most things get done, somehow or other, at the expense of the nerves of others. That is why most foreigners in Vietnam, diplomats or not, are on the verge of insanity. The invariable last ditch defence: 'we fought for thirty years'.

I am sending a copy of this despatch to Her Majesty's Representatives in Bangkok, Vientiane, Hong Kong, Peking, Moscow, Paris and Washington.

I have, etc.,

ROBERT TESH.

~

'In the event of your marriage you would be required to resign'

JULIET CAMPBELL, HM AMBASSADOR
TO LUXEMBOURG, OCTOBER 1991

After such interesting and enjoyable years here it was a difficult decision to leave the Diplomatic Service. The Service has of course changed greatly over the years I have known it, and to my mind mostly for the better . . . I naturally also appreciate the greater opportunities for women. I joined a Service in which women had not achieved equal pay, and my letter of appointment included a paragraph warning that 'in the event of your marriage you would be required to resign this appointment'. Now I head an Embassy (surely the first) in which the majority of DS spouses are male.

~

'Our predecessors earned more; and their day ended earlier'

SIR BRIAN FALL, HM AMBASSADOR
TO RUSSIA, JUNE 1995

When I joined the Service, a Grade I Ambassador was paid £7000 a year. Twice that then would have bought a lot more house than twice what I'm paid would today. Some handy allowances have been slipping too: when I first went to Moscow, as a married Third Secretary, we had a maid who could cook; the Head of Chancery had a maid, a cook and a driver. When I got back here as Head of Chancery, we had a maid who could cook. Civil Service pensions, which looked so good in the 1960s and 1970s, have now fallen behind private sector best practice. And Knighthoods, in those dear, dead days, were two a penny compared to now.

Admittedly, some of the cuts were into fat. Others were compensated by improved conditions of service: children's concessionary journeys; difficult post allowance (better the cash than the promissory note), opportunities for working wives, health care – even the furnishings in many of our houses and flats. But, at the end of the day, the balance seems clear: our predecessors earned more; and their day ended earlier.

My first boss in the Office, by reputation a martinet, was particularly keen that we should not skimp on the working day: by which he meant that we should not come in after 10.00, leave before 6.00 or spend more than two hours for lunch. I doubt that in those days there were Under Secretaries to be found searching the basement for their telegrams at eight o'clock in the morning, or key desk officers still hard at it twelve hours later. Nor, I suspect, were diplomatic staff in posts abroad so bound to their desks.

~

'Free housing, reasonable pay and not too much to do'

RICHARD THOMAS, HM HIGH COMMISSIONER
TO BARBADOS AND THE EASTERN CARIBBEAN,
FEBRUARY 1998

A snapshot of an earlier age and a slower pace, this is one of the editors' favourites: a gem of elegantly comical prose.

Before they were merged in 1968, two separate departments managed Britain's overseas affairs. The Commonwealth Relations Office conducted relations with countries that used to make up the British Empire; the Foreign Office dealt with the rest.

Further extracts from Thomas's despatch are on p.293.

One fine day in the summer of 1961 in the Scottish Highlands, on leave from the Army, and staying with my parents, I received a small brown envelope which contained news that I had gained entrance to the Civil Service by means of the Open Competition. I had been allocated to the Department of my choice, the Commonwealth Relations Office. I had chosen the CRO because I had a friend in it, who when I had last seen him was living comfortably, with free housing, reasonable pay and not too much to do, in Dublin. I told my parents the good news, and in answer to their enquiries explained that the CRO, as its full name implied, presumably looked after Commonwealth relations. 'Yes dear, but what does that mean?' asked my mother, herself the daughter of a Civil Servant and given to inconvenient bouts of intellectual rigour. I hadn't a clue, but so as not to let the side down I said that it presumably meant that I would be showing visitors from the Commonwealth around London. 'That sounds very interesting, dear,' replied my mother, in a tone that implied less than total conviction. My father, who earned a precarious living on the fringes of the theatre and who was appalled at the prospect of having a son in the Civil Service, merely shrugged. It was a beautiful day, and I was relieved to think that I would not have to look for a job when my National Service ended that November. We carried on with our holiday.

The reality, when it materialised one dreary late autumn day, was not much less off beam than my untutored expectations. Because of my National Service, I had missed the Induction Course and was thrown straight into the CRO's West and General Africa Department. There my duties were to fetch, twice a day, the telegrams on the current Congo crisis from the Foreign Office next door, sort them into date and time order, and give them to my immediate superior, a retired

Colonial Deputy Governor. What he did with them I never discovered. The room in which I was thus employed was an attic, and is now inhabited by three or four members of WIAD[1] – a neat irony, given my final appointment in the Service. My room-mates seemed busy enough, scratching away at manuscript drafts and occasionally dictating into astonishing machines that resembled tea-trolleys, recording on discs which were sent to Blackpool for transcription. (The results came back two or three weeks later, after one had forgotten what they were about, and in a form that did not encourage recall.) I did not have enough to do, but my colleagues advised me not to point this out. Instead they directed me to a makeshift bed, hidden behind a row of steel presses at the end of the room, for the use of anyone in need of a little rest.

After a few months of this curious existence, so far from my expectations and, frankly, so boring, I told the Head of Estabs that I was inclined to seek alternative employment if things did not look up. Without further ado I was made Private Secretary to the CRO's Parliamentary Under Secretary, who fortunately had a forgiving nature, and from then on things did indeed look up. Not least of the improvements was the successful hostile takeover bid, three or four years later, mounted by the FO on the CRO. I had put the FO second on my preference list because I believed it to be staffed by toffs with triple barrelled names who had been to Eton, and thus not a suitable milieu for a keen young radical like me, whose sole previous contact with it had been as a Suez demonstrator in 1956. But my forays into its Congo section had now disabused me of this exaggerated view . . .

1. *WIAD*: West Indian and Atlantic Department.

8. The Sun Sets on Empire

'When I was about ten,' writes Matthew Parris in 1959, 'and hoping at that time to be appointed rather than elected to the leadership of a country somewhere in the world, I wrote from Africa to what I think was then called the Colonial Office, expressing my wish to be a governor when I grew up, and inquiring about the possibilities of employment, and the appropriate career-path. I received a kindly reply pointing out (gently) that by the time I was ready to be a governor, there might not be many British colonies left to be governor of; and suggesting I redirect my inquiries to the Foreign Office. Which I did.

'Reading the despatches which follow, it may strike you that I was not alone in reposing in a diplomatic career the ambitions I had privately nursed for a more paternalistic role . . .'

~

'Sweetmeats, Christmas cakes and fat goats . . . a far cry from the Foreign Office canteen. All this will pass one day'

SIR JAMES CRAIG, HM POLITICAL AGENT
IN DUBAI, OCTOBER 1964

British diplomats come bearing a range of official titles which can be rather confusing. An outsider, ignorant of what they do, might be forgiven for failing to distinguish, say, a high commissioner from a vice consul, or a first secretary from a chargé d'affaires. But there is a gulf between their responsibilities. At one end of the scale, consuls look after British tourists who have lost their passports (an honorary consul in a particular city or region might even be – heaven forfend – a 'locally engaged' foreigner). At the other end of the hierarchy, ambassadors have in them vested the powers of Her Majesty the Queen, and can negotiate with foreign governments on Her behalf.

Such powers at the top of the modern diplomatic tree are mere trifles, however, compared with the astonishing leeway given to British diplomats and colonial administrators in the days of empire. Along with their greater power went an entirely different (and now obsolete) array of titles – such as political agent. James Craig describes the responsibilities of this long-forgotten role in his peerlessly evocative despatch from Dubai, below, which we have reprinted in full.

The Trucial States (comprising the sheikhdoms which today make up the United Arab Emirates, including Dubai) were British Protectorates created by a series of peace treaties in the nineteenth century. London saw fit to impose these treaties – which gave the protectorates their name – upon the sheikhs after repeated attacks by pirates in the Gulf on British ships bound for India. Britain assumed the power, through these successive alliances, to arbitrate in any local disputes. Tribal politics were complex, with sheikhs frequently facing challenges from within their own tribe; often from members of their own family. The British diplomat on the ground would throw in his lot – and, decisively, that of the Royal Navy, whose gunships cruised near by – with whichever brother looked most likely to run things in accordance with British interests.

As well as playing kingmaker, political agents often had full legal jurisdiction over non-Muslims in the territory. The Indian penal and civil codes were imported for the purpose.

Most strikingly of all, British envoys had the power to free slaves. Slavery had been abolished in much of the region but was still practised in conservative enclaves. In Oman any slave who touched the flagpole in the British compound won their freedom, and in the 1950s the political agent there was still freeing more than a dozen a year. Slavery was finally abolished in Oman in 1970, seven years after Dubai.

Craig is held in deep respect by colleagues as an Arabist from the very top drawer; he taught at the so-called 'spy-school' for languages, MECAS, in Lebanon. His Dubai posting came comparatively early on; Craig went on to be ambassador to Syria (1976–9; see p. 252) and Saudi Arabia (1979–84). His Saudi valedictory was briefly the subject of a media storm (see the Introduction to Chapter 5) involving several high court injunctions which remain in force today. Craig's 'Impressions of Dubai Post' was not strictly a valedictory – he was still in the job – but it is a farewell despatch all the same. The times were changing in 1964, as Craig saw, and the political agent's days were numbered. Four years later, Britain declared its intention to withdraw from the Gulf, against the wishes of many of the locals. Like other remnants of empire the Trucial States had become a political liability for the Labour government and an expensive burden. The flag was hauled down, with undue haste, in 1971.

BT 1891/1   *Foreign Office Distribution*

TRUCIAL STATES

IMPRESSIONS OF DUBAI POST

Mr. Craig to Acting Political Resident (Bahrain). (Received October 1)

(No. 8. CONFIDENTIAL)   *Dubai,*
September 27, 1964.

Sir,

The title of Her Majesty's Political Agent, I have the honour
to submit, is an exceedingly romantic one. Even the dourest
would not deny that it carries a less prosaic, less workaday
ring than Commercial Officer or Second Secretary
(Information). It has, to begin with (despite a lamentable
increase of one-third in our numbers over the past three
years) a growing scarcity value. To the best of my knowledge
only four of us survive; and there is at times an enjoyable
feeling of political agents *contra mundum*. The name, too,
is rich in associations. It belongs with those other old and
evocative titles: Collector, Resident, District Commissioner.
It suggests remoteness in time and in place. One feels that a
Political Agent is (or should be) at the end of the line, one
of those originals on whom the sun used never to set, the
final, executive blood vessel in the network of arteries that
stretched out, long, efficient and complex, from the distant
heart of empire; the true *ultima ratio regum*.[1] The ghosts of
dead colleagues rise up: in the club at Mandalay, saddling
their horses in Peshawar, haranguing the tribes in the
Kalahari. And the nostalgia grows with the awareness that

one is very nearly the last of that very long line, those thousand men who month by month sent back their despatches to the district headquarters, to the provincial capitals, and finally to the red boxes of Whitehall. Oh my Wilson and my Cox[2] long ago!

I take the view, it will now be evident, that, having been given a title, one might as well enjoy it. But the times are changing. There has been criticism, as your Excellency knows, of the imperialist flavour of the name, and talk of adopting something more consonant with our egalitarian world. The nature of the post is also changing. Already the functions of my colleagues in our sophisticated neighbours, Bahrain and Qatar, are inclining more to the ambassadorial and less to the pro-consular.[3] Dubai has begun to take the same well-trodden road and perhaps before long will be catching up. The gunboats still call, but they are less peremptory than before. The Political Agent still commands, but more often now he suggests or advises.

Yet on the Trucial Coast, more perhaps than anywhere else, the old regime persists. The atmosphere is on the one hand imperial India. The guard at the compound gate hoist the flag at sunrise, and all day long it looks down upon the dhows and ferryboats in Dubai creek. Below the windtowers the bazaars are crowded with Sindis and Baluchis, Bengalis and Pathans, *dhobi-wallahs*, *babus*, and *chokidars*. The Agent sits in court below the Royal Coat of Arms and sees the old procession of clerks and petition writers. His servants wear turbans and puggarees and long *shirwani* coats. He inspects gaols and pursues smugglers, runs hospitals and builds roads. He takes the salute from the Trucial Oman Scouts, on a sandy barrack square, amid ornamental cannon, pennants on lances, bugles and pipes and drums. He makes State tours with reception tents and dining tents and sleeping tents, trestle tables, carpets and military escorts. He is very much a *bara sahib*.[4]

But he is also a sheikh. All year round he sits and receives his callers: Rulers with business of State; tribesmen with pastoral complaints; conspirators with offers of partnership; wealthy merchants seeking agencies; gold smugglers seeking passports; schoolboys seeking scholarships to England. To each he offers, through his coffee-maker girt about with the great silver dagger, the tiny, handleless cups of black spiced coffee. Twice or thrice a year he sits in full *majlis*[5] while the visitors pour in with congratulations, sweetmeats, Christmas cakes and fat goats. His letters are addressed to 'His Honour, the Most Glorious, the Magnificence of Her Majesty's Trusted One in the Trucial States, the Revered'. He decides fishing disputes, negotiates blood-money, examines boundaries, manumits slaves. He presides over the Shaikhs' Council. He exempts, pardons, appeases; exacts, condemns, ordains. Over a large but undefined field he in effect rules. It is all a far cry from the third room and the Foreign Office canteen.

It is important, I may break off to remark, that the sheikhly nature of the Political Agent should be thoroughly appreciated in the department. It may well be difficult for his fellow clerks, who have often seen him – and will no doubt see him again – making the office tea in a drab Whitehall corridor, to picture him as an oriental potentate among the grey-haired dervishes. The effort, arduous and even comical though it may be, must nevertheless be made. Without it, not only will the Agent seem intolerably pompous when he goes home on leave; his colleagues for their part will fail to understand the curious necessities which his post involves. What can he be doing with two maunds of cardamom and a bag of charcoal? For what purpose has he had his censer repaired? Why does the coffee-maker need (of all things) a dagger? Such questions, Sir, are pardonable. But they must be asked from a deferential and an understanding heart.

The Political Agent has, forbye, more orthodox functions. He must persuade Rulers and influence public opinion. He must justify (stern task) the workings of the United Nations and intercept the policies of the Arab League. He must help to negotiate oil concessions. He must expound the need for a law on workmen's compensation and even, in settling sea frontiers, explain to an illiterate sheikh the principle of constant equidistance involved in the trigonometry of the median line. He must be severe and masterful when he feels insignificant and ill-assured. He must at times be as diplomatic as any conventional diplomatist.

But above all he must travel: in a long and ceremonious caravan or in a solitary Land Rover; in his own dhow or in an R.A.F. aeroplane; at speed across the gravel desert, slowly and painfully through a mountain wadi, or stuck altogether in the mud of the salt flats. This is his Crispin's Day[6] that will live into his old age. Long after the minutes and the submissions and the subcommittees have faded, he will remember waking on the great plateau to the scuffle and the mutter of the bedu at their dawn prayers; coming out of the tent to see them huddled in their skimpy cloaks round the fire waiting for the blackened coffee-pot to heat up; the hawks behind them on their perches, now huddling in against the cold, now fluffing out their feathers to dry off the night-dew. Or being called out from a party with a message of a shooting in the hills; the scurry round for a driver and a bed-roll and then out of the Agency gate and away across the salt flats into the dunes; sleep in the sand beside the track, then up at first light and through the mountains to where two groups of bandoliered tribesmen wait for him nervously. Nor will he forget the incense and the rose-water proffered by his host at the end of a stiff and dusty journey, or the chanted, stylized greetings, strophe and antistrophe, of the desert bedu, or the Agency dhow at anchor in the bay of Dibba with the Red Ensign fluttering improbably over those unheard-of fishermen.

All this will pass one day and we shall be centralised and standardised. The powers and the privileges, the discomforts and the eccentricities – all will vanish, and with them the fun. Meanwhile, Political Agent Dubai is a splendid job in a splendid place. When the name is changed and the first consul or Ambassador arrives, it will indeed be the end of a very auld sang.

I am sending copies of this despatch to all Gulf posts, to Her Majesty's Principal Secretary of State for Foreign Affairs and *en titre personnel* to Mr. Balfour-Paul at Her Majesty's Embassy in Beirut.

I have, &.

A. J. M. CRAIG.

Her Majesty's Political Agent

1. *ultima ratio regum*: 'The last argument of kings.'
2. *my Wilson and my Cox*: Sir Arnold Wilson and Sir Percy Cox, British colonial administrators of Iraq (then Mesopotamia) during and after the First World War.
3. *pro-consular*: A leader imposed by a foreign power; a jibe often thrown at ambassadors from superpowers (e.g. the United States) who try to lean on their neighbours (e.g. Canada).
4. *bara sahib*: (White) colonial master.
5. *majlis*: Formal sitting; legislature.
6. *Crispin's Day*: From Shakespeare's *Henry V*:

And Crispin Crispian shall ne'er go by,
From this day to the ending of the world,
But we in it shall be remembered,
We few, we happy few, we band of brothers.

Across the centuries, Crispin's Day (25 October) has by chance become famous for battles. As well as Agincourt, the Charge of the Light Brigade also fell upon it.

∽

'*If you asked the Chinese Singaporean why he was put on this earth he would without hesitation reply: "to make money"*'

SIR ARTHUR DE LA MARE, HM HIGH COMMISSIONER
TO SINGAPORE, OCTOBER 1970

A bittersweet farewell. Sir Arthur de la Mare used his valedictory from Singapore to state the case, as controversial then as it is now, for the British Empire as a force for good. De la Mare titled this despatch 'Farewell to the Lion City'. His valedictory from Thailand is equally striking (see p. 75).

With its affluent population, clean streets and ordered society Singapore remains a poster child for the potential of imperial rule to civilize and enrich its subjects; the strongest evidence among all Britain's former possessions in the case for the defence of empire. In material terms, Singapore today is an example to the rest of the world of how to run an economy. Politically, however, it is a case of arrested development, with democratic rule along one-party lines (the current Prime Minister, Lee Hsien Loong, is the son of the founder of the nation, Lee Kwan Yew, more of whom below).

De la Mare's pride in Singapore's development is badly

tainted by what he calls 'that hour of dishonour at the Ford Motor Works'. The car plant was the setting, on 15 February 1942, for the unconditional surrender of British forces in Malaya to the Japanese. In ten days of fighting, troops under the command of Lieutenant General Arthur Ernest Percival lost the supposedly impregnable Singapore peninsula to an invading Japanese army less than half their size. Sixty thousand British and empire troops became Japanese prisoners of war in what Winston Churchill called the 'worst disaster and largest capitulation in British history'.

The Straits Chinese – and that means Singapore, for the minorities who make up some 20 per cent of the population do not count – are self-made men who have gained power and affluence by hard work, tenacity and business acumen. They have been immensely successful, and success, particularly in a race naturally self-reliant to the point of cockiness, tends to make men overreach. The Singaporeans, with their minute power-base and a population of only 2 million, cannot expect to make such a showing in the world as do the Japanese, but while they dislike and fear the latter they feel a sneaking admiration for them for having, in a bare quarter of a century since total defeat, out-smarted, out-guessed and out-manoeuvred the rest of the business world. And if the Singaporeans concede to Japan the palm of Asian success story No. 1 they have no doubt at all that they are Asian success story No. 2. But just as, I suspect, many Japanese prefer not to face the fact that part at least of their success stems from good fortune, notably the guilt-complex of the United States, and that sooner or later the privileges and advantages thrust upon them will be withdrawn, so I believe many Singaporeans prefer to forget that it was one thing to make money while a benevolent foreign Power provided the necessary setting for the acquisition of wealth, but quite another thing now that they themselves have to shoulder the responsibility and financial burden of independence. To be fair, some of the more mature Singaporeans do realise this, and while lip-service is everywhere paid to the goddess of Sovereignty there are those among the older generation who secretly hanker after the good old colonial days when, while the complaisant British undertook the necessary but unprofitable tasks of administration, they themselves could address their single-minded devotions to the goddess of Mammon. If you asked the Chinese Singaporean why he was put on this earth he would without hesitation reply: 'to make money'. Independence and sovereignty are expensive, and the Singaporeans, like many other newly-independent nations, are discovering to their chagrin that their own tax-masters are harder on their pocket than were the much-maligned colonialists ...

People who work hard with brawn and brain deserve to succeed and the Singaporeans work hard with both. They make mistakes, they have a touch of arrogance and insensitivity, they are materialistic and grasping. But they have purpose, drive, vision and above all tenacity. Their simplicity has hitherto not been marred by spurious pretensions to culture, and they have no chips on their shoulder about being the sons of toil. Honest labour ennobles them, and their very industry commands respect. Some observers are repelled by their self-righteousness, but theirs is not the self-righteousness of the Indians, based on nothing but conceit, but rather that of the Americans before their confidence collapsed, and is based on the knowledge of achievement. It is brash but not nauseating and it is largely neutralised by their many qualities. With time and the march of so-called progress they will lose some of their simpler communal virtues: the working-man will adopt the still outlandish notion that Jack is better than his master: the new denizens of high-rise urban apartment buildings will not or ever remain the kindly, uncomplicated people so long inured to the life of the *kampong*.[1] With a few notable exceptions the rich have hitherto shunned the public ostentation of wealth, both to deflect the jealousy of the gods and to fool the tax-man. But the power of the gods is waning, and the tax-man is no longer easily conned. Elaborate, expensive, tasteless and crashingly boring entertainment at the 'de luxe' hotels and night-spots springing up all over Singapore is becoming widely regarded as the accepted way to consummate the union between wealth and 'gracious living'. Singaporean hostesses, may heaven forgive them, are beginning to read Emily Post.[2] The social homogeneity born of a common urge for self improvement is loosening. The 'rugged society' of Lee Kwan Yew's[3] ideal is already being eroded by hedonism, and the disorders of sophisticated urban society are not far away. I consider myself fortunate to have known the Singaporeans at their simple best: my successors may not, I fear, find them as likeable as I have.

It is now 34 years since I first saw Singapore, and though until I took up my present post I had never lived here for any length of time it has long exercised a strange fascination upon me, both attractive and repellent. Attractive because of its vigour, industry, bustle and thrust: repellent because every day I am reminded of the shame of 1942. It was as a diplomatic prisoner in Japan that, on my birthday, I heard of Singapore's surrender. Mercifully for all of us held captive in the enemy's capital we were then too numbed and too uninformed to realise that what had taken place was not only an appalling military disaster but the most shameful disgrace in Britain's imperial history. It was only later that we heard of the irresolution, the incompetence and the bungling of those charged here with the duty of defending not merely Britain's military interests, but her very name. One may or may not regret the passing of empire but no loyal British subject living in Singapore can forget that it was here that the hollowness of the imperial ethos was so cruelly and so shamefully exposed.

Reminders of that shame beset me daily. It is not the people of Singapore who remind me of it, for no Singaporean has ever mentioned February 1942 to me in criticism or reproach. But history is too near, and the smell of our ignominy still hangs in the air. The very house I live in was occupied by the Japanese Commander of Singapore Military District; every time I drive along the Bukit Timah Road I relive, in imagination possibly even worse than the actual reality, that hour of dishonour at the Ford Motor Works; the monument erected near the Padang[4] to the local Chinese victims of Japanese atrocity is a memorial not only of Japanese savagery but also of our betrayal of our trust. And it does not relieve me to recall that the military pomp and ostentation – not to say the arrogance – with which we reoccupied Singapore was a sham and a fraud, for we reoccupied it not by our own efforts, but by an American atom bomb dropped on Hiroshima . . .

. . . [I] am grateful to the Singaporeans. We have a national reason for being grateful to them: it is they, more than anyone else including ourselves, who have done most to restore the British image in East Asia. For, unlike the present rulers of many other former British possessions they have not only maintained the heritage we left them, they have improved upon it. In so many other places the governmental and civil structure we left behind has fallen into misuse, corruption and decay. Here it is kept in first-class working order, furbished and efficient, a tribute to Stamford Raffles, who remains the national hero, and to the able and dedicated civil administrators who followed him. It is a tribute to them, the people of Singapore, that they remember us, not as the military bunglers who brought upon them the agony of three and a half years of Japanese terror, but as the honest and just administrators who for almost a century and a half helped, guided and supported them as they transformed an uninhabited malaria-infested swamp into the model of peaceful and ordered prosperity which Singapore is today. They are justly proud of their own achievement, but they willingly bear witness that it was we who made it possible. The foreigner who now visits Singapore is heartened to see what Asians can do, but he cannot but reflect also on the colonial Power which created the setting, educated the present leaders, trained them in the arts of business, administration and self-government, and finally, when the time came, handed over power to them not reluctantly or with recrimination but in friendship and goodwill. And if that foreigner is himself a man of goodwill he must acknowledge that Britain too has reason to be proud of her handiwork.

1. *kampong*: Native village (Malay).
2. *Emily Post*: American author (1872–1960) of *Etiquette in Society, in Business, in Politics, and at Home.*
3. *Lee Kwan Yew*: Prime Minister of Singapore, 1959–90. Lee led Singapore into independence from Britain, into (and out of) federation with Malaysia, and on to prosperity as an Asian Tiger. 'In a matter of expediency,' says de la Mare of Lee elsewhere in this despatch, 'this most enigmatic of men . . . will brush aside all sentiment and all tradition, and will treat his best friends just as shabbily as he would his worst enemies.'
4. *Padang*: Green space in the heart of Singapore's business district.

∼

'For the first time since the Dutch swept the Medway, our country was despised'

SIR FRANK JOHNSTON, HM HIGH COMMISSIONER
TO AUSTRALIA, APRIL 1971

There is real anger in this swansong. Johnston's rage at the manner in which Britain shook off our colonial responsibilities in the Far East still resonates nearly forty years on. In the late 1960s Britain's distaste for the trappings of empire saw us rush our exit, which inevitably led to stumbles. In 1967 more than a century of British rule in Aden (now Yemen) ended in an ignominious 'scuttle', a full-scale military retreat under sniper fire ('without glory but without disaster', as Sir Humphrey Trevelyan, the last high commissioner put it). Elsewhere in the Middle East, Britain's unseeming haste to wash our hands of power damaged the nation's standing among the newly independent states we left behind, and contradicted assurances given by our ministers in London, and repeated by our diplomats on the ground, that local allies and clients would not be left high and dry.

Malaysia and Singapore proved to be another example. The trauma of separation was felt at the very extremes of the empire, as Johnston explains here. In the late 1960s British policy on maintaining troops in Malaysia and Singapore went through several evolutions – or 'phases' as Johnston calls them. The first was a commitment to stay for as long as those countries wanted to play host. The second phase was for withdrawal by the mid 1970s. The final phase was for accelerated withdrawal by the end of 1971. The manner in which these shifts were communicated to the Australians – each new position accompanied with an assurance of its permanence – made for a 'painful process' for the high commissioner, one in which he was powerless to do anything except 'watch our Government's credibility evaporate'.

Britain's relations with the Antipodes would be further stretched two years after Johnston wrote his despatch, when Edward Heath took the UK into the European Economic Community. Losing preferential access to the British market was hugely costly, wiping out (for example) much of the Australian butter industry overnight. Australia and New Zealand had been established as farming colonies – the larder of the empire – and the mother country was severing that link in order to sell goods to France and Germany. To add to the ignominy, Antipodeans arriving in London had for the first time to submit themselves to EEC border controls as 'foreigners'.

In the course of these proceedings there was a ludicrous episode which had such a disproportionately bad effect on our relations with Australia, and was also so symptomatic and characteristic of the period, that it should not be concealed from the historian. When we were preparing to give the Australians advance notice of the second phase, i.e., withdrawal in the mid-1970's, one of the reasons discussed in Whitehall for this change of policy was the argument that 'white faces' did more harm than good on the mainland of Asia. The posts concerned, including Canberra, advised strongly that our case should rest on the economic and financial arguments, and that the ideological point about white faces should not be used. It was clear that in this country it would have the worst possible effect, and would jangle nerves very deep in the Australian character; after all, if you come to think of it, the Australians themselves are 'white faces' on their own mainland. In accordance with this advice, an official communication was made to the Australian Government basing the new policy entirely on economics and finance. At the same time however an authoritative British source conveyed to the Australians the political arguments in favour of planning to remove white faces from the mainland. When this message was reported to them, Mr. Holt[1] and his Government simply exploded. I have never known the relations between the two countries more difficult. It was not only that the communication about white faces reflected seriously on the sincerity of the official British message, concentrating as it did exclusively on the economic and financial arguments. After all, it is nothing new for British Governments to be distrusted by their allies and associates; this has been a familiar situation to us at least since the Peace of Utrecht.[2] But, up to now, if we had been distrusted, we had at least been taken seriously. It was the inherent frivolity of the 'white faces' episode which was so regrettable. To Australians the defence of South-East Asia was and is a matter of national survival. For us to tell them that we were withdrawing our forces, and to offer them instead a piece of trendy left-wing theology, was like seeing a swimmer in difficulties and throwing him a pair of waterwings by Mary Quant. It all accentuated the flibbertigibbet impression which, during these years, our country all too often gave overseas. In the eyes of Australians Britain seemed to be dwindling to a minute island where there was practically nothing except 'swinging London' and in which Westminster and Whitehall were insignificant compared to Carnaby Street and the King's Road. We had lost our national reputation for gravitas and appeared as a giddy butterfly flitting unsteadily round the fringe of world politics. It was a heart-breaking period for British representatives on this side of the globe, a time of severe national humiliation. For the first time since the Dutch swept the Medway,[3] our country was despised . . .

Looking back over the past six years, I would say that they

have seen something like a pragmatic revolution in the Australian connection with Britain. The old relationship was predominantly a family one, and had that quality of boredom with which such relationships are too often attended. Each side took the other for granted: Britain was a dreary old Mum doing her knitting in the North Sea, Australia was a brash young daughter hopping about Down-Under; in theory they loved each other, in practice they regarded each other as part of the furniture. During these six years, with their dramatic and sometimes bitter developments, the relationship has evolved into something quite different: a consciousness of the strong common interest existing between mature and independent equals, living in different parts of the world, and confronted with different regional problems – but for that reason needing each other all the more in order to prevent regional influences from swamping the national identity. That seems a much sounder and healthier relationship to build on in the future.

1. *Mr Holt*: Harold Holt, Prime Minister of Australia, 1966–7. Holt's term in office came to an abrupt and untimely end one December day in 1967; taking a swim in heavy surf near Melbourne the Prime Minister vanished. His body was never recovered.
2. *Peace of Utrecht*: Signed in 1713 between the major European powers, concluding the War of the Spanish Succession. Putting an end to French territorial expansion, the treaty cleared the way for the growth of the British Empire.
3. *since the Dutch swept the Medway*: An audacious attack by the Dutch Navy in 1667. Sailing up the River Thames, and then up the River Medway to Chatham, they burned much of the English fleet at anchor, towing the flagship *Royal Charles* away with them.

~

*'The new niggers in the woodpile . . . must be the still
surviving colonialists'*

ARTHUR KELLAS, HM HIGH COMMISSIONER
TO TANZANIA, DECEMBER 1974

It is a fixed conviction in the Third World that aid is morally
owing from developed to developing countries, and from the
UK in particular to the liberated parts of the old British
Empire. A kind of atonement is demanded, in compensation
for conquest or for years of colonial oppression or neglect. If
conquest is hard to identify, if oppression was milder than
the practice of the liberated government themselves, if neglect was benign, or indeed outweighed by the efficient and
dedicated service of so many devoted colonial administrators, then it is argued that in any case human dignity was
impaired by the colonial relationship itself, which outraged
or frustrated indigenous values and positively obstructed
development. Thus if by virtue of aid we are now certainly in
better standing in Tanzania, nevertheless the Tanzanian Government in no way regard themselves as beholden, nor
inhibited from reviling our international policies . . .

. . . The issue of principal concern to Tanzania is residual
colonialism in Africa, apartheid, and the whole black–white
confrontation. In this context, for historical, political, economic and indeed racial reasons the British appear to
Tanzania to be on the wrong side and our policies suspect if
not hostile . . . From all this is derived an attitude on the part
of the Tanzanian rulers which disposes them against ourselves. Perceiving the relatively backward condition of their
country, they blame for it the Portuguese adventurers, the
Arab slave traders, the German imperialists, or the British
colonialists. If the British colonialists after 40 years' rule

quietly conceded power a dozen years ago to the leader of a popular movement, then somebody else, dear Brutus, must be to blame now. The new niggers in the woodpile, to quote my American colleague (himself a nigger of the highest quality), must be the still surviving colonialists, the neo-colonialists, the dollar imperialists, the Central Intelligence Agency, the Zionists, multi-national corporations, or British reactionaries. Above all somebody other than the Tanzanian people must be to blame. The ideology is ready made. Its vocabulary of invective and abuse is contributed by the disciples of Marx, Lenin and Mao Tse-tung. It is enriched, still ten years short of 1984, by a new 'double speak'; in which language, for example, employment is exploitation, investment is robbery, profit is a bad word (better say surplus), the people is the Party, propaganda is education, agitation is vigilance or nation building, and aid is more agreeably called a transfer of resources.

∾

'Neither the Minister nor the Permanent Secretary
have been educated beyond primary level'

TOM LAYNG, HM COMMISSIONER IN TUVALU,
SEPTEMBER 1978

GOVERNMENT HOUSE
FUNAFUTI
TUVALU
20 September 1978

Rt Hon David Owen MP
Secretary of State for Foreign and Commonwealth Affairs
Foreign and Commonwealth Office
London SW1A 2AH

Sir,

TUVALU – VALEDICTORY

I have the honour to forward my valedictory despatch on
Tuvalu. In it more farewells, perhaps, than usual are being
said. This is not only my own final report on the country,
but it will be, Sir – with independence now only a few days
away – the last despatch you receive on colonial Tuvalu. It
will also be the last formal civil service document from my
pen, as this is my final post after almost exactly twenty years
spent in five different sets of small islands . . .

. . . My job was initially to try and reconcile two opposing
philosophies: the local view that Tuvalu should rapidly be
equipped with a modern infrastructure comparable to that
existing in neighbouring territories, and the idealistic view
from afar that the territory should be set up cheaply along
traditional lines of yesteryear as a settlement of happy
smiling natives in leaf huts and lavalavas.[1] Inevitably in so

political a period, the wishes of the locals have prevailed. A stoneage oasis in the modern world is just not practicable. But the result has been a period of constant struggle to obtain the modest finance needed to make the administration work.

It would be pleasant to be able to go on to say that all the problems have been overcome and that in the short time available all the multifarious preparations for statehood have been satisfactorily completed. Regrettably this is far from the truth. Some will say that Tuvalu is the most unprepared nation ever to go forward to independence. Only two Tuvaluans working in the country have obtained university degrees. In one Ministry neither the Minister nor the Permanent Secretary have been educated beyond primary level. At the last Cabinet meeting which I attended it became clear that the Minister for Finance had little idea of what is meant by purchasing shares in a company, and the Minister of Commerce had no idea at all of the meaning of the word to 'subsidise'. There is certainly a truly alarming shortage of experience, competence and brainpower. But the situation is improving. Now that there are no expatriates in administrative or executive positions – and thus nowhere to pass the buck and no convenient scapegoats – the civil service is learning to make decisions and take responsibility . . .

I, Sir, have always supported Tuvalu's move towards early independence for two reasons – firstly because in all fields except top level government these tiny isolated islands have in effect always been independent, and secondly because the people genuinely want to do things in their own way. Independence brings with it the freedom to govern a country well or govern it badly. It is a basic human right to have the choice of making a success or a failure of one's life.

If a country wants to run its own affairs, and is happier doing this 'badly' than having it done more expertly by others, then a colonial power should not stand in its way.

Polynesians are a proud people, at times even arrogant. They regard themselves – and perhaps not without reason – as superior to the other races with whom they have come in contact. Tuvaluans are to Western eyes probably the most virtuous of the various Polynesian tribes. They set great store by family obligations, are not promiscuous and are by no means as light fingered as islanders are often reputed to be.

Tuvalus' Chief Minister, Mr Toalipi Lauti, is generously endowed with Polynesian virtue. He has concentrated his efforts to date on obtaining the independence of his country. To him this is an end in itself, and he has, I think, not yet given much thought as to how he will run things afterwards. 'We will do things in our own way' is a frequent phrase from his lips. He is not at all concerned when it is pointed out that in many technical fields there is only one way of doing things and this may require considerable expertise. To him, anything done in the colonial era is automatically bad, and must be changed. His immediate reaction to the question of treaty succession is 'scrap the lot, and we'll start again from scratch'. A completely new Public Service Commission had to be appointed simply because all the old members of Public Service Advisory Board had been appointed under the former regime. A recent Cabinet decision has been that General Orders – the bible of the civil service – should be abolished and all matters requiring decision be referred to the whole Cabinet . . .

I am also often asked how long Tuvalu will continue to depend on aid and whether the present appearance of being a 'begging bowl' nation will continue . . . Regrettably the present ministerial team seems more interested in spending money than in looking for ways to raise it. It has to be admitted that this is not a government which will have the courage to increase taxes or levy new dues. Indeed all moves since internal self government have been in the opposite direction. But this is understandable. The country is currently generously endowed with aid money. In recent months local officials have been exhorted time and time again to try and think of ways in which to spend the various grants. The New Zealanders are upset that the country is only using a quarter of the allocation from Wellington. The United Nations has sent several officials to draw up plans to spend the one and a half million dollar independence grant, and British officials keep pointing out how difficult it will be for the country to absorb its ordinary development aid allocation let alone the special (five million dollar) fund.

The result is that Tuvaluans, particularly the Ministers, are firmly convinced that the rest of the world is much too rich. This is emphasized by the treatment which they receive on overseas visits. Last year I accompanied a small delegation to Wellington and Canberra which was traveling at the invitation of the Australian and New Zealand governments: First class air travel, top class hotels, large limousines to take us everywhere, champagne before breakfast on Air New Zealand, exotic gifts on Canadian Pacific, far too much to eat and drink all the time. Naturally the overall impression taken back to the isolated atolls was that the Antipodeans have more money than they know what to do with. In Polynesia, even keeping surplus fish in the fridge for use next week is considered anti-social behaviour. Any excess should be given, now, to those without. So who can blame Tuvaluan ministers – firmly believing, Sir, that you and I and other Europeans drink champagne daily before breakfast – for thinking that it is their <u>right</u> to be given as much aid finance as they need from the bottomless pit in the outside world? Perhaps we should try to arrange that the next time the Chief Minister goes to London he stays with the Desk Officer and helps with the washing up ...

For all this – and what country is perfect? – Tuvalu is (almost) launched safely into the world as a sovereign state. Few colonies, Sir, can have caused you less trouble. There have been no riots, no bloodshed and no unfavourable publicity. If you had told officials retiring from Tarawa[2] in 1972 that the Ellice Islands would be separate and independent six years later, they would have laughed at you. In Tuvalu, fifty years of history has been compressed into five. It is scarcely surprising that everything is not as neat and tidy as one might like it to be. Tuvaluans are proud, but they are also an immensely likeable people. A colonial administrator tends to develop a love/hate relationship with the locals in whatever far away place he may work. One may be exasperated beyond words by Polynesian ministers during office hours, but charmed by their wives and children outside. And as companions on a fishing trip, opponents on the tennis court or hosts at a party, there can be no more delightful people. Which, Sir, is just as well, for without fishing, tennis and beer, life for your first, last and only Queen's Commissioner in Tuvalu and other expatriates serving in this remotest remaining outpost of empire could indeed have been dreary at times.

I am, Sir,

Your obedient servant,

T. H. Layng

1. *lavalavas*: Cloth skirt; a Polynesian take on the sarong.
2. *Tarawa*: Colonial capital of the Gilbert and Ellice Islands, a British Protectorate which split in 1976, shortly before independence, into Kiribati and Tuvalu.

∾

'We abandoned our subjects to a motley crew of mountebanks, criminals and even monsters'

SIR MARTIN EWANS, HM HIGH COMMISSIONER
TO NIGERIA, APRIL 1988

The last third of a century has not been the easiest period in which to represent Britain overseas, particularly for one whose career has lain mostly in the so-called developing world. For much of the time, it has meant trying to help manage, and mitigate the consequences of, our retreat from Empire, against the background of a loss of sense of national purpose and relative economic decline. Some of the manifestations of this decline have been particularly galling, in particular our consistent failure, through a penny-pinching approach, to make the best of those incomparable sources of influence overseas, the BBC, the British Council, and our educational and military training institutions. It has therefore been all the more pleasant, in my last few years, to have been able to take some pride in the beginning of economic resurgence and of a positive role in the European Community, where we manifestly belong.

I have strongly-held views about our withdrawal from Africa. Several generations of Britons devoted their lives, and sometimes died, in trying to do something worthwhile for the people of this continent. Over a good many years, we assumed a responsibility for the well-being of millions of

Africans. Then we about-turned, broke faith with our predecessors and abandoned our charges to what has, for the most part, been a miserable and often tragic fate. Of course, we had to go. But overwhelmingly, the path we followed towards the independence of our African colonies was that of least resistance. The institutions we established – the civil service, army, police, judiciary and so on – were, unlike their Indian counterparts, insufficiently deep-rooted to sustain coherent states against tribal and other forces. Some of our African colonies we even abandoned against their will. One of my vivid recollections is being at the receiving end of an impassioned plea by Jimmy Mancham of the Seychelles that his country should remain under British rule. Not so long afterwards, I was the person who had to go round to the Savoy and break it to him that he had been overthrown by a small band of squalid left-wing usurpers, backed by Tanzania.

For me, the moment of truth came when that incompetent humbug, Julius Nyerere,[1] quixotically invited a number of former colonial administrators to come back on the tenth anniversary of Tanzanian independence in order to see what had been achieved since their departure. They came; they saw; and they were appalled. Not only were they themselves being crudely lampooned in the schools they had founded as blood-sucking imperialists but much of their development work was in ruins. In retrospect the only surprising thing about this is that it should have been surprising. Less than ten years before independence a UN Commission had advised that twenty-five years would be needed before Tanganyika could be self-governing. I suppose that we saw no alternative but to saddle our colonies with Westminster-type Parliaments, with all the trappings of Speakers, maces and copies of Erskine May,[2] but their irrelevance and futility were soon painfully obvious. (But this is not to say that Africans are unfit for democracy. I would strongly dispute that proposition: and just about the one perceptive thing which I heard the Nigerian Foreign Minister, Bolaji Akinyemi, say, was that the view that Africans could operate democratic institutions was proved by the fact that they had almost never been allowed to do so!)

At the end of the day, therefore, we abandoned our subjects to a motley crew of mountebanks, criminals and even monsters. In post-independence anglophone Africa, I can think of only two leaders of real stature and integrity, Sir Abubakar Tafawa Balewa[3] and Sir Seretse Khama.[4] And of these, the former was never master in his own house and was murdered within a few years. Of course, our subsequent record is by no means wholly bad. Live Aid and its successors have, for example, provided heartwarming examples of genuine concern. But as a nation, we have in recent years not really wanted to know, and we have done pitifully less than we could have done to help our former colonies along. Whatever one may say about the French (and who does not), at least they have done better for their ex-colonies than we have.

1. *Julius Nyerere*: The first President of Tanzania (1964–85).
2. *Erskine May*: The rule book of parliamentary procedure.
3. *Sir Abubakar Tafawa Balewa*: Prime Minister of Nigeria 1960–66; overthrown in a coup.
4. *Sir Seretse Khama*: President of Botswana, 1966–1980.

9. Envoi

Many despatches title their final section 'envoi' – a literary term; in poetry an envoi is a short stanza at the end used either to address the reader or to comment on the preceding verses. Some ambassadors would confine their outspokenness to this final section, having devoted the remainder of their valedictory to serious foreign policy reporting; some of these envois are therefore parting shots in miniature.

Valedictories followed a certain format – part of the tradition was the format. Sir Peter Ricketts, the former Permanent Under Secretary at the Foreign Office, insisted to us that 'over time I think it's true to say the valedictory despatch risked becoming a caricature of itself. Some were excellent, and very sharp, and of course stay in the mind like Nicko Henderson's famous despatch, but many tended to conform to the stereotype of a few paragraphs of analysis of the country, something about how successful the ambassador had been, then quite a long passage on the various grievances and gripes that had been stored up over a career, and finishing with an encomium to the spouse.'

Thanks were effusive, and not just to the spouse – rare was the ambassador who did not thank the other members of the Diplomatic Service on their staff (who in a tough post would share the downs with the ambassador but not always the ups). And ambassadors would typically thank their locally engaged staff – foreigners working within the embassy – often with a note of regret that the pay and conditions verged on the exploitative; which they did.

But the spouse – almost always the wife – was typically the

centrepiece of this section. Thanks were more than mere routine. Wives gave up their careers to follow their globe-trotting spouse; their sacrifices and years of unpaid labour spent playing hostess and entertaining guests (and often doing secretarial work too) are an abiding theme. The fact they were not paid was an abiding gripe. The FCO's own historians, in a study written in 1999, explained that 'besides balls, receptions and dinners for foreign diplomats and statesmen, the Ambassadress had to be prepared for a constant stream of house guests ranging from personal family and friends to visiting dignitaries and even members of the Royal Family'.

Lord Tyrrell, British Ambassador to Paris in 1933, observed that 'there is no career in the world in which a man's work is so much shared by a woman as is a married diplomat's by his wife'. In 1964, the Plowden Report acknowledged the great contribution by diplomatic wives, 'to the work, welfare and way of life of an overseas Mission'. Its consequent recommendations were to improve the conditions of service (more generous representation allowances, boarding-school allowances, etc.) so that a wife could cope better with the special family problems inherent in a life of movement.

But times were changing, and so was the nature of professional people's marriages. How could both partners have a career? It's a question the Diplomatic Service has struggled to answer satisfactorily. In the 1990s efforts were intensified to find paid work for spouses at missions abroad. When husbands and wives were both career officers, joint postings were where possible arranged. The Office was also prepared to help with training and retraining. The post of Residence Manager has been created in some embassies – well suited to a spouse. And the existence of a male spouse to a female ambassador has ceased to be the oddity it once was.

In more than a few of these despatches the reader senses that the author knows this 'envoi' is supposed to be the final drum-roll, but cannot quite find the words to do justice to the moment. In the small hours of a hot, tropical night, more than a few moistened eyes will have stared at more than a few chewed pens, as the ambassador struggled for the words with which to end a career of public service. As often as not, the note is wistful rather than fulsome. In the air hangs the question 'Is that it, then?'

It was. And four years ago, that was it, too, for the Valedictory Despatch as an institution. With this chapter, it's *vale* to the Valedictory. The casual use of Latin in a book, like the casual use of Latin in a diplomat's despatch, like the very institution of the despatch itself, is on its way to oblivion.

~

'Those doughty but elderly denizens of Whitehall, Sir Awkward Precedent and Sir Sacrosanct Principle'

SIR PAUL WRIGHT, UK AMBASSADOR
TO LEBANON, APRIL 1975

On looking back over my career in the Diplomatic Service, I realise that for me it has been something of a love affair. Indeed, it was love at first sight, exemplified in the improbable person of Sir Gladwyn Jebb (now Lord Gladwyn), my first Ambassador. Since then I have served under many distinguished men; from all of them I have learned much and to all of them I owe a great deal. But my debt is at least as great to those who have served with or under me and particularly to my present staff, whose loyalty and friendship in a difficult and sometimes dangerous post will always be one of my principal and proudest memories. But, as in all properly conducted love affairs, there has been and is criticism – doubtless mutual in my case. The Service has changed drastically since the day nearly 25 years ago when I, as a third room dogsbody, felt that I was on Christian name terms with everyone from the PUS down. This may sound nostalgic but I deplore the fact, inevitable though it is, that we are less eclectic, less personal a service. I find it hard to believe that we need these large and often cumbersome missions abroad in which the art of diplomacy is now often the least of our activities. I cannot understand why Heads of Mission, held responsible as they often and rightly are for matters affecting our vital national interests, cannot be trusted to authorise small expenditures on simple administrative needs without reference to London. I regret the continued influence of those doughty but elderly denizens of Whitehall, Sir Awkward Precedent and Sir Sacrosanct Principle. I realise with a start that I have suddenly become old-fashioned enough to believe that the word 'service' means what it says, that one's duty comes before anything; and that not all our younger colleagues share these ideals, however far short of them I have fallen myself. But these are as lovers' tiffs compared with the pride and exhilaration which I have derived over the years from belonging to what remains, in spite of its defects, demonstrably the best instrument of its kind in the world and, in spite of pressures from within and without in this age of bureaucracy, the best and most efficiently administered. And if my old master Gladwyn, were to pop the same question now that he did 25 years ago, my answer would again be, 'Yes, sir, yes – a thousand times yes.'

I am sending copies of this despatch to Her Majesty's Representatives at Cairo, Tel Aviv, Amman, Damascus, Jedda, Paris, Washington, UKMIS New York and UKDEL Brussels.

I have, etc.,

P. H. G. WRIGHT.

∽

'To her courage . . . I owe my life'

RONALD BAILEY, HM AMBASSADOR
TO MOROCCO, MARCH 1975

In conclusion I would like to express my warm thanks to all those with whom it has been my privilege to work over the years. I have met nothing but friendship, understanding and consideration.

My last words must be a tribute to my wife who has shared all the pleasures and hardships of diplomatic life in many distant capitals. To her courage in attacking and expelling my would-be assassin when he had seriously injured me in Taiz in 1962 and her calm resourcefulness in the hours which followed, I owe my life.

I have, etc.,

R. W. BAILEY.

~

'My valedictory is: "Thank you"'

SIR EWEN FERGUSSON, HM AMBASSADOR
TO PARIS, DECEMBER 1992

It would be silly, whatever the occasional frictions in our relationship, not to enjoy oneself in this Embassy and, over five and a half years, my wife and I have done so – enormously. My valedictory is:

'Thank you'

and my envoi:

'Adieu, kind friends, adieu,
I can no longer stay with you.'

I am Sir,

Yours sincerely,

Ewen Fergusson

~

'I don't want my last words . . . to be words of complaint'

HUGH ARBUTHNOTT, HM AMBASSADOR
TO DENMARK, 1996

Denmark has not been only the pretty, quiet but dull country it seemed to be at first (even if it is unremittingly flat). There have been unexpected things to discover, the people are friendly and the work has been fun. I have enjoyed it here and it has been a good place in which to end my career in the FCO. I am very grateful to my staff for their help, friendship and hard work. I am also grateful to my wife who has helped me enormously and worked long hours but has had to make do with only a share of my pay as she will have to make do with only a share of my pension, both of which she would have got anyway by doing nothing for the Diplomatic Service. A change here would be one change that everyone would surely welcome.

To have been in the British Diplomatic Service during the last 36 years, as the country's wealth and power has steadily declined in relative terms, has been nothing if not a challenge. It has seemed particularly daunting in the years since 1974 during which I have spent much of the time involved in EEC/EU affairs, as the Diplomatic Service has tried to explain to our European partners why almost everything they want to do is wrong and everything we want to do is right. During the same period, numbers in the Service have declined in line with the country's economic strength. But even as the economy has improved, our numbers continue to decline ... I think the number of staff here has gone below the level needed to pursue our interests in Denmark as effectively as they need to be pursued. Do the cuts in numbers mean we are no longer trying to pursue a global foreign policy? It is difficult to see how they can be compatible ...

But I don't want my last words, as I leave the Service, to be words of complaint about it. It has been a good way to make a living and a good deal better than most. I was lucky and proud to be in it and I am sure I shall miss it even if what I shall miss will inevitably be something rather different from what it is becoming.

I am copying this despatch to HM Ambassadors in EU countries, the Baltic States, Norway and Switzerland; and to HM Permanent Representative to the EU in Brussels.

I am, Sir

Yours faithfully

H. J. Arbuthnott

∼

'*Without her nothing would have been possible*'

SIR PERCY CRADOCK, HM AMBASSADOR
TO CHINA, DECEMBER 1983

And now '*Lusisti satis*'.[1] It is time to put away the telegrams and the despatches and the great generalisations and return to the serious business of life in London. This is not only my last despatch from Peking but my last in the Service. I would not have wished to bow out from any other post. This battered caravanserai, so unlike the Embassy of popular imagination, which I have seen burned down, rebuilt, and now extended, has been my home at various times for altogether some nine years and one cannot leave a place where one has laboured so long, however unprofitably, without a certain emotion . . .

I am sorry to leave the Service at a time when it is still beset by criticism. Though I have met, very occasionally, sharper minds at the Bar and greater accumulations of learning at universities, for a general assemblage of intelligence and professional skills, flexibility and loyalty, the Diplomatic Service is surely unsurpassed. Its trouble lies in its function: accurately reporting a world less responsive to our wishes than a generation ago, it has often met the fate of the messenger with bad tidings. But it may, to some degree, have been itself to blame. I recall it at certain periods in the past as perhaps too supple, too anxious to please, too much like the sharp pencil ready to inscribe any message on the blank paper, perhaps even a little lacking in courage. The duty to execute faithfully policy once Ministers have decided it is, of course, clear. But the duty before that decision, to present the choices and consequences plainly and unequivocally, is equally imperative. And to aim off in that presentation out of some misplaced sense of diplomacy or in order to meet political or personal considerations in Ministers' minds which can only be a matter of surmise is to commit the one unforgivable sin. That for us is the *'trahison des clercs'*.[2]

But this is to be ungrateful. The Service has been very kind to me, has borne with my foibles and given me the postings I sought, as Head of the Planning Staff, which I still regard as the best job in the Office, the bonus of the Assessment Staff, an Embassy in Europe and finally Peking. I record my thanks. I must also thank all those who have worked with me. Above all, my wife who, apart from the last few weeks, has been with me throughout, in times of considerable strain and sometimes physical danger, always braver and always wiser than I was. Without her nothing would have been possible. Next the staff at Peking, who have maintained high standards under great pressure, particularly over the last year. And finally the wider group of young men and women who have assisted me at various posts, whose intelligence I have greedily drawn on and whose resilience and sense of humour have sustained me in the necessary business of arguing against the other side and the sometimes necessary and even more difficult business of arguing against my own. With these abilities to hand the Service should have little to fear in the future.

I am sending copies of this despatch to Her Majesty's Representatives at Washington, Moscow, Tokyo, Singapore and to the Governor of Hong Kong.

I am, Sir
Yours faithfully

PERCY CRADOCK

1. *'Lusisti satis'*: From Horace: 'Lusisti satis, edisti satis, atque bibisti, tempus abire tibi est' – 'You have played enough, eaten enough and drunk enough; it's time for you to leave.'
2. *'trahison des clercs'*: 'Betrayal by the bureaucrats.'

~

'Marriage turned out to be a package deal that included a job'

SIR WILLIE MORRIS, HM AMBASSADOR TO EGYPT, MARCH 1979

The three missions I have headed in the past eleven years – Jedda, Addis Ababa and Cairo – have all in some degree been hardship posts, but posts where the Head of Mission tended to get more than his proportionate share of the interesting action to compensate for the hardships that fell more heavily on his staff. I would like to pay tribute here to the support I have had from my staff in Cairo, as in those other posts. I was once snubbed by a Head of Personnel Services Department for suggesting that the FCO Administration should commit itself to the factual statement that Diplomatic Service wives performed duties in support of their husbands: I failed, he said, to appreciate that a growing minority of members of the Service wanted their wives to live at arm's length from their husbands' work and would resent such an assertion. I will nevertheless take my courage in both hands and express my thanks to the wives of the allegedly shrinking majority, who have greatly helped my wife and me. And among them, my own wife, who finding that marriage turned out to be a package deal that included a job, did not repent or repine but put into it all she had.

I am sending copies of this despatch to HM Representatives at Amman, Baghdad, Beirut, Jedda, Khartoum, Tel Aviv, Tripoli, Washington and Jerusalem.

I am, Sir,
Yours faithfully,

Willie Morris

'A witness of the mischief of the times'

SIR ROBIN HOOPER, HM AMBASSADOR
TO GREECE, NOVEMBER 1974

'To live retired,' wrote an ambassador who left the service of Charles II just over three centuries ago, 'was ever safe and to studious minds never unpleasant, but now by so much the better as the world is worse. It is a happiness not to be a witness of the mischief of the times nor liable to the allurements of common evils which of necessity must either vex or infect us.' Whether the world is really worse than when I joined the Service in mid-Munich is a question no prudent man would care to answer. I doubt whether Lord Fauconberg, when he left Italy in 1669 for his broad acres in Yorkshire, took a very cheerful view of the prospects of Restoration England. A cynical, amoral and disillusioned society reflected in a theatre seeking only to mock traditional values; dependence, financially, politically, and militarily on more powerful neighbours; a navy that can't even keep the Dutch out of the Medway; the chance to build a monumental new London frustrated by private greed: one can almost hear his lordship banging on. But he lived on past 1688 to see the foundations of Britain's 18th century greatness laid; and it is in the hope of seeing a similar revival that I now, for the last time,

have the honour to be,
Sir,
Your obedient Servant,

R. W. J. HOOPER.

'A miserable reward for 32 years of hard work'

RICHARD THOMAS, HM HIGH COMMISSIONER TO
BARBADOS AND THE EASTERN CARIBBEAN, FEBRUARY 1998

My wife, and spouses in general

Finally, my wife, the traditional theme of the last paragraph
or two of all Valedictory Despatches since time immemorial.
There is not much which I can add to the many pages which
have accumulated on this subject in the last few years. Not
only am I profoundly grateful to my wife, I am also ashamed
on the Service's part that she will 'retire' no better off, and no
more acknowledged, than her analogues of earlier years.
While I was trying to work out what we would be living on in
retirement, I learned from an office in Newcastle that my
wife would be entitled to the princely sum of £16.24 per week
from age 60 (the price of a hair-do), reducing to £1.49 a week
when I become 65, provided she (repeat, she) paid £3,126
in arrears of unpaid national insurance contributions by
this coming April. This derisory future 'income' financed by
her from zero current income, would be all that she would
have in her own right, which strikes me as a miserable reward
for 32 years of hard work in support of HMG's interests
abroad – work that became steadily harder the more senior
her husband became. Many was the time that the show had
to go on even if the caterer had let us down or whatever
other crisis had intervened. She has been cook, cleaner, and
hotel manager since I first became Ambassador in (servant-
less) Reykjavik in 1983, and before that. She has also been a
shoulder for innumerable members of staff and spouses to
cry on, and a very concerned and hard working 'charity'
worker, mainly in support of the mentally handicapped,
in several posts. She has gladly done her bit week in week

out, for the BDSA[1] and for various British expatriate women's groups. And yet she is not even British, as on occasions of particular frustration she reminds me. The Service has collectively and individually taken her for granted ever since I had the good fortune to be accepted by her as her husband. I am immensely grateful to her, and the Service should be too.

Perhaps it is time to drop some of our pretensions. Is it really necessary to go on behaving as though Residences abroad, even small ones with only part-time domestic help, are regarded by the Service as some kind of Edwardian country house, but with all mod-cons, available for the repose of all travelling Ministers and senior officials? In reply to a point in a recent questionnaire issuing from somewhere in the FCO (yes, my wife gets them too!) she wrote, 'I now detest official guests, who treat me as though I were part of the furniture. Can't these people be put in hotels?' I felt for her, and I wish her successors a fairer deal. Spouses who elect to give up their own careers and private lives for the furtherance of HMG's business, especially spouses of Heads of Mission, should be paid or allowed to opt out.

Envoi

But it would be wrong to end on so carping a note. I have had an enjoyable and, I hope, productive career, much of it spent in exotic places and in exciting times. Gripes about the hotel management remuneration aspect apart, my wife and I have been fortunate to be able to spend almost all our married life together, unlike colleagues in the armed services and many other occupations that require overseas travel. We have been supported by a system and by colleagues who cared, and we have made lasting friendships all over the world, in and out of the Service. Our three children have had a tremendous launching pad for their adult lives. I would like to be starting all over again.

THOMAS

1. *BDSA*: British Diplomatic Spouses Association (nowadays called the Diplomatic Service Families Association).

∾

'For thirty five years, at home and in eight countries overseas, we have done everything together'

LORD MORAN, HM HIGH COMMISSIONER
TO CANADA, JUNE 1984

Like others I have been sad to see the Office decline in public esteem. Much that is said about us is unfair but I think the Office is now often perceived (I hope not irrevocably) as having no gut feeling for our own people, as insufficiently zealous for British interests, as seeking agreement with foreign governments at almost any cost, as unreasonably obsessed with Europe, and as knowing and caring little about Britain north of Potter's Bar. It was not always so. I recall a former Chief Clerk telling a startled candidate that you did not join this Service because you liked foreigners but 'to do the foreigner down'. I regret too that our administrative procedures are now so Byzantine and, in this age of computers and microprocessors so extraordinarily slow.

But, nevertheless, much has gone well. I am grateful for all the help I have had from my staff in Ottawa . . . I pay tribute, as I have done in some of my speeches, to the incalculable contribution made to our efforts by a good many of our wives, unpaid but often making all the difference between success and failure. And in this, my last despatch, I should like to say thank you to my own wife. For thirty five years, at home and in eight countries overseas, we have done everything together. Mine has been an easier job than hers. But her contribution has been enormous. Doing it all together has made it fun. Indeed to have done it without her would have been inconceivable.

I am sending copies of this despatch to the Secretary of State for Trade and Industry, the Governor of the Bank of England, the Secretary of the Cabinet, Heads of Mission at NATO posts and Canberra, to the United Kingdom Representatives at NATO and the United Nations, and to Consular Posts in Canada.

I am Sir
Yours faithfully

Moran

~

'Farewell then, Valedictory Despatches'

CHARLES CRAWFORD, HM AMBASSADOR
TO POLAND, SEPTEMBER 2007

Finally – proof that the tradition lives on. Charles Crawford left the Foreign Office in 2007, having served as ambassador in Bosnia, Serbia and Warsaw. At an earlier posting in South Africa, Crawford had as a mentor Robin Renwick, a future ambassador in Washington whose singular dry wit clearly made an impression on the young diplomat.
Crawford ended his career as ambassador in Warsaw. Valedictory despatches had been abolished the year before but Crawford neatly sidestepped the ban by sending his

parting shot by email to colleagues (or eGram, in Foreign Office lingo) instead. His valedictory took the form of an awards ceremony for lifetime achievement. Crawford now writes an entertaining blog (www.charlescrawford.biz); he describes his Career Oscars as 'a self-indulgent but droll list of the best and worst moments of 28 years' service'.

En route to the exit, Crawford also wrote a more serious valedictory, about the historical fallout from the Katyn massacre. In 1943 the Nazis discovered mass graves in Russia's Katyn forest containing the bodies of more than 20,000 Polish prisoners of war. They had been killed by Russian security forces, but for the next fifty years Moscow denied responsibility, blaming the murders on the Nazis. Right through to the modern era the international community, Crawford believes, has failed to hold former Communists to account for their crimes in Eastern Europe. To many Poles, and outsiders familiar with this largely forgotten atrocity, Katyn remains unfinished business.

THOSE FCO CAREER OSCARS! IN FULL!

Summary
So, Farewell then, Valedictory Despatches. Welcome instead . . . FCO Career Oscar Awards. In no special order:

Best Suppression of Hostile Reviews
In 1986: As Resident Clerk from a standing start at midnight helping secure an injunction at 0400 hrs against the Glasgow *Herald* to stop the printing presses and block their publication of Sir James Craig's valedictory despatch on The Arabs.

Best Droll Repartee with Future Head of State
Soon after he was released from Robben Island in 1990

Nelson Mandela unexpectedly appeared at the Embassy in Pretoria. I (First Sec Internal) was running the shop. He abruptly asked, 'Do you people want [Zulu leader] Buthelezi to be President?' I said, 'If he wins a free and fair election of all South Africans, why not?' Long silence. Mandela: 'Good answer.'

Best Action Sequence
The deafening gunfire outside our Moscow flat late into the night as the attempted 1993 Communist counter-coup against President Yeltsin ran out of steam. My teethmarks were visible in the carpet under the bed at the Skatertny Pereulok flat many years later.

Best Wildlife Sequence
Borrowing two wallabies from a Vojvodina zoo for a reception at the Residence in Belgrade to promote Fosters Lager (Note: as brewed in and exported from the UK).

Best Child Prodigies Scene
In Sarajevo early one morning in Spring 1997 when James and Robert Crawford (6 and 4 respectively) shouted 'Wake up Mr Potato-Head' through the keyhole of the bedroom of visiting Chief Clerk Rob Young, whose career never really recovered thereafter.

Most Appalling and Bewildering Balkan Stupidity Ever
(Note: a record number of nominations in this category)
Winter Olympics, Sarajevo 1984: Tasked with the seemingly banal task of opening and closing a briefcase belonging to a member of the Royal Family, I somehow bent the internal brass hinge. My Belgrade Embassy Serb driver obligingly tried to twist it back into shape – but *snapped it off*, saying 'Don't worry, he won't notice . . .' . . .

Best Slapstick Sequence
Energetically knocking a full champagne glass across the table in No 10 Downing St at the start of talks between Tony Blair and President Kaczynski (2006).

Most Heroic Attempt at 'The Italian Job: 3'
2006: Using a crane to lift a Mini Cooper S into the first floor reception room at the Warsaw Residence for a New Mini launch event . . .

Hottest Sex Scene Involving a KGB Attempt to get an Embassy Maid to Entrap Me
No entries (so to speak) in this category, alas. But we must always be alert to KGB penetration of our most secret places.

Finest Russian Existentialist Analysis of International Relations
Moscow 1996: Russian Ministry of Foreign Affairs Head of Baltic Section Alexander Udaltsov, in response to my argument that Russia should not link energy supplies to the problems facing Russian-speaking minorities in Estonia: 'Meester Crawford: nothing is leenked. But everything is leenked.'

Sir R. Renwick's Old Ambassador's Strategic Priorities
'That's very important. But it doesn't matter.' (Note: oddly tricky to translate this into Slav.)

Best Ever Supporting Actress
Helen Crawford (numerous glamorous leading roles in HMG productions overseas, mostly unpaid).

Notes on the Material

FREEDOM OF INFORMATION
AND THE NATIONAL ARCHIVES

British diplomats' despatches are classified documents. They are not supposed to be read outside of government. Many ambassadors' working reports contain information which could, if revealed at the wrong time or to the wrong audience, wreck Britain's relations with foreign countries at a stroke. At the extreme end, secrecy is a matter of life and death; the most sensitive despatches can touch on the work of the intelligence services, and confidentiality is essential if foreign agents and informers are to avoid being compromised.

Valedictory despatches rarely contained information of quite such mortal importance, but as the extracts in this collection show, they still had ample potential to cause considerable shock and embarrassment. As a result, they were restricted. Most of the despatches which feature in this book were graded 'Confidential', the third-highest security level, behind 'Top Secret' and 'Secret'. Valedictories were often distributed widely across Whitehall, but when stamped 'Confidential' (or 'Restricted', the next level down) they could go only to people who had passed a rigorous security-clearance check. All sorts of precautions and penalties exist in the Foreign Office to stop this kind of material being read by unauthorized eyes, let alone published in a collection like this.

This chapter explains how we overcame that obstacle. In doing so, I hope it will offer some reassurance to any who may feel – as at least one listener did – that broadcasting some choice extracts from valedictories on BBC Radio 4 amounted to a national security threat (an argument which, by extension, would make publishing this book tantamount to treason).

Various laws exist in the UK which set a balance between protecting the government's need for confidentiality and the public's right to information. That balance shifted markedly in the public's favour in 2000 with the passage of the Freedom of Information Act. The legislation enables any member of public to request, for whatever purpose, any information held by an astonishing range of government departments and agencies. The Act introduced for the first time a bias for disclosure – all government information was to be deemed releasable, in the event of a request, unless it fell under certain defined exemptions. Crucially, the legislation applied retroactively. For the first time, anyone who was curious might obtain confidential files written in the recent past by civil servants who had no idea at the time that their scribblings would one day reach a wider audience.

Journalists had already made many significant discoveries using the Freedom of Information process, but when I fired off our first requests to the Foreign Office in 2008 it was with low expectations. I thought the project was likely to founder on the so-called 'qualified' exemptions built into the legislation. These included provisions for government departments to withhold information where disclosure might prejudice international security, or defence, or the 'formulation of government policy' or – crucially – 'international relations between the UK and any other state, international organization or court'. Ominously, there was also an exemption which could stop disclosure in order to protect the 'free and frank provision of advice and exchange of views for the purposes of deliberation'.

The other obstacle was that in trying to identify which diplomats had written entertaining valedictories we were mostly shooting in the dark. The tradition of valedictory despatches was strong in the Foreign Office but not every diplomat wrote one – and of those that did many were routine reports; only a minority were likely to be really interesting. In order to narrow the field I set about researching ambassadors' biographies, looking for interesting characters, high-flyers and mavericks among the many hundreds of men and women who had passed through the overseas service. I drew on obituaries, news reports and on a collection of 'oral histories'; transcripts of recorded interviews with diplomats held at Churchill College, Cambridge. These transcripts were invaluable; the interviews were generally done shortly after retirement, and gave a good indication as to the preoccupations and temperament of the author around the time they would have written their valedictory. I also tried to identify diplomats who worked in interesting times and key posts, such as the embassies either side of the Berlin Wall before reunification, and posts in the Middle East around the time of the first Gulf War.

Altogether, I made Freedom of Information requests to the Foreign Office for nearly sixty valedictories written between 1979 and 2006. The results were pleasantly surprising. Forty valedictories were eventually released to me. Only five were withheld altogether because of exemptions. These included a valedictory from Israel (by John Robinson, 1981) and from South Africa (Dame Maeve Fort, 2000). Despatches from recent envoys to the superpowers were also, perhaps unsurprisingly, deemed too sensitive to release, including

Sir Roderick Lyne's valedictory from Russia in 2004 (although two other Moscow valedictories, from 1988 and 1992, passed the censors intact.) Sir Christopher Meyer's parting shot from Washington in 2003 was also withheld. (This should be worth a read once it is eventually declassified. Meyer told us that when he sat down to write it, after five years in the most high-profile job in the service, 'it all came out like a dose of salts'.) Meyer's 1997 valedictory from Bonn was, however, released to us and appears in Chapter 1.

Most of the despatches which emerged from the process were censored with some sections obscured, commonly because of the exemption regarding 'international relations'. The Foreign Office seemed particularly sensitive about releasing despatches written by ambassadors to conservative societies. One valedictory from Jordan (Peter Hinchcliffe, 1997) bore some particularly heavy redactions and another from Saudi Arabia (Sir James Craig, 1984) was withheld outright. In both cases the Foreign Office wrote me a letter which made much of the need to maintain 'trust and confidence' in relations with the countries concerned. They seemed more relaxed about hurting the feelings of other mature liberal democracies when assessing the material for release; Lord Moran's wonderfully scathing 1984 valedictory from Ottawa being a case in point.

Sometimes only a sentence or a few phrases would be hidden by the censors' pen. In other despatches whole pages were obscured. Robin Renwick's (now Lord Renwick) final telegram from Washington in 1995 bore some particularly swingeing partial edits which were fatal to the meaning. The ambassador began a section with some remarks on the first George Bush: 'As President, he was an anomaly, devoting two thirds of his time to foreign affairs . . .' The next three or four sentences, however, are redacted, and the next legible lines read: 'I have got to know him well over the past three years. He is highly intelligent, pragmatic to the core, a good debater and has been personally very friendly to us. But there are few fixed points on his compass.' A memorable phrase, which at first glance seems to give an insight into Bush's character. But here Renwick was in fact summing up Bill Clinton, who succeeded Bush in 1993. It was a perceptive analysis and, given that Clinton's ability to twist with the political wind became his hallmark, a far-sighted one. (A year after Renwick wrote his despatch, the Democrat known as 'Slick Willy' retook the White House, outmanoeuvring his opponents by 'triangulation' – stealing popular Republican policies.) It would be interesting to see what else Renwick had to say of Clinton beyond those foreshortened remarks, but the censor also struck out what remains of the section.

Renwick's despatch did not make this collection. Most of it is serious in tone, and what remained of the livelier sections of text after filleting by the censors was rather bitty. Historians may note, however, that this despatch may have helped to erect a central pillar of British economic policy: writing two years before New Labour came to power, Renwick argued that the Bank of England should be set free of government control. In Washington the ambassador in fact took Gordon Brown (then Shadow Chancellor) to meet Alan Greenspan, the chairman of the US Federal Reserve, to learn of the merits of central bank independence.

The parting thoughts of Sir Robin Fearn, who retired in 1994 while ambassador in Madrid, are also absent from these pages. I had high hopes for this valedictory. Fearn had seen interesting service as head of the South American Department during the Falklands War. He was 'lucid ... and very funny' according to his obituary in *The Times*, which drew a colourful picture; Fearn once set fire to his suit while giving a lecture to other diplomats, having absent-mindedly put his lit pipe into his pocket. It all sounded promising.

The Foreign Office released the despatch, and most of the document passed the censors relatively unscathed. It is well drafted, if routine, stuff, describing the state of Spain's economy and the ebb and flow of the regional tensions which dominate its politics. But the final three sections are entirely obscured with the thickest of marker pens. Clues in an earlier passage indicate that much of the missing text concerns the tussle between Britain and Spain over Gibraltar. Whatever Fearn had to say on the issue in 1994 obviously still retains a charge today. The centuries-old dispute burst into the open three years after his retirement, with Spain making a fresh demand for joint sovereignty. In 2002 Jack Straw, then Foreign Secretary, actually agreed to back the idea, subject to an eventual referendum. The idea was roundly rejected by 98 per cent of Gibraltarians in a poll hastily organized by enterprising local officials and the plan was quickly dropped.

The final paragraph, usually the place where a diplomat thanks his wife and staff, is also rendered as a solid block of black ink in Fearn's despatch; only the heading 'Envoi' remains legible. This was not unusual; other valedictories also had the personal touch stripped away, with the censors invoking the Data Protection Act in order to withhold private information about individuals. Like the other restrictions, however, censorship on data protection grounds was inconsistently applied. In other despatches, many of the touching tributes to wives were, happily, not struck out. Varying results are, of course, only to be expected when civil servants attempt to follow legislation drafted with such lofty aims (and numerous loopholes) as the Freedom of Information and Data Protection Acts.

The modern extracts that feature here are what trickled through the censors' net. We cannot know what was held back, but it is possible to make an educated guess. Most of the entertaining valedictories in this book are basically rants, and they fall into one of three broad categories: rants about foreigners, about living conditions, and lastly about the Foreign Office itself. Compared with the older (pre-1980) despatches, the material released under FOI is slanted more towards the third category with a little less of the first two. This is consistent with the exemptions in the FOI Act. The legislation gives the Foreign Office ample opportunity to censor colourful tirades which might offend foreign governments but less cover to withhold gripes about (for instance) how the Diplomatic Service is run. It is entirely likely, therefore, that in the paragraphs which have been redacted the authors of modern valedictories harangued foreigners just as strongly as their predecessors once did. Although one expects the sweeping racial generalizations of old may nowadays be expressed more seldom, or at least more subtly. The Foreign Office has after all moved with the times.

All in all, the Freedom of Information process performed satisfactorily. The Information Rights Team at the FCO dealt with my voluminous requests with laudable thoroughness and patience, although not always with haste. The Act obliges public bodies to make an initial response after twenty days, but it sometimes took months to get a final result. When the decisions went against us I chose not to challenge them (the appeals process is rather tortuous and can take years; although at its apex the independent Information Commissioner can force disclosure). For their part, the Foreign Office did not invoke against me, as I feared they might, a clause in the legislation barring 'vexatious or repeated requests'. Of course these days the Foreign Office, like most government departments, is geared up to handle a high volume of FOI traffic; in 2009 it received 1,136 FOI requests, or roughly three a day.

Nosiness seems to have found an equilibrium; previous years have shown a remarkably similar total number of requests. Public access to information does not come cheap, however; the Foreign Office employs a team of about ten to manage the process. Central government auditing shows that they answer just 31 per cent of requests in full, which makes the FCO one of the strictest censors in Whitehall; among the other Departments of State only the Cabinet Office had a lower response rate. Given the sensitivity of the material that goes into the diplomatic bag, this is perhaps understandable. If you include partial responses, almost 50 per cent of public requests received by the Foreign Office meet with some degree of success.

The FOI legislation includes a 'cost cap'. Central government departments can refuse to answer requests where the cost in time and manpower to process the information would exceed £600. (Usefully, this amount does not include time spent *assessing* whether the material can be released, only actually processing it.) In this respect, it helped that my requests were for specific documents rather than for general information which might have to be pulled together from different sources. The Foreign Office has indeed had to scramble to answer some opaque and spurious FOI requests over the years. At the time of writing, the last submission answered on the department's Access to Information website concerned the number of personal items reported stolen in the past two years from FCO buildings in London. Past topics of inquiry have included the cost of running the FCO wine cellars and – that tabloid favourite – the budget for toilet roll (February 2008 was a particularly heavy month, should anyone care: home-based diplomats at King Charles Street tore their way through 190 rolls, at a cost of £2,500).

The experience of fielding all these requests – be they from academics, interested members of the public, time wasters or hostile journalists – has left its mark on Whitehall, and the chill has been felt particularly keenly in the Foreign Office. The main provisions of the Freedom of Information Act came into force in 2005. Denis MacShane was Minister for Europe at the time; he remembers 'people began to get very worried' as the first FOI requests arrived at the Foreign Office, suddenly realizing that anything they put in writing would no longer be protected as before.

The Diplomatic Service has for centuries run almost entirely on paper and its modern equivalents. (Nowadays, compared with countries of comparable size Britain has a relatively small number of diplomats, spread thinly across the globe; email is the only way they can keep in touch.) And, while diplomats posted abroad may be thousands of miles away from their colleagues, the network in which they communicate and share reports is a close one, in which confidentiality is essential in order to allow a frank exchange of views. FOI, thinks Mac-Shane, is 'seriously challenging' that culture. He thinks Freedom of Information 'is reducing the quality, and the frankness, and the brutal honesty of what very clever men and women are sending back to their masters in London. And that may begin to affect the quality of decisions that government takes.'

The culture of the Diplomatic Service is wrapped up in its prose; it is through their written reports that members of the tribe communicate, praise and chastise one another, argue and share jokes. The results often make terrific reading, as the extracts in this book hopefully show. But the possibility of disclosure brought by Freedom of Information creates a 'chilling effect' which works against the spirit of like minds locked in common endeavour, sharing stories. It may well be that the sort of entertaining indiscretion and refreshing honesty contained in some of these despatches is now going to disappear.

Fortunately, there is a wealth of material still to be discovered. The richest seam of material for valedictories remains the National Archives, which is where the bulk of the despatches in this book were unearthed. Government departments send their old files to Kew and, after thirty years, most get declassified and opened up to the public. The Foreign and Commonwealth Office records series is, along with the Cabinet Papers, one of the most popular resources among the professional researchers and academics who nowadays have to fight for a desk in the reading rooms with a noisy crowd of amateur genealogists inspired by television programmes. Every Christmas the opening of a fresh set of government files provides historians with new discoveries and broadsheet journalists with whimsical picture stories. Among the valedictories from 1979 most recently declassified under the thirty-year rule which feature in this collection are Sir Nicholas Henderson's famous telegram from Paris and Sir Anthony Parson's forlorn apologia from Tehran after the fall of the Shah.

The electronic catalogue at the National Archives admits the existence of about 350 valedictories. There are doubtless many, many more in the vast stacks behind the scenes: valedictories indexed under a different heading, in files with other papers, and in series of despatches bound in books (the so-called 'Confidential Print'). Finding good despatches in this Alexandria of Libraries was simply a numbers game; about one in every five or six of the documents I read was interesting. Many of the despatches – most, in fact – were too much 'of their time' to mean much to the modern reader. Foreign policy analysis tends to date quite quickly.

Most of the Kew valedictories were written between 1960 and 1979. Things picked up – from a records-keeping point of view – in 1968, when the Foreign Office merged with the

Commonwealth Office. One of the first innovations in the modern, combined FCO was a common file registry, a great asset which helps today's researchers delve among thousands of individual despatches, reports and other correspondence, all of which are bound together with the minute sheets upon which ministers and Whitehall clerks would scribble their comments. Similar records exist for most government departments. Taken *en masse* this is nothing less than the nation's memory.

Not everything sees the light of day at Kew after thirty years. Some of the valedictories in this collection (notably Sir Arthur de la Mare's from Bangkok in Chapter 1) still carry redactions many decades after they were written. Having been deemed exceptionally sensitive, this material is protected under the Public Records Act of 1958 which gave the Lord Chancellor sweeping powers to withhold information 'with the approval, or at the request' of another minister 'or any other person who seems to him to be primarily concerned'. There is no time limit. Or rather, there was; that legislation has now been superseded by the Freedom of Information Act, which allows members of the public to request a review of any missing information with a mind to releasing it; although one imagines that in most cases the reasons for keeping it under lock and key will still stand.

The movement towards greater disclosure which began with FOI continues to inch forwards, however, and in 2009 Gordon Brown announced that the thirty-year rule would be relaxed. A review into the issue chaired by the *Daily Mail* editor, Paul Dacre, backed halving the delay to fifteen years. The government settled on moving to a twenty-year rule. The change will happen in stages over the next decade, in order to give the National Archives time to process the necessary two million extra files to support it. The Foreign Office, incidentally, argued for twenty-five years. As the new rule comes in there will also be 'strictly limited' new exemptions, in order to protect 'particularly sensitive material', including records on the Royal Family.

Researching this project has been something of an adventure, and I would like to end with thanks to the many people who gave me help, guidance and pointers along the way. They shall remain (for I hope obvious reasons) individually nameless. Particular thanks are also due, for their expertise and for their time, to the staff at the National Archives and to the Information Rights team and records keepers at the Foreign Office. Martin Rosenbaum at the BBC deserves a special mention for backing the idea and nurturing it through two series of radio programmes.

Lastly, thanks are owed in abundance to the authors of the despatches, whose parting shots are captured here. We have been shameless in purloining their material, and ruthless in cutting out most of the serious stuff. There was lots of serious stuff; even in their valedictories. For them, duty always came first; having read many of their reports I found British diplomats as a class to be possessed of a strong and distinct sense of public service, an idea that has become a little old-fashioned. They considered life in the Diplomatic Service to be a privilege. They tolerated its downsides – 'distance, dirt and danger' as David Gore-Booth put it – with equanimity and with a certain *sang-froid* unique to the Foreign Office. They are the best of British.

Andrew Bryson

Index of Diplomats

Index of Countries